Practical Considerations in
Computer-Based Testing

Springer
New York
Berlin
Heidelberg
Barcelona
Hong Kong
London
Milan
Paris
Singapore
Tokyo

Cynthia G. Parshall   Judith A. Spray
John C. Kalohn   Tim Davey

Practical Considerations in Computer-Based Testing

With 17 Illustrations

Springer

Cynthia G. Parshall
University of South Florida
4202 E. Fowler Avenue, EDU 162
Tampa, FL 33620-7750
USA
parshall@tempest.coedu.usf.edu

Judith A. Spray
ACT, Inc.
2202 N. Dodge Street
Iowa City, IA 52243-0168
USA
spray@act.org

John C. Kalohn
ACT, Inc.
2202 N. Dodge Street
Iowa City, IA 52243-0168
USA
kalohn@act.org

Tim Davey
Educational Testing Service
Rosedale Road
Princeton, NJ 08540
USA
tdavey@ets.org

Library of Congress Cataloging-in-Publication Data
Practical considerations in computer-based testing / Cynthia Parshall . . . [et al.].
   p. cm.
  Includes bibliographical references and index.
  ISBN 0-387-98731-2 (pbk. : alk. paper)
   1. Educational tests and measurements—Computer programs. 2. Educational tests and
measurements—Data processing. I. Parshall, Cynthia G.
  LB3060.5 .P73 2001
  371.26′0973—dc21   2001032008

Printed on acid-free paper.

Production managed by Michael Koy; manufacturing supervised by Jeffrey Taub.
Camera-ready copy prepared from the authors' Microsoft® Word files.
Printed and bound by Sheridan Books, Inc., Ann Arbor, MI.
Printed in the United States of America.

9 8 7 6 5 4 3 2 1

ISBN 0-387-98731-2   SPIN 10708448

Springer-Verlag New York Berlin Heidelberg
A member of BertelsmannSpringer Science+Business Media GmbH

To my children, Daniel, Sarah, and Stefanie Angela
　　　　　　　　　　　　　　—C.G.P.

To my sister, Jan
　　　—J.A.S.

To Tom, Jake, and Kacey
　　　　—J.C.K.

Preface

This book introduces computer-based testing, addressing both nontechnical and technical considerations. The material is oriented toward practitioners and graduate students. The practical emphasis will be useful to measurement professionals who are or will be responsible for implementing a computerized testing program. The instructional information is also designed to be suitable for a one-semester graduate course in computerized testing in an educational measurement or quantitative methods program. While certain theoretical concepts are addressed, the focus of the book is on the applied nature of computerized testing. For this reason, the materials include such features as example applications, figures, and plots to illustrate critical points in the discussions.

A wide range of nontechnical issues need to be considered in implementing a computer-based testing program. Separate chapters are provided on test administration and development issues, examinee issues, software issues, and innovative item types. Test administration and delivery issues include the location of exam administration, selection of hardware and software, security considerations, scheduling of administration frequency and time limits, cost implications, and program support as well as approaches for addressing reliability, validity, comparability, and data analysis. Examinee issues include the influence of examinees' reactions to adaptive testing, the effect of computer-based task constraints, and the impact of examinees' prior computer experience. Software issues include usability studies and software evaluation as tools in selecting and developing appropriate software, based on the test program needs. Additional software issues include critical features of the user interface and software design. Finally, innovative item types are items that use some feature or function of the computer (such as audio, video, interactivity, or alternative response actions) to enhance their measurement capacity. Issues with innovative item types include the measurement purpose, the innovative dimension, and the effect of task complexity on test development.

One strong feature of this book is the exposition of a number of test delivery methods. Computer-based testing can be conducted in a variety of ways, beyond simply "linear" or "adaptive" methods. A test delivery method should be selected based on the characteristics of a specific examination program, as each method has particular strengths and weaknesses. A full chapter is provided on each of the delivery methods: computerized fixed testing (CFT), automated test assembly for online delivery (ATA), computerized classification testing (CCT), and computerized adaptive testing (CAT). Additional technical aspects of computer-based testing are addressed in a chapter on item pool evaluation and maintenance. Finally, the book concludes with a comparison of test delivery methods in terms of both technical and nontechnical considerations.

We would like to acknowledge Rose Cahill, Jane Coppernoll, and Jan Peters at ACT, Inc., for their clerical support, and Chi-Yu Huang, Chuan-Ju Lin, and Tianyou Wang for their psychometric assistance with several chapters. We would also like to thank ACT, Inc., the Educational Measurement and Research Department at the University of South Florida, and the Institute for Instructional Research and Practice, also at the University of South Florida, for their support and assistance.

Tampa, Florida, USA   Cynthia G. Parshall
Iowa City, Iowa, USA   Judith A. Spray
Iowa City, Iowa, USA   John C. Kalohn
Princeton, New Jersey, USA   Tim Davey
June 2001

Contents

1
Considerations in Computer-Based Testing

In recent years, many tests have begun to be administered on computer. In some cases, the tests are developed for or converted to a computer-based format for no better reason than the trend value. Computerized exams frequently are perceived as being "state of the art" or automatically better than traditional, standardized, paper-and-pencil exams. These clearly are not accurate assumptions, and a testing program should not elect to computerize an exam without stronger reasons than these. Indeed, there are many challenges inherent in computer-based testing, and development of a computerized exam program should not be undertaken lightly. However, while computerized tests are not intrinsically better than paper-and-pencil tests, there are some distinct advantages available in computerized test administration.

There are benefits to the testing agency from administering an exam on computer. These include cost savings on printing and shipping and some improvements in test security, due to the relative ease in handling and protecting electronic files as opposed to stacks of test forms and booklets. The fact that the test data are collected automatically by the computer during test administration is another advantage, in that it can simplify the process of scoring the exam.

Other features of computerized test administration are primarily seen as advantageous to the examinees. For example, many computerized testing programs offer immediate test scoring. Computer administration also makes greater measurement efficiency possible, and this usually translates into shorter tests. Another advantage for examinees is that most computerized exam programs offer tests more frequently than is common for paper-and-pencil testing. In fact, this so-called *continuous testing* approach results from limited numbers of computer stations typically available for testing at any given time, and it actually creates certain challenges to the testing program. Nevertheless, it is a highly valued examinee benefit.

Another benefit of testing on computer is the opportunity to use innovative item types. Computer administration provides for expansions in the forms of measurement and in the types of cognitive skills and processes measured. Computers also allow additional data to be collected during an exam. For example, an accurate distinction between "omitted" items and "not reached" items can be made. The amount of time an examinee spends on an item, or the *response latency*, also can be collected. If an item is designed appropriately, process data as well as product data can be collected.

Computer administration of tests also has potential for some important technological provisions for handicapped examinees. Examples include the provision of large print or audio for vision-impaired examinees, alternate input devices for examinees who are unable to write, and other accommodations.

These are only some of the potential benefits of computer-based testing. However, a number of challenges for the development and administration of a psychometrically sound computer-based test accompany them. It is important for any agency considering a computer-based testing program to study the critical issues or features of computer-based testing in order to design a program that best suits its needs. These features or issues of computer-based testing are presented briefly in this chapter and discussed more thoroughly in those that follow.

Issues in Test Administration and Development

The processes of test administration and development are critical elements in any testing program. While the terms are more commonly paired as "test development and administration," when an exam program is being considered for computer-based delivery it is often the administration issues that are of immediate concern. A number of important issues for both administration and development are introduced here and discussed in further detail in Chapter 2.

Test Administration

When an exam will be administered on computer, a number of new or different administrative procedures are needed. An obvious, but nevertheless important, need for computer-based tests (CBT) is the test administration sites. Given that CBTs need to be administered on computer, provision needs to be made for a sufficient number of computers to manage the test volume. A test program may elect to manage the administration of the exams in their own computer labs or to use a chain of commercial computer test centers. Decisions must also be made about the software and hardware platforms for the computer-based test. Consistency needs to be maintained across test administrations in order to ensure comparability and to avoid any attacks on the validity of test scores. New test security procedures must also be implemented for computer-based test programs. Test security concerns with computer-based exams need to address secure methods for the storage and transmission of electronic test data. Scheduling changes are also needed for computer-based tests. The time limits for individual exams and the frequency with which exam administrations are held must be set under conditions that differ considerably from paper-and-pencil test administrations. Finally, new procedures may also be needed in the staffing of test program support personnel. Given more frequent exam administrations, support personnel need to be available to respond to problems on a more constant basis.

Test Development

A range of test development activities is needed to produce a computer-based test. For tests that already exist in paper-and-pencil form, the first test development task is likely to be an evaluation of the current pool of items. This evaluation may address several assumptions of computer-based testing, the adequacy of the items in the pool, and the extent of the need for additional item development. For both exam programs that are brand new and those that are new to the computer, investigations of test reliability and validity need to be conducted. The optimal methods for estimating reliability and validity will depend on aspects of the test program. For exams that will be administered as both computer-based and paper-and-pencil tests, additional investigation into score comparability will also be needed. Finally, new schedules for the analysis of test data will need to established, given the changes in test administration frequency for computerized test programs.

Examinee Issues

The perspective of the examinees taking computer-based tests needs to be considered as well. Issues related to examinees include their affective reactions to computer-based test administration, the impact of prior level of computer experience on their test performance, effects of the user interface, effects of task constraints, effects of the test administration process, and examinees' mental models as they test. A few of these topics are introduced in the following sections.

Examinee Reactions

Many early studies in the field of computerized testing found that examinees had very positive reactions to the experience of taking an exam on computer. However, the majority of these studies were conducted on tests under unmotivated conditions, that is, the examinees had little reason or motivation to perform well. As the number of operational computerized tests has increased, a somewhat less optimistic picture has developed. Examinees tend to be more cautious about offering positive reactions under any genuine test condition and are sometimes very concerned or even negative about the experience under high-stakes conditions (i.e., tests with critical educational or career implications).

Examinees have expressed some concerns about the use of the computer itself. Generally, these include a fear that their prior experience is insufficient for the task or a sense that the task constraints will be more binding. Different, less familiar test-taking strategies appear to be optimal for the process of taking a computerized test. Scanning the test or quickly moving about the exam is difficult or impossible when only a single item can be displayed on the screen at a time. Note taking or marking an item for later review is also more difficult when entering responses with a keyboard or mouse than when using a pencil.

In addition to the general effect of testing on computer, examinees are concerned about certain specific aspects of adaptive testing. For example, a typical computerized adaptive test (CAT) may result in an examinee getting only about half of the items administered correct. This may provide a more difficult testing experience than is the norm for many test-takers. Some examinees are also frustrated by constraints on adaptive tests, such as the lack of opportunity to review or change their responses to previous items. Also, given that adaptive tests frequently are shorter than the traditional format, examinees can become much more anxious about their responses to each and every item. Finally, examinees may be made more anxious, to the extent that they are aware of their interaction with the computer. That is, because answering an item correctly causes the computer to select and administer a more difficult item but answering incorrectly causes the computer to select and administer an easier item, examinees may become anxious about their perceived performance, based on the "feedback" of the current item's difficulty level.

Impact of Prior Computer Experience

The impact of an examinee's prior computer experience depends on the type of item (and item interface) in the computerized exam. For example, a test consisting solely of multiple-choice items will be easier to learn and use than an exam that includes several item types that are more innovative, departing from the traditional, discrete, text-based, multiple-choice format. An important equity consideration is that the level of prior computer experience in the test population may be systematically different across examinee subgroups. Prior to testing, different examinee subgroups may have had different opportunities for computer access and computer experience.

Additionally, the extent of the examinees' prior computer experience has implications for instructional components of the test administration software. Every computer-based test should include at least a minimal level of instruction screens, practice items, and help options. In addition to general test-taking instructions, specific instruction is needed for every item type included on the test. Furthermore, when the target population for the exam has little computer experience, more extensive instructions (and practice opportunities) are often necessary.

Effects of the User Interface

While test developers must consider every aspect of the computerized exam, the only aspects of the computer-based test with which the examinee is directly concerned are the item screens and the information screens. In both cases, examinees need to know clearly to what part of the screen they must attend, how to navigate, and how to indicate a response. The user interface comprises those elements of a software program that a user sees and interacts with. The more "intuitive" the computer test software is, the less the examinee needs to attend to it, rather than to the test questions. A good interface is clear and consistent and should be based on sound software design principles in order to support the overall goals of the program.

Typically, it is more difficult to read from the screen than from paper. This fact has particular implications for longer reading passages, multiscreen items, and items that require scrolling. Scanning an entire test and skipping, answering, or returning to items may also be easier in pencil-and-paper mode. On the other hand, some advantages for presenting items on screen have been found. For example, the presentation of one item per screen has been seen as helpful to distractible examinees. In addition, several potential sources of measurement error are removed. For example, an examinee is only able to select a single response to a multiple-choice item; no double-gridding can occur. Further, an examinee cannot mistakenly provide an answer to the wrong question; if item 14 is displayed on screen, there is no possibility of gridding item 15 instead.

Effects of Task Constraints

Although testing on computer provides many features not available in paper-and-pencil testing, it typically includes some constraints or restrictions as well. The most prominent of these is present in adaptive test delivery methods such as CATs. Adaptive tests generally restrict examinees from omitting, reviewing, or revising items. Adjusting an adaptive testing program to include this flexibility may be problematic and, at the least, may reduce measurement efficiency. This restriction on item reviewing is probably the aspect of CATs that examinees complain about most frequently.

There are additional task constraints related to examinee responses and other interactions with the test. Further discussion of these topics is provided in Chapter 3.

Software Issues

The selection or development of software to administer computer-based tests is an important step in the process of developing an online exam program. Usability studies and software evaluations help test developers ensure that the software program is well designed and meets the needs of the exam. Critical aspects of the software's interface include navigation, visual style and writing for the screen. These topics are introduced in the following sections and discussed in greater detail in Chapter 4.

Usability Studies

Usability studies are the means by which software developers evaluate and refine their software programs. Potential users of the program are asked to interact with and comment on early versions or prototypes of the software. In this way, the software developers obtain information about the program's value, utility, and appeal.

Usability studies help ensure good software design; making decisions without obtaining user input often leads to design flaws and operational problems. Testing successive versions of the interface on actual users and making changes based on the feedback provided have been shown to contribute to a program that meets users' needs, and one that functions well in practice. For computerized testing software, one important effect of good software design is that examinees are able to spend less time and attention on how to take the test and more on the actual test itself. This may remove a potential source of measurement error and a limitation on test score validity. Testing programs that develop their own software for computerized test delivery are well advised to incorporate usability testing into the development process.

There are several different approaches to usability testing, ranging from very expensive to very inexpensive. Usability studies can be conducted using very elaborate, high-fidelity prototypes of the actual software interface. However, they can also be conducted quite effectively using inexpensive, simple mockups of the interface. The studies themselves can be conducted in numerous ways, including direct observations, interviews, and talk-aloud protocols or focus groups.

Software Evaluation

Software evaluation is a process through which users can, somewhat formally, consider a potential software program in terms of specific criteria. Test developers who intend to purchase commercial software for computerized test administration may use the software evaluation process to analyze and compare existing commercial programs. A thorough evaluation of competing software programs ensures that a testing agency will select the program that best meets its needs and the needs of the examinees. Those testing agencies that are producing their own computerized testing software can benefit from software evaluation. Checklists and usability heuristics can be used to aid in the evaluation process.

Navigation

Navigation refers to the methods provided in a software interface by which users move through the program. With instructional screens, for example, users are often asked to click a mouse button or press the Enter key to advance to the next screen. Occasionally examinees are provided with a button or keystroke option to move back to the previous screen. A program that has simple navigation typically will be easy to learn and will minimize the impact of the interface on test performance.

Under flexible test conditions (i.e., test administrations in which examinees are free to omit items and to review and revise their responses), navigation might include menus to test sections, a means of "marking" items for review, and buttons or keystrokes to allow examinees to return to previously viewed items to review or revise them. Even under nonflexible conditions, navigation might include options for moving to the next item, a way to access Help screens, and a way to end testing early. Software design principles recommend that navigation buttons be placed in the same location on every screen and keyboard commands be consistent across displays. And, although they should be unobtrusive, their purpose should be apparent.

Visual Style

The visual style of the software interface is reflected in all of the individual visual elements on the screen, from the choice of background color to the shape and label of navigation buttons to the type and size of text fonts. The visual style of the program is displayed through the use of borders, spacing, and the physical layout of screen elements. The style and detail of any graphics included, as well as any animation or video, also contribute to the program's visual style. Finally, the visual effect of all of these elements combined contributes to the overall visual style of the interface.

In any software package, the visual style should be appropriate for the target audience and for the subject matter of the program. It also should be designed to match the style and tone of the written communication. For computerized testing, a simple uncluttered style is best. Clear, legible text with few screen windows open at one time is the least confusing to novice users of the testing software. Soft colors, with a good level of contrast between the font and the background, are easiest on the eyes and thus help reduce potential examinee fatigue during the exam.

Writing for the Screen

The topic of "writing for the screen" refers to important facets of written communication with the software users. The term applies to the information on software screens such as the introductory screen, instructional and tutorial screens, any practice item screens, help screens, and closing screens. It does not refer to the writing of the actual test items.

The (nonitem) textual information included in a program should be well written, communicating information clearly and at an appropriate reading level for the target users. Reading extensive information on screen is more taxing to the reader than reading the same information from print, so brevity is a critical concern in writing for the screen. Concise communication also can be aided by the use of formatting techniques, including physical layout, spacing, and bulleted text.

The font used for textual information should be selected carefully, to be visually pleasing on screen, large enough to be seen from a reasonable distance, and fully legible. Next, the display of text should be carefully designed. It should be formatted with attention to aesthetics and attractive placement on the screen. Legibility and readability are improved when text is left-justified rather than centered or full-justified. The information is easier to read if the text is not overly cluttered; instead, visual breaks should be used, and the text should be surrounded by white space.

Issues in Innovative Item Types

Innovative item types constitute the most promising arena in the field of computer-based testing. Administering a test on computer allows items to utilize some of the computer's features and functions, potentially offering new and better forms of assessment. The term *innovative item types* is used to refer to items that are enhanced, due to their use of capabilities provided by the computer. Aspects of innovative item types in the following sections include their potential benefits, the dimensions of item innovations, and effects of task complexity. Further discussion of each of these topics is provided in Chapter 5.

Potential Benefits of Item Innovations

Items may be innovative (or depart from the traditional, discrete, text-based, multiple-choice format) in many ways. Innovative items may include some feature or function not easily provided in paper-and-pencil testing. This can include the use of video, audio, or graphics in the item stems or response options. Examinees might respond by clicking on or moving a screen graphic, entering a free response, highlighting text, or another action. Other innovations relate to the computer's ability to interact with examinees and to score complex responses by the examinees.

The overarching purpose of innovative item types is to improve measurement, through either improving the quality of existing measures or through expanding measurement into new areas. In other words, innovative item types enable us to measure something *better* or to measure something *more*. Innovative item types may offer improved measurement by reducing guessing or allowing more direct measurement than traditional item types provide. Innovative item types also may improve measurement by expanding an exam's coverage of content areas and cognitive processes.

Dimensions of Innovation

Item innovations can be categorized in terms of five dimensions. Although these dimensions are not completely independent, any given item is usually innovative in only one or two dimensions.

The five dimensions of item innovation are: item format, response action, media inclusion, level of interactivity, and scoring method. *Item format* defines the sort of response collected from the examinee; major categories of item format are *selected response* and *constructed response*. *Response action* refers to the means by which examinees provide their responses to the questions or items on the test. This includes key presses and mouse clicks. *Media inclusion* covers the addition of nontext elements within an item, including graphics, sound, animation, and video. *Level of interactivity* describes the extent to which an item type reacts or responds to examinee input. This can range from no interactivity through complex multistep items with branching. Finally, *scoring method* addresses how examinee responses are converted into quantitative scores.

Task Complexity

Innovative item types span a very wide range of *task complexity*. Task complexity summarizes the number and type of examinee interactions within a given task or item. The level of task complexity has implications for item development as well as for implementation within a test delivery method.

Items with low task complexity are the most similar to traditional, text-based multiple-choice items in terms of the amount of examinee response time required and the amount of measurement information the item may be expected to provide. The modest differences between these innovative item types and more traditional items mean that items with low task complexity can be incorporated into an existing test structure fairly easily. Innovative item types with high task complexity, however, are another matter. Items with high task complexity tend to require far more examinee response time, whether they consist of an online essay prompt, a computerized simulation of a performance-based task, or another extended assignment. Assessments of high task complexity are often developed for a specific exam program to satisfy particular needs for coverage of content knowledge and cognitive skills within the domain of interest. High-complexity tasks and items are often administered in a "stand-alone" fashion rather than incorporating them into an existing test. The majority of the research and development of innovative item types has been conducted at these two extremes of task complexity. Comparatively little work has been accomplished in terms of developing item types of *moderate* task complexity.

The specific type of item innovation under consideration has implications for item and item-type development as well as for implementation within a test delivery model. The use of novel item formats may require an extensive effort in the development and evaluation of appropriate scoring algorithms. Construct validation of the alternative assessment may need to be conducted. Appropriate means of combining information from innovative items with that obtained through traditional items may also need to be developed. Finally, tests in which only a few high-complexity tasks are administered may have problems with memorization, task specificity, low generalizability, and item exposure.

Test Delivery Methods

There are a number of distinctly different ways in which tests may be assembled and administered on computer. These different approaches can be termed *test delivery methods*. Each test delivery method has some advantages and is the best choice for some testing programs. In this section several delivery methods are introduced. Each method introduced here is discussed in greater detail in a separate chapter later in this book.

Computerized Fixed Tests

The simplest test delivery method is the computerized fixed test (CFT). This nonadaptive computer test design has a format similar to the conventional paper-and-pencil test on which it is modeled. The CFT is sometimes referred to as a "linear" computerized test, or simply as a CBT (although that term has come to mean *any* computerized test). The computerized fixed test has a fixed length and consists of a fixed test form; the fixed set of items can be administered in either fixed or random order. The computerized test forms are usually constructed based on classical item statistics (p-values and point-biserial correlations), and the tests typically are scored by number correct or scaled number correct. When necessary, alternate forms can be equated by conventional means, or a passing score can be determined for each test form if a classification decision needs to be made.

In this delivery method, tests can be administered several times yearly on fixed dates, during fixed testing *windows* (i.e., fixed periods of time in which testing may take place), or under continuous test availability. Official test scores may be provided immediately upon test completion. Alternatively, provisional scores may be provided at the time of testing, with official scores reported at a later date. Finally, the exam program can be self-sustaining through embedded pretest item sections.

Automated Test Assembly for Computer Delivery

Under the automated test assembly (ATA) test delivery method, computerized exams are constructed by selecting items from an item *pool* in accord with a test plan, using both content and statistical constraints. Like the CFT, ATA tests have a fixed length and are not adaptive. In fact, although many examinees receive a different test, the forms may be constructed in advance of the test session. Multiple tests for examinees make formal equating following administration impossible. However, forms are usually constructed under constraints that render them *equivalent* by a predetermined set of criteria based on content and psychometric specifications.

Tests constructed with this method can be administered frequently on fixed dates or during fixed windows. Item pools can be used for several administrations before the item pool is set aside or restocked, and the exams may be scored by classical test theory methods or estimates of each examinee's ability as measured by the test. Either official or provisional test scores may be provided at the conclusion of the test session, as discussed previously. The test program is often self-sustaining through embedded pretest sections. More information item development and pretesting is provided in Chapter 2.

Computerized Adaptive Tests

In the computerized adaptive test (CAT) delivery method, items are individually selected for each examinee based on the responses to previous items. The goal of this type of test is to obtain a precise and accurate estimate of each examinee's proficiency on some underlying scale. The number of items, the specific items, and the order of item presentation are all likely to vary from one examinee to another. Unique tests are constructed for each examinee, matching the difficulty of each item to the examinee's estimated ability. Immediate scoring is provided. Examinee scores are put on the same scale through reliance on item response theory (IRT) latent ability estimates. (More information on IRT is provided in the *Basics of IRT* appendix and in Chapter 8.)

CAT test programs usually provide either continuous testing or frequent testing windows. The item pools need to be refreshed regularly and the exams are scored by IRT ability estimates. The official scores therefore can be reported immediately. The test program is self-sustaining through embedded pretest sections.

Computerized Classification Tests

The computerized classification test (CCT) delivery method, like the CAT, is adaptive. However, the goal in this delivery method is to classify examinees into two or more broad categories, rather than to obtain an ability estimate for each examinee. That is, examinees are placed into groups, such as pass or fail, but may not be provided a score. This model is more efficient for making classification decisions than a full CAT exam, although less information about the examinee's ability is obtained. Both classical and IRT versions of the test are possible.

Testing programs using the CCT delivery method often provide continuous or year-round testing, and item pools may be changed or refreshed several times annually. The official scores, or classification decisions, are often reported immediately. The program is typically self-sustaining through embedded pretest sections.

Organization of the Book

The material introduced in this chapter provides the framework for the book as a whole. Chapters 2 through 5 deal with issues in test administration and development, examinees issues, software issues, and issues in innovative item types in greater detail. Chapters 6 through 9 present the details of the four test delivery methods: computerized fixed tests, automated test assembly for Online administration, computerized adaptive tests, and computerized classification tests. Chapter 10 is devoted to item pool evaluation and maintenance. Chapter 11 presents a comparison of the four delivery methods on a number of non-technical and technical issues. Additional materials include an appendix on the basics of IRT and an index.

2
Issues in Test Administration and Development

The processes of test administration and development are both critical elements in any testing program. Chronologically, the development of any test occurs before its administration, and thus the two are more commonly paired as "test development and administration." However, in discussing computerized testing programs, it is often useful to address the administration issues first and then turn to the development considerations. This is the approach followed in this chapter.

Test Administration Issues

With any test delivery method, certain administrative issues must be addressed. These include selection of the computerized test delivery sites, computer test software and hardware considerations, test security provisions, time limits, administration frequency, cost concerns, and test program support. These issues are each discussed briefly in the following sections.

Computer Test Sites

Depending on the test program, an agency might decide to administer computerized exams at its own sites, arrange to use computer labs at community colleges and universities or other such locations, or have the exams administered at sites managed by a commercial chain of computer test centers. For low-stake and practice tests, another option is Web-based tests delivered without restriction to any computer with Internet access. The choice of test site has implications for exam cost, security measures, and aspects of the storage and transmission of test data. In addition, it may affect the test registration processes, the administration procedures, and the responsibilities of proctors and other testing personnel. Furthermore, certain test sites may be limited in the test administration software (and thus, software features) available.

For a standardized test, it is particularly important that the setting be conducive to testing. That is, the environment should be quiet, comfortable, and without distractions, and it should be consistent across sites (APA, 1986; ATP, 2000). The hardware and software used should also be consistent across sites. The administration procedures should provide for secure delivery of exams (Rosen, 2000). The test sites should also be set up to provide reasonable accommodations for examinees with disabilities (e.g., computer carrels that are wheelchair accessible). Finally, examinees should have easy access to information about the test site's environment in advance of testing, so that no lack of awareness on their part will impact their test performance.

Software for Computer-Based Testing

There are a number of options for obtaining access to a computer-based test administration software package. Some testing agencies have their own propriety software that can be used to develop computer-based tests for their clients. Another alternative is to purchase a commercial software program. Several commercial software publishers sell off-the-shelf computerized testing programs. These vary in terms of the features available, cost, and ease of use. Another alternative is to actually develop software for computer-based testing. If a testing program has requirements that are not met by commercial software, custom software may need to be developed, either in-house or through external consultants. As mentioned earlier, the choice of test administration software may be impacted by the selection of test administration site, as some sites are restricted to the use of their own proprietary software.

The selection (or development) of a software program for computerized test administration should be based on the inclusion of essential software features, in a useful and usable manner. A given test program may have specific needs for software features related to measurement model, test delivery method, innovative item types, and more. In addition to these test-specific elements, any administration software program should include the facility for providing examinees with practice tests (APA, 1986) and clear instructions in how to take the test and respond to items (AERA, APA, & NCME, 1999). The software should also afford accommodations, such as large type for visually impaired examinees (APA, 1986). Finally, the software should be designed with recovery from technical problems in mind; that is, it should have the capability of recovering any data entered by an examinee prior to a hardware, software, or power failure (ATP, 2000).

Additional aspects of computerized test administration software, including guidelines for software evaluation, are addressed in Chapter 4.

Hardware for Computer-Based Testing

A minimal hardware configuration should be identified and specified for any test program that will be administered on computer. The specifications for hardware will usually include at least: type of computer, operating system, processing speed, random access memory (RAM) available, hard disk storage space available, monitor size and resolution, and response input devices (ATP, 2000). The test program's hardware platform should be identified early enough in the test development process so that items can be written, and reviewed, on the hardware platform that will be used in operational testing.

The operational hardware platform should be used consistently across test administrations and sites. If there is a lack of consistency in hardware devices (e.g., monitor size, keyboard, or mouse input devices), this could affect the comparability of test scores across examinees or the appropriateness of test norms (APA, 1986; Clauser & Schuwirth, in press).

Examinees should be provided with information about the computer hardware on which they will be tested and should be provided with opportunities in advance of testing to become familiar with the testing platform, including practice testing.

Reasonable accommodations should be provided; this may include extended testing time, larger monitors for visually impaired examinees, or the use of alternative entry devices for examinees with physical impairments (APA, 1986; ATP 2000). The test program may also consider the use of alternative response entry devices, such as touch screens and light pens, for particular applications or examinee populations (APA, 1986).

Security

Under paper-and-pencil administrations test security is primarily concerned with the protection of physical test booklets. For computer-based exams, however, a primary security concern is software. Transmission of data, both to and from the test site must be handled securely. Often, password protection along with data encryption and fragmentation are used. For example, at the test site encryption procedures are typically used in conjunction with limited access to the software to ensure the security of the items and their keys (Rosen, 2000; Shermis & Averitt, 2000; Way, 1998). The test program must ensure the security of test data, such as updated item pools, as well as examinee data, including personal registration information and test records (APA, 1986).

An additional test security issue concerns the procedures used to identify examinees that register for an exam. In some instances, this includes limiting permission to take an exam to those candidates listed in a roster or database (as occurs in some certification programs). In addition, computerized testing sites are often equipped with digital cameras; a photograph of each examinee may be stored along with his or her test record. Fingerprinting and possibly even retinal scans may be required by some high-stakes exam programs (Rosen, 2000). Additional security measures taken by the computer test site sometimes include video and audio taping of test administrations, along with monitoring by proctors to discourage or detect cheating (Rosen, 2000).

A problematic test security issue related to new technology concerns the increasing availability of miniature recording devices. Miniature cameras and video recorders (Colton, 1997; O'Neal, 1998) may put CBT text, graphic, and audio information at risk. A high-stakes exam may need to consider additional security approaches (Shermis & Averitt, 2000), including electronic countermeasures such as scanners and recorder nullifiers (Colton, 1997).

More frequent test administrations may also affect item security. Continuous testing exposes items over time in ways that are not entirely predictable. Actions to address this overexposure of items include administering exams only during limited testing windows, adjusting the test's item selection procedures to include exposure control parameters, and rotating or replacing entire item banks (e.g., Way, 1998). Exposure control in particular is an important item security topic. It is addressed in more detail later in this book.

Examinee Time

There is an inherent conflict in the imposition of time limits on test administrations. On the one hand, measurement concerns emphasize untimed conditions, particularly for IRT-based (i.e., Item Response Theory–based) exams, given that speededness can change the dimensionality of the test. On the other hand, scheduling examinees in and out of a computer lab necessitates some time limits. Furthermore, commercial test sites often bill the testing agency by *seat time*, or the amount of time the examinee uses the test site computer. Additionally, under untimed conditions, some anxious examinees will spend far more time than they need, making the exam more stressful and exhausting than it might otherwise be. A satisfactory compromise or resolution to this conflict is obviously needed, and most test programs elect to set a time limit that research suggests is no more than minimally speeded for the majority of examinees.

Beyond these general issues are several more subtle timing concerns that may arise. For example, exam times might need to be recorded separately for each test component, including registration and sign-on screens, instructional screens, and each exam in a battery of tests. Timing may also be a concern at the item level, particularly when tests are somewhat speeded. Even minor item presentation delays, such as those that can occur with graphical items or when testing over the Internet, need to be controlled. This time can be constrained so that it is equal across all administrations, or the exam's time limit can be computed without including the time for items to display on screen (ATP, 2000). Finally, in adaptively administered exams that are variable-length, a time limit that is sufficient for the maximum test length must be established.

Administration Frequency

The number of exam dates a computer-based test is available for administration should be based on several factors. First, the testing program must consider the overall number of examinees who are likely to test. Next, the number of test computers available needs to be determined, along with the amount of time those computers will be available to the testing program. This available time will be based on the hours and days a week when computer labs are open, availability of proctors, and the computers that are not being used for other test programs or activities. These figures provide a baseline for test administration frequency.

For security purposes, an exam program may want to further limit the availability of a test. That is, rather than allowing examinees to test on any day throughout the month or year, test administrations may be limited to "testing windows." Testing windows limit the scheduling availability of an exam; for example, a test may be available for administration two days per week or only one week per month.

Conversely, the times examinees are likely to consider most desirable for administration must also be considered. For some testing programs (including many certification programs), examinees will naturally disperse their scheduled administrations throughout the calendar year. In other instances (e.g., college admissions), a majority of examinees will want to schedule their exams within a fairly short time period. Under this more demanding situation, it may be necessary to ensure the availability of many additional computers for a short period of time in order to meet the demand.

Cost Concerns

The costing structure for a computerized exam is likely to be very different from that of a paper-and-pencil exam. There may be cost savings due to reduced printing and shipping costs. Test programs where paper-and-pencil exams have been administered individually may save on salaries for exam proctors after switching to computerized administration. In general, however, computer-based testing is more expensive. This higher cost is the result of such elements as the test administration software (whether purchased or developed internally), the additional items that must be developed, the psychometric research to support the program, and the computer test site fees. Part or all of the additional cost is often passed along to the examinees. Given this higher cost to the examinee, it is helpful to ensure that examinees see advantages to the CBT, particularly when both paper-and-pencil and CBT versions of an exam are offered. Otherwise, very few examinees may choose the less familiar and more costly CBT version. The most common advantages that examinees perceive are more frequent test dates and immediate scoring. Additional discussion of CBT economics (and other logistical matters) is provided in Vale (1995) and Clauser and Schuwirth (in press).

Test Program Support

Administrative support of test programs is very different for computerized tests, particularly those offered under continuous testing. Changes need to be made in program procedures such as registration, proctoring, and scoring. More frequent test dates necessitate a change in support from intensive but occasional support, associated with a few test administration dates per year, to a near-constant trickle across continuous test dates. In addition to direct support for test registration and proctoring, test program support includes provision of information and problem resolution. Pertinent information about procedures for registering, scheduling, checking in, taking a practice test, and taking the actual test should be made fully available to examinees, along with any relevant aspects of test security (ATP, 2000). Finally, under continuous test administration, test problems arise more frequently, but when they do arise, they only affect a small number of examinees. This is different from paper-and-pencil administration problems, which are likely to affect large numbers of examinees when they occur. Fortunately, many of the problems that do arise in CBT administration are considerably lessened due to the ease in rescheduling exams.

Test Development Issues

In addition to the test administration issues just addressed, a number of test development issues must be considered. Issues in the psychometric planning of a computer-based test occur in several stages, discussed in detail herein. In addition, appropriate measures of reliability and evidence of test validity need to be obtained. Finally, new schedules for conducting data analyses must be determined, and comparability concerns may need to be satisfied. Each of these issues is addressed here.

Planning the Test

There are a number of psychometric issues related to planning the test, including developing the test blueprint, defining the test characteristics, developing the item pool, obtaining the item statistics, and conducting computerized simulations. These stages in CBT development are introduced next.

1. Determine the composite of traits that the test should measure in order to develop *the test blueprint*. This process will vary depending on the subject matter being assessed. For example, developing the

test specifications for an algebra test is fairly simple. The domain of knowledge to be assessed is well defined and easily identified. A more complex situation is the development of the test specifications for a certification or licensure test. These types of tests generally require a job or task analysis to determine the appropriate domain of content that should be included in the test specifications. The result is a content blueprint, which facilitates item development and defines how many items should be included from each content area.

2. Define *the test characteristics* desired. At minimum, this should include test length, measurement precision, and the maximum acceptable rates at which items can be used or exposed to examinees. Technical properties such as rules and procedures for item selection, scoring methods, and the characteristics of reported scores should be tentatively specified.

3. Develop or identify the set of items that might comprise a suitable *CBT item pool*. An extensive item-writing and pretesting effort is often needed.

4. Depending on the delivery method to be used, one may need to obtain *item statistics* (classical or IRT–based) to facilitate the construction of tests. For adaptive tests (CAT or CCT) item statistics are required.

5. Some test delivery methods (e.g., ATA, CAT, and CCT) use software to select items either to construct test forms prior to online administration or for administration in real time. It is imperative for tests of this nature to conduct a series of *computerized simulations* to predict how the test might perform operationally. A computerized simulation considers many different factors that can impact the efficiency and accuracy of a test. The simulation process permits a test developer to select the best set of controls to strike a balance between competing factors. Simulations are discussed in greater detail in Chapter 10.

6. Compare predicted test performance to the desired characteristics. Adjust test specifications, testing procedures, or outcome expectations as required.

7. Finalize the operational specifications and procedures.

Steps 1 through 5 are discussed in more detail next. The remaining steps are discussed further in Chapter 10.

The Test Blueprint

Test specifications are the details that define what a test is designed to measure and how the assessment will be accomplished. The test specifications for many testing programs moving from a traditional paper-and-pencil examination to a

CBT require little or no revision. For new testing programs, test specifications need to be developed.

The first steps in developing any CBT are identical to those undertaken when conventional tests are developed. Determining what a test is to measure and developing items to effectively do so are processes well described in other references (e.g., Crocker & Algina, 1986) and will not be detailed in this book. One of the differences for CBTs results from the expanded range of item types made possible by computerized test administration. More information about these possibilities can be found in Chapter 5.

The product of these steps is a blueprint that specifies the type, format, and content characteristics for each item on the test. The options and flexibility are almost endless. The test can comprise discrete items, stimulus-based units, or a combination of the two. Even discrete items can be formed into bundles that are always administered collectively (see Wainer, 1990, for a discussion of the benefits of these bundles, called *testlets*). Items can allow for any means of responding, provided scoring is objective and immediate. Although multiple choice is currently the dominant item type, alternatives are available and are becoming more prevalent. Lastly, the content characteristics of the items and the proportion of the test devoted to each content domain are specified. This in turn specifies the constraints under which items are selected during test administration.

The Test Characteristics

The decisions made at this point in time are also much like those made during the conventional paper-and-pencil test development process. These decisions are driven by intended uses of the test and practical and economic circumstances. The test developer frequently encounters these complicating matters that are either confounded or in conflict with one another. Consider, for example, the matter of test length. Test length primarily depends on how precise or reliable the test needs to be. Item quality enters into the equation at this point because adaptive tests comprising more discriminating items can afford to be a bit shorter than those based on less discriminating items. Item exposure control restricts access to the most discriminating items, thereby complicating the matter. This is a function of how secure the test needs to be and how frequently the test will be administered using the same item pool. Other aspects of item selection and test scoring also are relevant, including pool size, composition, and how strictly content must be balanced. Practical considerations put a limit on the amount of time an examinee can reasonably be asked to devote to the test. Finally, economic concerns are significant if test administration costs depend on the amount of time the examinee is seated in front of the computer. Sorting out all of these competing priorities can be a difficult and often contentious process. However, by the end of the process, decisions are required to balance all of these factors so that a test that meets the desired test characteristics is produced.

During the development of specifications, the following questions should be considered:

1. How reliable must the test be? Often, a CBT is required to match the reliability of the existing paper-and-pencil test that it is replacing.
2. Will the test length be fixed or variable? If a test is to be a fixed length, how long must it be to reach the required level of reliability? If a test is to be variable in length, what are the minimum and maximum test lengths and the required precision?
3. How large should the item pool be? What should its composition be?
4. What content specifications should be imposed on item selection?
5. What item selection rules or procedures will be used? How will the first item be selected for administration?
6. How frequently will items be permitted to be administered to examinees? What methods will be used to protect item security?
7. How will the test be scored? How will scores be reported to examinees?

The CBT Item Pool

An item pool is a collection of test items that can be used to assemble or construct a computer-based test. The item pool should include sufficient numbers of items of satisfactory quality, appropriately targeted to examinee ability. Requirements for the item pool are related to the test purpose, the test delivery method, the measurement or statistical assumptions of the model used to obtain the item characteristics within the pool (i.e., the model used to describe the interaction of an examinee with an item), the test length, the frequency of test administrations, and security requirements. In other words, the item pool should be developed with the size and composition best suited to the test's content and technical requirements; however, compromise of some sort on this ideal may be necessary.

The items in the pool usually have been administered previously so that they have some data or item characteristics associated with them. These are called *operational items*. For example, it is typical for each operational item within a CBT item pool to have a difficulty index or value, as well as some measure of the item's ability or potential to discriminate between examinees. In addition, items within an item pool typically are associated with certain content classifications or categories.

Most standardized testing programs routinely add items to the available pool through regular item writing and pretesting efforts. The operational items in the pool can be contrasted with *pretest* or *tryout items*. Pretest items are usually administered on a trial basis during an operational exam and are not scored. Typically, pretest items are administered fewer examinees than operational or scored items. Therefore, the statistics computed for the pretest items often suffer from larger standard errors of estimate than their operational counterparts and may not reliably represent the item's performance on an operational form.

Nevertheless, if item analyses show that the items are performing adequately, they subsequently can be used operationally.

An item pool that has been used for a paper-and-pencil assessment program may need additional items to be developed before it can go online, particularly if any kind of adaptive test is planned. Further, CBTs often have a continuing need for many more new items to be written and pretested. In fact, for some testing programs the need to satisfy the voracious requirement for items has become one of the most challenging aspects of computerizing the exam. One cause of the increased need for items in computer-based testing is the more frequent administration of tests. The continuous test administrations cause items to be exposed over time, potentially affecting test security. Furthermore, in the adaptive test delivery methods, items are individually administered at differing frequencies. The most desirable items (e.g., for many CATs, items of middle difficulty and high discrimination) tend to be exposed most frequently and may need to be retired from the item pool particularly quickly. These requirements for additional items are especially relevant for high-stakes exams, less so for low-stakes test programs. In low-stakes applications, an item pool only needs to be large enough to provide good measurement, without the additional need to address test security.

The need for large numbers of items in many computer-based testing programs is often coupled with a need for examinee response data from a large number of appropriate examinees. In addition, continuous testing results in a slower, more gradual accumulation of sufficient numbers of examinees to compute item statistics. The number of pretest examinees needed is related to the measurement model in use; test programs using classical test theory are less demanding than those using IRT. Item parameter estimates that are computed using an insufficient number of examinees are likely to be poor, leading to lessened test score precision (Hambleton & Jones, 1994).

For these reasons, computerized fixed test programs, or CFTs, that use classical methods and are applied in low-stakes settings have fewer demands than other delivery methods. The automated test assembly method, or ATA, requires a greater item writing and pretesting effort, due to its use of multiple forms. The adaptive methods, computerized classification testing and computerized adaptive testing (CCT and CAT) also experience greater demands for additional items. An adaptive exam program often requires a large initial set of items and a greater need to replenish the item pool regularly. Furthermore, pretesting large numbers of items can be a particular issue for short adaptive tests, given the proportion of pretest-to-operational items. These demands typically are greater for a CAT than a CCT. Further discussion of pretesting accommodation is provided in each of the chapters covering test delivery methods. More discussion of the issues in CBT item development and pretesting is provided by Parshall (2000).

Prior to implementing computer-based testing, it is important to conduct an evaluation of the existing item pool. This evaluation includes an assessment of the quality of the current items and, if a measurement model is assumed, a test of the goodness-of-model-fit. It should also include a computer-simulation phase, in which the adequacy of the pool can be further examined. Simulations can assist in the determination of the extent to which the pool can support different test delivery methods. More information regarding computer simulations is presented next, while both computer simulations and pool evaluation are discussed in more technical detail in Chapter 10.

The Item Statistics

There are several important assumptions that must be met before a testing program can migrate from traditional paper-and-pencil testing to a computer-based program. These assumptions include those that relate to the test items and the quality of their item statistics.

Most pools consist of items with content identification and statistical or psychometric characteristics. It is rare that items in a CBT item pool have no data at all. Usually, it is assumed that the statistical data have been obtained from similar examinee populations. This is especially true when the statistical characteristics consist of the more traditional p-values (i.e., the item's difficulty index or proportion of correct responses to the item) and point-biserial correlation coefficients (i.e., the item's discrimination index).

It is also assumed that the statistics represent the performance of the item free from context effects. Context effects may include such things as page breaks, test speededness, and item-response dependency. Most of these effects are due to conditions that can occur within a paper-and-pencil test administration. For example, an item whose stem or stimulus might appear in its entirety on one test form but appear broken or on two pages in another form may have different characteristics simply due to the page-break effect. If these statistical characteristics of that item are then used in a CBT situation where the item will appear unbroken on the computer monitor, then the statistics obtained when it appeared on two pages may not reflect the operating characteristics of the item as part of a computer-based test.

Similarly, items that have appeared on a paper-and-pencil test that is *speeded*, (i.e., one in which not all examinees reach those items near the end of the test with enough time to be able to provide thoughtful responses that reflect their true ability) may not have statistics that accurately describe the item's performance on a computer-based test.

Finally, items that appear together on a paper-and-pencil form in such a way that some items interact with others to modify the responses to those items may exhibit certain statistical characteristics that may not reflect the item's performance when it appears without the other items. In these situations, the items are said to be *dependent* in the sense that the correct response to an item may depend on other items in addition to the ability of the examinee. However, as part of a CBT item pool, the item may or may not be administered to an examinee in the same order or with the other items that appeared with it on the paper-and-pencil form. Thus, its characteristics again may not accurately describe its performance on a CBT.

All of these are situations in which the examinees in the calibration sample may not have responded to the items in the same ways or under the same circumstances that operational CBT examinees eventually will. Some general points to consider in this regard include the following:

1. Were the data gathered under computerized or pencil-and-paper test administration? If the latter, is it reasonable to assume that items will perform similarly across modes? This assumption is reasonable if computerized presentation of the items closely parallels conventional administration. For example, items should not have to be scrolled to be fully viewed on screen. Items should not require or even invite extensive notations on the test booklet.
2. Were the data gathered from motivated examinees? An example of unmotivated examinees might be those asked to participate in a special study to pretest items.
3. Were the data gathered under conditions approximating operational testing? For example, were items administered in a fixed or random context? The former would be true if the data were based on fixed forms. But with a CAT or CCT, a given item may be preceded by any other item in the pool. An item also may appear at the beginning, middle, or end of a test rather than in the same fixed location. This distinction is particularly important if the prior administration is more or less speeded than the operational CBT.

In summary, items within a CBT item pool are assumed to have statistical characteristics associated with them that are valid for CBT situations. The best way to ensure that this condition is met is to obtain the statistical item data under CBT conditions. When this cannot be done, then some caution must be made regarding the decisions obtained with CBTs assembled from item pools that have been transferred directly from paper-and-pencil programs. This is also true of item pools that are IRT-based. Item calibrations obtained from paper-and-pencil forms will not necessarily reflect the performance of the items within a CBT context.

Once an item has been calibrated *online* however (i.e., as part of a CBT program), it is usually assumed that these online calibrations *will* represent the true performance of that item, even though the item will most likely appear in a different order and with different items for each examinee. It is assumed that these effects will cancel out across examinees so that an item's characteristics as measured online will accurately reflect that item's performance overall (i.e., over all examinees and over all possible computer-based tests).

The Computerized Simulations

Simulations are often used to answer questions that are difficult or impossible to approach more directly. For example, a flight simulator might be used to observe a pilot's performance in situations that would be dangerous to actually experience. Other uses of simulations are motivated by considerations that are more mundane. Such is the case with the evaluation of adaptive testing procedures.

Simulations are, first and foremost, much cheaper, faster, and more convenient to conduct than studies using actual examinees. However, their appeal is not simply practical; they also offer compelling theoretical advantages, such as complete experimental control. Simulated examinees do not drop out of studies before the conclusion. Simulated examinees can be assigned to exactly equivalent groups. In addition, simulated examinees can be tested repeatedly without the process of measurement changing the traits that are measured. An even more important theoretical advantage is that simulated examinees have known true abilities. Knowing the true ability of an examinee makes it easy to evaluate whether a test is measuring accurately.

An important benefit of IRT is the convenient process it offers for generating simulated data. Simulated data consist of sets of item responses that appear to have been produced by actual examinees. Once item parameters are set, simulated examinees and responses can be generated using the following process.

First, choose and define an "examinee" by assigning an ability value. This can be done in one of two ways for one of two purposes. First, examinees can be assigned specifically chosen ability values. For example, if the focus is on how a test measures able examinees, a high ability value would be assigned. A special case of this is to assign each of several examinees ability values that evenly span a given range. A common choice is to use the values −3.0, −2.9, −2.8,…,0.0, 0.1,…2.9, 3.0, resulting in 61 evenly spaced ability levels. This is useful for evaluating how a test's measurement properties change across the ability scale. (An example is also provided in Chapter 8 in which larger increments are used over the θ range [−4, +4].)

A second way of assigning abilities is by randomly drawing values from some plausible distribution. This is analogous to randomly drawing examinees from some population. This would be done to evaluate a test's aggregate properties in a target population. For example, in order to predict a test's score distribution, examinees would be randomly sampled, each would be tested, and the score results tallied. Randomly sampling examinees would also be used to determine how frequently a given item might be administered during an adaptive test.

Once the examinee parameters are assigned, they can be used along with the item parameters to simulate examinee responses to items. The probability of a given examinee correctly answering a given item is computed by evaluating the response function for that item at the ability level for that examinee. A right or wrong answer is then determined by comparing that probability with a random draw from a uniform distribution between zero and one. A uniform distribution is one in which each value has an equal probability of occurring. If the uniform value falls below the response probability (the chances of which are equal to that probability), then the answer is marked correct. If, instead, the uniform draw is greater than the response probability (the chances of which are one minus the probability), the answer is marked as wrong. This process is repeated for every item administered to every examinee.

This process makes it easy to simulate the administration of thousands of adaptive tests. The resulting data are then analyzed to predict how the test will perform once it is operational. Of primary interest is the complicated interaction of test length, test precision, item pool size, and the extent to which pool usage is balanced. Finding the proper compromise among these competing priorities is often a matter of trial and error.

Summary of Planning the Test

Each of the stages in the planning and development of a CBT is important to good measurement. However, as noted previously, differing requirements for a testing program tend to serve as competing goals, and a compromise across these competing goals or targets is often necessary. Some of the topics introduced here are addressed further in this book, particularly within the context of specific test delivery methods (e.g., CFT, CAT).

Further test development needs, and how they may differ for computer-based tests, are discussed next.

Reliability

Reliability, or the precision or consistency of test scores, is important for any testing program, whether exams are administered via paper and pencil or computer (Crocker & Algina, 1986; AERA, APA, & NCME, 1985). There is nothing inherent to computerized administration that automatically aids or limits test reliability. A well-designed computer-based test is as capable as a paper-and-pencil test of demonstrating adequate reliability. However, the appropriate measure of reliability depends on the test purpose and design and on the test delivery method used. For example, for classically scored computer-based tests (e.g., CFT, ATA), traditional methods of estimating reliability, such as KR-20, are appropriate. For computer-based tests that are designed to classify examinees into classes or categories (e.g., CCT), an appropriate measure of reliability is an estimate of the proportion of examinees consistently classified on more than one test administration. Adaptive tests that use IRT methods for item selection and scoring (e.g., CAT) can use the standard error of measurement (SEM) to estimate reliability at any given ability estimate. Adaptive exams tend to have greater reliability for examinees with extreme abilities than traditional tests composed of a fixed set of items. An average reliability measure over all examinee ability levels, sometimes referred to as a *marginal reliability*, can also be estimated for CAT. Depending on the test application, it may be important to investigate and report separate reliability estimates for examinee subgroups, for different test platforms (e.g., computer-based or paper-and-pencil tests), or for variable administration conditions (ATP, 2000). Reliability is addressed further in each of the chapters in this book addressing the specific test delivery methods.

Validity

To demonstrate validity, any test instrument (whether administered in paper-and-pencil or computer mode) must be designed according to a clear construct definition, use appropriate test specifications, and be composed of well-written items. For any computerized test that represents a newly developed exam program, evidence of validity can be obtained using the standard methods for establishing validity in paper-and-pencil assessments (see Crocker & Algina, 1986). Alternatively, when a computer version has been designed to parallel an existing paper-and-pencil test (for which the validity of test scores has already been established), equivalence between the two delivery methods can be used as evidence of comparable estimates of validity for the computer version (Green, Bock, Humphreys, Linn, & Reckase, 1984).

Given the foundation of a well-developed exam program, the test administration mode should not be critical to test validity. However, for some applications, some item types, or some examinee groups, it is conceivable that computer-based administration could serve as a source of construct-irrelevant variance. Thus, an investigation of potential test mode effect (i.e., paper-and-pencil versus computer) may be appropriate and even necessary (ATP, 2000). This topic is addressed further under Comparability later.

For an adaptive test delivery method, a specific concern for content validity may arise. The adaptive exam may administer items from differing content levels very unevenly across examinees. When balanced administration of subcontent areas is a concern, then content-based requirements can be added to the exam's statistical item selection procedures.

One additional type of validity evidence may be necessary. If the test includes an alternative scoring approach, perhaps to an innovative item type, it may be important to investigate and establish the appropriateness of the scoring approach. Scoring methods may be more or less well aligned with an optimal measure of the construct of interest and should be documented to the extent that they do not conflict with the testing program's need for security. A rationale or theory for the scoring approach used, along with research evidence as to its efficacy, should be provided (APA, 1986; ATP, 2000; NCME, 2000).

Of course, the results of any validity studies must be reported with sufficient details about the examinee sample, hardware, software, and administrative procedures to inform test users adequately. Examinees and potential examinees should be informed about adaptive item selection (if present) and appropriate score interpretation (APA, 1986; ATP, 2000; AERA, APA, & NCME, 1985).

Data Analyses

For testing programs that administer exams periodically (e.g., the traditional paper-and-pencil format), as opposed to continuously, data analyses are easily scheduled and performed. After each periodic, large-group administration, a number of psychometric procedures are routinely conducted using the full set of examinee test data (Crocker & Algina, 1986). Item performance can be examined through computation of the classical item statistics measuring difficulty (p-values$)$ and discrimination (point-biserial correlation coefficient$)$, or through IRT calibration. Distractor analyses can be performed to determine the proportion of examinees selecting each response option. The possibility of item bias is usually investigated through an analysis of *differential item functioning* (DIF). For fixed-form exams, the mean performance of examinees and the reliability of each test form can be computed, and if necessary, each test form can be equated to a base form, and standard setting can be conducted.

Conversely, for most computer-based testing programs, exams are administered far more frequently and to far fewer examinees on any given test date. Each of these CBT exams can be scored as soon as each individual examinee has completed testing. However, the change to continuous test administration necessitates a change in the procedures for the analysis of test data. The testing program can establish regular intervals (e.g., quarterly) for item and test data analysis. All test data accumulated during each of these periods can be collapsed, and various group-level analyses can be conducted. Reports can then be generated, summarizing the results of item, subtest, and test analyses for the testing period (as opposed to the single test-administration date used in more traditional test programs). For some analyses, particularly analyses on examinee subgroups, an insufficient number of examinees may test during a reporting interval. In these instances, data should be collected over time until sufficient samples are available, at which point the additional analyses can be conducted (ATP, 2000).

This delayed approach to item and test analysis is not entirely satisfactory. In less frequently administered, standardized, paper-and-pencil testing, these analyses can be conducted prior to the release of test scores. If problems are found (e.g., a negative discrimination or a high DIF value), then the problematic items can be removed before the test is scored. However, when these analyses are delayed, as is the case in most CBT applications, the possibility exists that flawed items remain in the operational pool for a much longer period and will be included in many examinees' final test scores.

Comparability

There are a number of circumstances under which the comparability of test scores needs to be established. An example in which comparability might be a concern is the situation in which a computer-based test and a paper-and-pencil version of the same test are offered for simultaneous administration. This situation is referred to as maintaining an exam program across *dual platforms*. There may also be versions of the CBT in multiple languages. In addition, for security reasons a testing program may use more than one item pool. Finally, the maintenance of a single item pool may produce substantive changes in the pool over time, as the items in the pool are removed and new items used to replenish the pool. In all of these cases, it may be important to investigate test comparability (Wang & Kolen, 1997).

The initial concern for comparability was that of *mode effect* (APA, 1986). Numerous studies compared examinee test scores obtained across computer and paper-and-pencil test administration modes. Reviews of many of these early comparability studies were conducted by Mazzeo and Harvey (1988) and by Mead and Drasgow (1993). The overall results of these early comparability studies suggested that test administration mode did not result in significant differences for most power tests, although differences were found for speed tests. However, some items and some item types did produce mode differences. It is therefore recommended that any test program using scores as though they were equivalent across dual platforms document the results of a comparability study (APA, 1986; ATP, 2000). In fact, most of the early comparability studies investigated tests comprised of discrete, single-screen item types. There is a concern that multiscreen items, graphical items, and innovative item types may be more subject to mode effect differences. This issue is related to the potential effect that specific item presentation elements may have on item performance. (Godwin, 1999; Pommerich & Burden, 2000). Pommerich & Burden (2000) provide an example of research into the impact that subtle item formatting differences may have across modes.

Another aspect of comparability may arise when two or more pools are used for the construction of adaptive tests. If more than one pool is used to assemble tests or if the items in a single pool change over time, then differences in item content or statistical characteristics could create a lack of comparability (Wang & Kolen, 1997). Within adaptively administered exams, an additional comparability issue is that of content balancing across individual examinees. Content rules can be incorporated into the item selection algorithms to address these issues, but comparability studies may be needed to document the level of their effectiveness.

Summary

Table 2.1 provides a list of highlights from the topics related to test administration and development introduced in this chapter. Several of these topics are further addressed later in this book, particularly as they are related to specific test delivery methods and other aspects of computer-based testing.

Table 2.1 Highlights of Test Administration and Development Issues

Test Administration	*Recommendation*
Test sites	Ensure an environment that is quiet, comfortable, and conducive to testing.
Software	Select software that has the necessary features for the test program.
Hardware	Maintain consistent hardware configuration across test administrations.
Security	Use data encryption procedures to protect the test data.
Examinee time	Establish a maximum time limit that avoids speededness but allows scheduling.
Administration frequency	Set an administration frequency that meets the testing volume need with the computers available.
Cost concerns	Provide benefits to examinees to offset additional fees.
Test program support	Schedule staff support to meet program needs across continuous test administrations.

Test Development	*Recommendation*
Test blueprint	Specify what the test will measure and the type, format, and content of the items.
Test characteristics	Define such test characteristics as test length, measurement precision, and exposure rates.
CBT item pool	Evaluate the current items and initiate pretesting to increase the pool.
Item statistics	If possible, collect statistical item data by administering items on computer.
Computerized simulations	Conduct simulations to predict how the test will perform operationally; revise the test as necessary.
Reliability	Estimate the test reliability, using an appropriate measure.
Validity	Investigate test validity using standard means, or correlate CBT to existing paper-and-pencil version.
Data analyses	Conduct test analyses at regular intervals on all data accumulated during that time period.
Comparability	If the test program maintains dual platforms, investigate the comparability of scores across the two modes.

References

American Educational Research Association (AERA), American Psychological Association (APA), and the National Council on Measurement in Education (NCME). (1985). Standards for educational and psychological testing. Washington, DC: APA.

American Educational Research Association (AERA), American Psychological Association (APA), and the National Council on Measurement in Education (NCME). (1999). Standards for educational and psychological testing. Washington, DC: AERA.

American Psychological Association Committee on Professional Standards and Committee on Psychological Tests and Assessment. (APA). (1986). Guidelines for computer-based tests and interpretations. Washington, DC: Author

Association of Test Publishers (ATP). (2000). *Computer-Based Testing Guidelines.*

Clauser, B. E., & Schuwirth, L. W. T. (in press). The use of computers in assessment. In G. Norman, C. van der Vleuten, & D. Newble (Eds.), *The International Handbook for Research in Medical Education.* Boston: Kluwer Publishing.

Colton, G. D. (1997). High-tech approaches to breaching examination security. Paper presented at the annual meeting of NCME, Chicago.

Crocker, L. & Algina, J. (1986). *Introduction to Classical and Modern Test Theory.* Ft. Worth: Holt, Rinehart & Winston.

Godwin, J. (1999, April). Designing the ACT ESL Listening Test. Paper presented at the annual meeting of the National Council on Measurement in Education, Montreal, Canada.

Green, B. F., Bock R. D., Humphreys, L. G., Linn, R. L., & Reckase, M. D. (1984). Technical guidelines for assessing computerized adaptive tests. *Journal of Educational Measurement*, 21, 347–360.

Hambleton, R. K., & Jones, R. W. (1994). Item parameter estimation errors and their influence on test information functions. *Applied Measurement in Education*, 7, 171–186.

Mazzeo, J., & Harvey, A. L. (1988). The equivalence of scores from automated and conventional educational and psychological tests: A review of the literature (College Board Rep. No. 88-8, ETS RR No. 88-21). Princeton, NJ: Educational Testing Service.

Mead, A. D., & Drasgow, F. (1993). Equivalence of computerized and paper-and-pencil cognitive ability tests: A meta-analysis. *Psychological Bulletin*, 9, 287–304.

NCME Software Committee. (2000). Report of NCME Ad Hoc Committee on Software Issues in Educational Measurement. Available online: http://www.b-a-h.com/ncmesoft/report.html.

O'Neal, C. W. (1998). Surreptitious audio surveillance: The unknown danger to law enforcement. *FBI Law Enforcement Bulletin*, 67, 10–13.

Parshall, C. G. (In press). Item development and pretesting. In C. Mills (Ed.) *Computer-Based Testing.* Lawrence Erlbaum.

Pommerich, M., & Burden, T. (2000). From simulation to application: Examinees react to computerized testing. Paper presented at the annual meeting of the National Council on Measurement in Education, New Orleans.

Rosen, G.A. (2000, April). Computer-based testing: Test site security. Paper presented at the annual meeting of the National Council on Measurement in Education, New Orleans.

Shermis, M., & Averitt, J. (2000, April). Where did all the data go? Internet security for Web-based assessments. Paper presented at the annual meeting of the National Council on Measurement in Education, New Orleans.

Vale, C. D. (1995). Computerized testing in licensure. In J. C. Impara (Ed.) *Licensure Testing: Purposes, Procedures, and Practices.* Lincoln, NE: Buros Institute of Mental Measurement.

Wainer, H. (Ed.) (1990). *Computerized Adaptive Testing: A Primer.* Hillsdale, NJ: Lawrence Erlbaum.

Wang, T., & Kolen, M. J. (1997, March). Evaluating comparability in computerized adaptive testing: A theoretical framework. Paper presented at the annual meeting of the American Educational Research Association, Chicago.

Way, W. D. (1998). Protecting the integrity of computerized testing item pools. *Educational Measurement: Issues and Practice,* 17, 17–27.

Additional Readings

Bugbee, A. C., & Bernt, F. M. (1990). Testing by computer: Findings in six years of use. *Journal of Research on Computing in Education,* 23, 87–100.

Buhr, D. C., & Legg, S. M. (1989). *Development of an Adaptive Test Version of the College Level Academic Skills Test.* (Institute for Student Assessment and Evaluation, Contract No. 88012704). Gainesville, FL: University of Florida.

Bunderson, C. V., Inouye, D. K., & Olsen, J. B. (1989). The four generations of computerized educational measurement. In R. L. Linn (Ed.), *Educational Measurement* (3rd ed., pp. 367–408). New York: Macmillan.

Eaves, R. C., & Smith, E. (1986). The effect of media and amount of microcomputer experience on examination scores. *Journal of Experimental Education,* 55, 23–26.

Eignor, D. R. (1993, April). Deriving Comparable Scores for Computer Adaptive and Conventional Tests: An Example Using the SAT. Paper presented at the annual meeting of the National Council on Measurement in Education, Atlanta.

Greaud, V. A., & Green, B. F. (1986). Equivalence of conventional and computer presentation of speed tests. *Applied Psychological Measurement,* 10, 23–34.

Green, B. F., Bock, R. D., Humphreys, L. G., Linn, R. L., & Reckase, M. D. (1984). Technical guidelines for assessing computerized adaptive tests. *Journal of Educational Measurement,* 21, 347–360.

Haynie, K. A., & Way, W. D. (1995, April). An Investigation of Item Calibration Procedures for a Computerized Licensure Examination. Paper presented at symposium entitled Computer Adaptive Testing, at the annual meeting of NCME, San Francisco.

Heppner, F. H., Anderson, J. G. T., Farstrup, A. E., & Weiderman, N. H. (1985). Reading performance on a standardized test is better from print than from computer display. *Journal of Reading,* 28, 321–325.

Hoffman, K. I., & Lundberg, G. D. (1976). A comparison of computer-monitored group tests with paper-and-pencil tests. *Educational and Psychological Measurement,* 36, 791–809.

Keene, S., & Davey, B. (1987). Effects of computer-presented text on LD adolescents' reading behaviors. *Learning Disability Quarterly*, 10, 283–290.

Lee, J. A. (1986). The effects of past computer experience on computerized aptitude test performance. *Educational and Psychological Measurement*, 46, 721–733.

Lee, J. A., Moreno, K. E., & Sympson, J. B. (1986). The effects of mode of test administration on test performance. *Educational and Psychological Measurement*, 46, 467–473.

Legg, S. M., & Buhr, D. C. (1990). Investigating Differences in Mean Scores on Adaptive and Paper and Pencil Versions of the College Level Academic Skills Reading Test. Presented at the annual meeting of the National Council on Measurement in Education.

Linn, R. L. (Ed.). The four generations of computerized educational measurement. *Educational Measurement*, 3rd ed., pp. 367–408, NY: MacMillan.

Llabre, M. M., & Froman, T. W. (1987). Allocation of time to test items: A study of ethnic differences. *Journal of Experimental Education*, 55, 137–140.

Mason, G. E. (1987). The relationship between computer technology and the reading process: Match or misfit? *Computers in the Schools*, 4, 15–23.

Mills, C. (1994, April). The Introduction and Comparability of the Computer Adaptive GRE General Test. Symposium presented at the annual meeting of the National Council on Measurement in Education, New Orleans.

Olsen, J. B., Maynes, D. D., Slawson, D., & Ho, K. (1989). Comparisons of paper-administered, computer-administered and computerized adaptive achievement tests. *Journal of Educational Computing Research*, 5, 311–326.

Parshall, C. G., & Kromrey, J. D. (1993, April). Computer testing vs. Paper and pencil testing: an analysis of examinee characteristics associated with mode effect. Paper presented at the annual meeting of the American Educational Research Association, Atlanta.

Raffeld, P. C., Checketts, K., & Mazzeo, J. (1990). Equating Scores from Computer-Based and Paper-Pencil Versions of College Level English and Mathematics Achievement Tests. Presented at the annual meeting of the National Council on Measurement in Education.

Sachar, J. D., & Fletcher, J. D. (1978). Administering paper-and-pencil tests by computer, or the medium is not always the message. In D. J. Weiss (Ed.), *Proceedings of the 1977 Computerized Adaptive Testing Conference*. Wayzata, MN: University of Minnesota.

Stocking, M. L. (1988). *Scale Drift in On-Line Calibration*. (Report No. 88-28-ONR). Princeton, NJ: Educational Testing Service.

Sykes, R. C., & Fitzpatrick, A. R. (1992). The stability of IRT b values. *Journal of Educational Measurement*, 29, 201–211.

Wise, S. L., & Plake, B. S. (1989). Research on the effects of administering tests via computers. *Educational Measurement: Issues and Practice*, 3, 5–10.

3
Examinee Issues

A computer-based testing program has numerous psychometric needs, and it can be easy to get so involved with these psychometric details that other essential points of view are lost. It is important to remember that every time an exam is given there is a person on the other end of the computer screen and to consider the reality of the testing experience for the examinee. Various steps can be taken to reduce examinee stress and make the experience more pleasant (or at least less unpleasant). Hopefully, these steps will reduce confounding variance and help produce a test that is as fair as possible. Those testing programs that are elective (i.e., that examinees are not required to take) have a particular need to ensure that the computerized testing experience is not onerous. There is little benefit in developing a wonderful test that no one chooses to take. This chapter will briefly address some computerized testing issues from the examinees' point of view.

Overall Reactions

Examinees' overall reactions to computer-based tests have been obtained under both motivated and unmotivated conditions. The pilot-testing stage of CBT development often includes a survey of the potential examinees. The examinees are asked about their reactions to the experience of testing on computer and about their preference for testing mode (e.g., "Would you prefer to take a test: on computer; on paper; no preference"). In those studies that involved unmotivated conditions, examinees overall were quite positive about testing on computer, and results frequently showed examinees expressing a preference for CBT over paper-and-pencil testing (e.g., O'Neill & Kubiak, 1992). These results certainly are encouraging. However, it should not be surprising that examinees are more critical under operational conditions in which they receive actual test scores that may impact their academic or career opportunities. This section will highlight some of the most commonly offered reactions by examinees to testing on computer.

First of all, examinees tend to be positive about certain aspects of computerized testing. In general, they are particularly positive about the increased frequency of test-administration dates and the availability of immediate scoring typical of many CBT programs. They are also positive about the shorter testing times possible under adaptive test-delivery methods. Many examinees prefer responding to multiple-choice items on a CBT, where they can click or select an answer, rather than having to "bubble in" a response on a scannable paper form. Examinees may also indicate that certain innovative item types seem to provide for more accurate assessment of their knowledge and skills in a given area.

Examinees have also reported negative reactions to computerized testing. Some examinees have a general anxiety about the computer itself, while others are more concerned about whether their level of computer experience is adequate for the task (Wise, 1997). Sometimes examinees object to computer-based tests because of built-in task constraints. They find it more difficult or awkward within a CBT environment to do such things as take notes or perform mathematical computations. More specifically, examinees may have difficulty with certain aspects of the user interface, or they may object to particular elements of adaptive test delivery.

The primary examinee objections are discussed in somewhat more detail later, along with suggestions for alleviating their potential negative impact.

Reactions to Adaptive Delivery Methods

Although computer-based tests provide many features not available in a paper-and-pencil environment, they may also include some restrictions. One critical example of this is that adaptive tests generally restrict examinees from omitting items and reviewing or revising their responses to previous items. Examinees tend to object strongly to these restrictions. They dislike the inflexibility of test-delivery methods that do not allow them to omit items or to review and change their responses to previous items (Wise, 1997). In fact, some examinees have indicated that their willingness to take a test on computer hinged on the inclusion of review flexibility (Pommerich & Burden, 2000). Although it is possible to structure an adaptive exam to include this flexibility (e.g., Kingsbury, 1996; Lunz & Bergstrom, 1994), it can be problematic. At the very least, it is likely to reduce measurement efficiency somewhat and may result in artificially inflated ability estimates (Lunz, Bergstrom, & Wright, 1992; Vispoel, Rocklin, Wang, & Bleiler, 1999). One option that may have merit is to allow examinees review within limited numbers of items, whether a testlet in a computerized mastery test (CMT; Way, 1994) or a short (e.g., 5-item) set. This approach appears to satisfy examinees' desire for review without impacting ability estimation (Pommerich & Burden, 2000; Stocking, 1997; Vispoel, Hendrickson, & Bleiler, 2000).

Examinees have also expressed a desire to preview upcoming items in order to estimate the number or difficulty of items remaining on the test and appropriately monitor their testing time (Pommerich & Burden, 2000). Very few operational CAT programs currently provide review and response change, although some computerized classification testing programs do. Most adaptive tests cannot allow examinees to preview items; at any point in an adaptive test upcoming items have not yet been identified.

Examinees may have affective reactions to other specific aspects of adaptive test designs. For example, a typical CAT may result in an examinee responding correctly to only about half the items administered. Thus, an adaptive test is likely to present a more difficult testing experience than many examinees expect (Lunz & Bergstrom, 1994), particularly very able examinees. Also, given that most adaptive tests do not allow items to be reviewed or changed, examinees may be overly anxious about giving a response. And, because most adaptive tests are shorter, examinees may be more concerned about the effect of each response. If an adaptive test does not fully address the content of an exam program, examinees may feel disadvantaged, to the extent that their content-knowledge strengths are not fully represented or even measured. Variable-length tests can be disconcerting to examinees, because they do not know how long the test will be or how to responsibly allocate time and energy (Wise, 1997). Examinees may also feel that they are not given a full opportunity to demonstrate their skill levels when a variable-length exam concludes quickly. Finally, examinees may be made anxious by their awareness and interpretation of the exam's adaptivity; that is, if an examinee perceives that he or she has suddenly been presented with an easier item, then the assumption that the previous response was incorrect could be stressful.

When possible, a testing program might be well advised to allow item omits, reviews, and changes by the examinee. Another action test developers may consider is to adjust the target difficulty of the exam, so that the probability of a correct response is greater than .5. A related adjustment is to administer an initial set of items that are easy for the target test population. Both of these test-design adaptations tend to lessen the efficiency of a test, but only to a modest degree. Examinees also may need to be educated about some aspects of adaptive testing in order to reduce their anxiety. This may include some assurances about the scoring model and the sufficiency of the content coverage. The rationale and effects of variable-length testing can also be explained to the examinees.

Impact of Prior Computer Experience

The level of computer experience that examinees possess as they take an exam can be of critical importance due to its potential impact on test-score validity. Obviously, to the greatest extent possible, the test should be designed so that examinees' level of computer experience does not affect their test scores.

When an exam consists solely of simple, discrete multiple-choice items, computer experience is likely to be only a minor issue for the majority of examinees. In this type of application, there are no multiscreen items, no need for scrolling, and no complex response actions required from the examinee. Examinees with even minimal prior exposure to computers will usually be able to respond to these item types without error, although not necessarily without anxiety. Under these conditions, a computerized version of an exam is likely to demonstrate similar performance to a paper-and-pencil version, and no mode effect may be in evidence.

However, even a modest level of computer experience may be too much to expect of some examinees. For example, a testing program with examinees from countries with low levels of technology will need to be particularly concerned about the potential detrimental effects of limited computer experience on examinees' test scores.

A concern for test equity suggests that whenever different examinee sub-groups have very different levels of opportunity for computer access and experience, it is important to ensure that the CBT is designed to minimize these differences (Gallagher, Bridgeman, & Cahalan, 1999; O'Neill & Powers, 1993; Sutton, 1993). In other words, the skills and content knowledge of interest ought to be measured in such a way that no more prior computer experience is needed than the least experienced examinee subgroup may be expected to have.

Prior computer experience may also be a greater issue when more complex item types are used. Some innovative item types require greater computer skills than those needed to select a multiple-choice response option (Perlman, Berger, & Tyler, 1993). Although it is often desirable to use these additional item types in order to expand the test coverage, test developers need to be attentive to the expected levels of computer experience in their test population as the item types are developed and field tested (Bennett & Bejar, 1998).

In general, test developers can best address the issue of prior computer experience by first obtaining a clear understanding of the computer experience levels in their test population. That information should then be utilized as the test is designed and developed. This will help ensure that the item types and test-user interface are designed appropriately and that the resulting test scores will not include measurement error arising from differing background computer skills. The CBT typically should also include specific instructions and practice items for each item type included on an exam. In some exam programs, more extensive practice tests can be included with the advance test-preparation materials to give examinees additional opportunity to become comfortable with the CBT software. Taken together, these steps will help ensure that a modest level of computer experience will be adequate to the task and that individual examinees will not be unfairly disadvantaged.

Effects of the User Interface

The more "intuitive" the computer test software is, the less attention an examinee needs to give to it—and the more attention he or she is free to give to the test items instead. It is this point that makes user interface design in computer-based tests so important.

The user interface primarily consists of the functions and navigation features available to the user, along with the elements of screen layout and visual style. The interface can be thought of as those components of a software program that a user sees and interacts with. A good user interface should demonstrate consistency and clarity and generally reflect good interface design principles.

While examinees may be unaware of the underlying psychometrics of an exam, they will be aware of and immediately concerned with the test's interface. In fact, an examinee is likely to perceive a CBT as consisting simply of the test items and the software's user interface. If the user interface is confusing, clumsy, or simply time-consuming, examinees will experience more frustration and anxiety. Beyond these affective reactions, extensive research has shown that a well-designed user interface makes software easier to learn, easier to use, and less prone to user error (Landauer, 1996; Tullis, 1997). When these facts are applied to CBT, they suggest that a good user interface can reduce measurement error (and conversely that a poor interface can increase it).

The goal in CBT interface design is to make the user interface as transparent as possible, so that only the test items remain consequential (Harmes & Parshall, 2000). Examinees primarily interact with a test's item screens and information screens. As the examinees encounter these screens, they need to know clearly what part of the screen to attend to and how to navigate from one screen to another. For item screens, they also need to know how to respond. The interface design can be used to guide the examinees to these elements in a clear and simple manner. A user interface that successfully communicates this information to the examinees will reduce the dependence on verbal instructions, practice items, and help screens. It will also help reduce examinee frustration and anxiety. (More information about user interface design, and the process of usability testing to ensure a successful design, is provided in Chapter 4.)

Effects of Task Constraints

In any assessment, there are elements that constrain the kinds of actions an examinee may take and the kinds of responses that he or she is able to give. Some task constraints are directly and intentionally built into the task, perhaps for content or cognitively based reasons or perhaps for reasons of scoring convenience. In other cases, a task constraint arises more as a by-product of some other aspect of the test mode environment. It is therefore evident that task constraints can have more or less construct relevance. Ideally, test developers want to design a test so that construct-relevant task constraints appropriately guide the examinee's process of taking a test and responding to items, while the effects of task constraints that are construct-irrelevant are reduced as much as possible (Millman & Greene, 1989).

A familiar example of task constraints can be seen in standardized paper-and-pencil tests. In this setting, examinees usually respond to items in a test booklet by filling in ovals on a separate, scannable sheet. This process has become a familiar activity, but it includes a number of construct-irrelevant task constraints. Examinees must keep track of which set of numbered ovals on one form is associated with which item on the separate booklet. Then they must fully "bubble in" a selected oval, and they must manage these activities quickly so that they can maximize their testing time. These task constraints are unintentional, construct-irrelevant aspects of the paper-and-pencil test environment. Unfortunately, these are challenging constraints for some examinees.

Computer-based tests also have task constraints, although some of them are very different from those found in paper-and-pencil testing. For example, responding to a computerized multiple-choice item is a somewhat different, and often simpler, task. Typically, only a single item is displayed onscreen at a given time. The response currently selected by the examinee may be highlighted or otherwise clearly marked on the current item. These features imply that there is no need for the examinee to keep track of two separate forms or lists, and there is little possibility of responding to the "wrong" item (Bunderson, Inouye, & Olsen, 1989). In another relaxation of task constraints, some test software programs allow examinees to use either the keyboard or the mouse to indicate response choices. Examinees have tended to respond positively to these changes in task constraint across test modes.

In other cases, the task constraints in a CBT may be more problematic. For example, on some constructed response items, the manner in which examinees must respond can produce objections that are as strong as those to "bubbling in" scannable ovals on answer sheets. Examinees who are unskilled at typing may object to use of the keyboard for providing text-based responses. On the other hand, examinees that regularly use word processors may object to the more limited set of editing features likely to be provided in CBT software. When examinees must type full essays on computer they feel particularly constrained by the necessity of using an unfamiliar word processor.

In addition to the task constraints on item responses, there are task constraints on other examinee actions. For example, CBT programs may require examinees to use computerized calculators to compute or estimate responses to some items. In some cases, examinees have complained that the CBT online calculators are more awkward to use than their own handheld calculators. In other applications, examinees have indicated that they feel the need to take notes or write on the items themselves as they work through a particular problem. For these types of problems, some examinees have expressed frustration with the computer environment, given that paper-and-pencil testing more easily lends itself to this type of note-taking. (In fact, examinees have even been known to write directly on the computer screen, in a remarkably poor attempt to circumvent this particular task constraint.) Mathematical computation items (and other numerical constructed response items) also have a task-constraint advantage for paper-and-pencil testing. Some CBT programs provide scratch paper at the test site to help address this issue, although this does not address the inconvenience of switching between paper-and-pencil tools and computer input devices.

Task constraints can also be seen on the test-taking experience as a whole. Examinees have access to one set of test-taking strategies with paper-and-pencil tests, where scanning the entire test, placing a pencil mark next to an item for later review, and jumping directly to another item type section, are all actions easily taken. None of these facilities were intentionally designed into the paper-and-pencil mode, although test-preparation materials frequently suggest that examinees make use of them. With a CBT, viewing the entire test is difficult, placing a computerized mark is possible only indirectly, and jumping to a given section may not even be feasible if sections do not exist. Some of these task constraints on CBT test-taking strategies are the result of test design elements, such as item selection rules and navigation elements of the user interface. Others are simply the by-product of the limitations on screen resolution compared to print (i.e., more items at a time can be clearly displayed in a print format).

In brief, task constraints shape the ways in which examinees can respond to items and tasks. They can focus and limit examinee response actions in ways that are cognitively appropriate and that make the scoring process easier and more reliable. Task constraints can also limit the types of questions that can be asked or confound a task and make it inappropriately more challenging. More subtly, they may even affect the ways in which examinees are able to conceptualize the tasks (Bennett & Bejar, 1998). In any of these cases, they diminish the value of the assessment.

To address CBT task constraints, test developers should first ensure that the items and the test as a whole include those task constraints that are endorsed for construct-relevant reasons. These intentional task constraints might apply to the ways in which examinees respond to items, other actions the examinee must make, and the test-taking process as a whole. A more challenging second step is to thoroughly examine all the tasks an examinee is asked to do in the CBT in order to identify additional sources of task constraints. These unintentional task constraints should be analyzed for their potential negative impact on examinees and their test performance. Once such problem areas are identified, the test developers need to either change the task to make it more appropriate or find ways to prepare the examinees to deal appropriately with the construct-irrelevant elements.

Effects of the Administrative Process

In addition to aspects of the test delivery method, the software interface, and the task constraints, examinees are impacted by, and have reactions to, aspects of the test-administration process. While examinees tend to be pleased with certain aspects of CBT administration such as the greater frequency of testing opportunities, they may be less pleased with other logistical matters.

The administration process at computer-based test sites is very different from that of paper-and-pencil settings; typically there is a much greater individualization of the process (ATP, 2000). Examinees are able to schedule their testing dates and times. They take their tests in rooms with perhaps only a handful of other test-takers. The rooms are usually quieter and possibly more comfortable than those often used for standardized paper-and-pencil test administrations. No group instructions are imposed on the test-takers. These are all positive logistical elements to many examinees. However, testing is never a truly positive experience, and examinees have expressed objections to other aspects of the CBT administration procedures (Rosen, 2000). Given that a specific test time has been scheduled, some examinees have negative reactions to any delay in the process. And, although there are very few examinees testing at any given time, some examinees are quite distressed when another examinee starts or finishes a test, and thus enters or leaves the room, during their scheduled testing time.

Aspects of the CBT registration process may also lead to some examinee complaints. Some CBT applications utilize a registration process that includes examinee passwords. Examinees, like other users of passwords, sometimes have trouble remembering or retaining their passwords, resulting in a logistical frustration. Additionally, administration at a dedicated CBT site allows for some new test security procedures to be easily implemented. Some exam programs have implemented the photographing of each test-taker. The examinee's digital photo is then stored electronically along with his or her test record. Not surprisingly, some examinees are vociferous in their complaints about what they perceive as a privacy intrusion. However, further security procedures utilizing digital storage are on the horizon. Both digital fingerprints and retinal scans can be collected and stored fairly easily. It will be important for a testing program to weigh the potential security advantages over the examinees' offense about these types of measures (Rosen, 2000).

In general, test developers can best address administrative concerns by making the logistical processes as smooth as possible and by completely preparing examinees for the CBT experience. To the extent that the process is well run, and to the extent that examinees are aware of the process, problems can be avoided—or at least minimized.

Examinees' Mental Models

Many of the examinee reactions, frustrations, and anxieties discussed in this chapter can be partially addressed by considering the examinees' mental models. A *mental model* is the user's internal explanation, theory, or belief about an underlying process (Norman, 1990). People can and will develop mental models for themselves, even when they only have very sketchy information. In the case of computer-based tests, examinees hold mental models about the testing processes that the computer follows. An examinee's reactions to computerized testing can be conceptualized as partially resulting from the accuracy of his or her mental model. Some mental models are inaccurate; there is a conflict or discrepancy between what the examinee perceives as transpiring and the actual process underway. Some negative reactions on the part of examinees are actually due to these inaccurate mental models.

As mentioned previously, some examinees have expressed concern about their own apparent poor performance when other examinees at the same test administration site ended their exams and left the room early. An incorrect mental model in this instance is that all examinees were being administered the same test and the same number of items. Because of this internal misrepresentation of the CBT administration process, some examinees felt unnecessarily anxious about their "slower" performance—when in fact they were likely to have been taking different tests of different lengths and difficulties.

Another example of distress caused by an inaccurate mental model was the anxiety felt by some examinees when their variable-length exam ended quickly. Some of these examinees assumed that they failed the test and had not been given an adequate opportunity to "show what they knew." In fact, testing may well have ended quickly because their performance was very strong, and they had already passed.

Another mental model that could cause examinees difficulty is related to adaptive item selection. Examinees are sometimes made anxious by trying to use the difficulty of the current item as a form of feedback about the correctness of their previous response. That is, when the current item appears to be easier than the last, they assume the previous answer was incorrect. This assumption may well be wrong, however, because item selection is usually complicated by content constraints, exposure control, and other factors unknown to the examinee. In fact, examinees may not be particularly good at determining the relative difficulty of one item from another. Given these additional elements of item selection, an examinee's guesses about his or her test performance based on the perceived difficulty ordering of the items is likely to be in error, although it still has the power to create anxiety and distress.

Often, the best way to address examinees' mental models is to ensure that they have accurate ones. This will be the result of giving the examinees accurate information, correcting misrepresentations, and directly addressing particular areas of concern.

Summary

Table 3.1 provides a summary of some of the affective reactions examinees have expressed toward computer-based tests as discussed in this chapter, along with some of the recommendations for developing computerized tests that address examinees' concerns. Tests are likely to remain unpopular with their primary audiences, even when they are administered on computer. However, they can be constructed to be fair and reliable and to produce valid test scores. Furthermore, they can be designed to minimize examinees' frustrations and to limit the sources of examinee anxiety. These additional test design steps are well worth taking, because of the affective and measurement improvements they offer.

Table 3.1. Some Examinees' Concerns about CBTs and Possible Courses of Action

Concern	Examinees' Reaction	Course of Action
Overall	Concern about testing on computer	Provide instructional materials, sample items, and practice tests
Adaptive tests	Dislike lack of flexibility on item omits, reviews, revisions, and previews	Provide flexibility, either in total test or short sets
	Concerns about average difficulty of test	Target the item selection to greater than .5
	Concerns about test progress under variable-length exams	Develop progress indicators to provide information to examinee
Prior computer experience	Anxiety about the potential impact of insufficient prior experience	Provide good informational materials, both in advance and during testing
User interface	Difficulty learning and using the CBT administration software	Thoroughly test the exam and item user interfaces on the target population
Task constraints	Frustrations with constraints on the test-taking process	Carefully evaluate the test and item types for construct-irrelevant constraints
Administrative process	Anxiety when other examinees start or end during their tests	Inform examinees that others are taking different tests of different lengths
Mental models	Concern about the correctness of an item response, when the following item is perceived to be easier	Inform examinees about the numerous factors used in item selection, beyond item difficulty

References

Association of Test Publishers (ATP). (2000). *Computer-Based Testing Guidelines.*

Bennett, R. E., & Bejar, I. I. (1998). Validity and automated scoring: It's not only the scoring. *Educational Measurement Issues and Practice,* 17, 9–17.

Bunderson, V. C., Inouye, D. I., & Olsen, J. B. (1989). The four generations of computerized educational measurement. In Linn, R. (Ed.) *Educational Measurement,* 3rd edition. New York: American Council on Education and Macmillan Publishing Co.

Gallagher, A., Bridgeman, B., & Cahalan, C. (1999, April). The Effect of CBT on Racial, Gender, and Language Groups. Paper presented at the annual meeting of the National Council on Measurement in Education, Montreal.

Harmes, J. C., & Parshall, C. G. (2000, November). An Iterative Process for Computerized Test Development: Integrating Usability Methods. Paper presented at the annual meeting of the Florida Educational Research Association, Tallahassee.

Kingsbury, G. G. (1996, April). Item Review and Adaptive Testing. Paper presented at the annual meeting of the National Council on Measurement in Education, New York.

Landauer, T. K. (1996). *The Trouble with Computers: Usefulness, Usability, and Productivity.* Cambridge, Mass: MIT Press.

Lunz, M. E., & Bergstrom, B. A. (1994). An empirical study of computerized adaptive test administration conditions. *Journal of Educational Measurement,* 31, 251–263.

Lunz, M. E., Bergstrom, B. A., & Wright, B. D. (1992). The effect of review on student ability and test efficiency for computer adaptive testing. *Applied Psychological Measurement,* 16, 33–40.

Millman, J., & Greene, J. (1989). The specification and development of tests of achievement and ability. In Linn, R. (ed.) *Educational Measurement,* 3rd edition. New York: American Council on Education and Macmillan Publishing Co.

Norman, D. A. (1990). *The Design of Everyday Things.* New York: Doubleday.

O'Neill, K., & Kubiak, A. (1992, April). Lessons Learned from Examinees about Computer-Based Tests: Attitude Analyses. Paper presented at the annual meeting of the National Council on Measurement in Education, San Francisco.

O'Neill, K., & Powers, D. E. (1993, April). The Performance of Examinee Subgroups on a Computer-Administered Test of Basic Academic Skills. Paper presented at the annual meeting of the National Council on Measurement in Education, Atlanta.

Perlman, M., Berger, K., & Tyler, L. (1993). An Application of Multimedia Software to Standardized Testing in Music. (Research Rep. No. 93-36) Princeton, NJ: Educational Testing Service.

Pommerich, M., & Burden, T. (2000, April). From Simulation to Application: Examinees React to Computerized Testing. Paper presented at the annual meeting of the National Council on Measurement in Education, New Orleans.

Rosen, G. A. (2000, April). Computer-Based Testing: Test Site Security. Paper presented at the annual meeting of the National Council on Measurement in Education, New Orleans.

Stocking, M. L. (1997). Revising item responses in computerized adaptive tests: A comparison of three models. *Applied Psychological Measurement,* 21, 129–142.

Sutton, R. E. (1993, April). Equity Issues in High Stakes Computerized Testing. Paper presented at the annual meeting of the American Educational Research Association, Atlanta.

Tullis, T. (1997). Screen Design. In Helander, M., Landauer, T. K., & Prabhu, P. (eds). *Handbook of Human-Computer Interaction*, 2nd completely revised edition, (503–531). Amsterdam: Elsevier.

Vispoel, W. P., Hendrickson, A. B., & Bleiler, T. (2000). Limiting answer review and change on computerized adaptive vocabulary tests: Psychometric and attitudinal results. *Journal of Educational Measurement,* 37, 21–38.

Vispoel, W. P., Rocklin, T. R., Wang, T., & Bleiler, T. (1999). Can examinees use a review option to obtain positively biased ability estimates on a computerized adaptive test? *Journal of Educational Measurement,* 36, 141–157.

Way, W. D. (1994). Psychometric Models for Computer-Based Licensure Testing. Paper presented at the annual meeting of CLEAR, Boston.

Wise, S. (1996, April). A Critical Analysis of the Arguments for and Against Item Review in Computerized Adaptive Testing. Paper presented at the annual meeting of the National Council on Measurement in Education, New York.

Wise, S. (1997, April). Examinee Issues in CAT. Paper presented at the annual meeting of the National Council on Measurement in Education, Chicago.

Additional Readings

Becker, H. J., & Sterling, C. W. (1987). Equity in school computer use: National data and neglected considerations. *Journal of Educational Computing Research*, 3, 289–311.

Burke, M. J., Normand, J., & Raju, N. S. (1987). Examinee attitudes toward computer-administered ability testing. *Computers in Human Behavior*, 3, 95–107.

Koch, B. R., & Patience, W. M. (1978). Student attitudes toward tailored testing. In D. J. Weiss (ed.), *Proceedings of the 1977 Computerized Adaptive Testing Conference*. Minneapolis: University of Minnesota, Department of Psychology.

Llabre, M. M., & Froman, T. W. (1987). Allocation of time to test items: A study of ethnic differences. *Journal of Experimental Education*, 55, 137–140.

Moe, K. C., & Johnson, M. F. (1988). Participants' reactions to computerized testing. *Journal of Educational Computing Research, 4*, 79–86.

Ward, T. J. Jr., Hooper, S. R., & Hannafin, K. M. (1989). The effects of computerized tests on the performance and attitudes of college students. *Journal of Educational Computing Research*, 5, 327–333.

Wise, S. L., Barnes, L. B., Harvey, A. L., & Plake, B. S. (1989). Effects of computer anxiety and computer experience on the computer-based achievement test performance of college students. *Applied Measurement in Education*, 2, 235–241.

4
Software Issues

The principles discussed in this chapter should be addressed early in the computerized test development process in order to reap the maximum benefit from them. The test administration software interface defines much of an examinee's test-taking experience; examinees' reactions to software programs often are strongly related to the quality of the interface. The user interface (i.e., the visual style of the software, the written instructions and communication, and the means provided for navigating through the test) is of critical concern. Software considerations should *not* be an afterthought on the part of test developers.

There are three primary software options for test developers preparing computerized exams. One is to have the software programmed either in-house or by a consultant. The second is to work with a testing agency that has or will develop proprietary testing software for the use of its clients. The third is to purchase and use existing commercial software. Obviously those who choose to develop their own software need to be very concerned with principles of good software design. Perhaps less obviously, these principles are also very important for test developers who choose to use existing software programs. Familiarity with software design principles enables test developers to make better, more informed decisions about the software program they should purchase. These design principles can also guide test developers as they produce those aspects of the computerized exam that are under their direct control, even if they are using a commercial software program. These may include certain aspects of the screen design and layout, the graphic files that may be included with some items, and the features of the written communications with the examinees.

The design of software interfaces is a specialized field that most psychometricians and test developers do not know well. There are books, conferences, and associations devoted to software design and the development of user interfaces (see, e.g., Helander, Landauer, & Prabhu, 1997; Kirakowski & Corbett, 1990; Nielsen, 1993; and Schneiderman, 1998). Software programs differ enormously in their usefulness and usability, that is in the total set of features provided and in the ease with which they can be used. One advantage to testing programs is that computerized test software typically represents very constrained software applications (with the relatively infrequent exception of innovative item types) offering a minimal set of features. Because of this, there are comparatively few critical aspects of software design that apply to computerized testing programs.

This chapter does not cover everything that could, or should, be known about software design, but it provides an overview of some of the most important issues for the development of good software testing programs. The references and additional readings listed at the end of the chapter include a number of valuable resources that can guide the interested reader further in these topics. The chapter begins with an introduction to the concept of the user interface, particularly as it applies to CBTs. This is followed by a discussion of the importance of usability studies and software evaluations. Principles of good interface design as they apply to the visual style, writing for the screen, and navigation are covered next. Specific interface issues relevant to Web-based tests are also addressed. Finally, the software evaluation phase of quality control (QC) is presented.

User Interfaces

The user interface can be thought of as those components of a software program that a user sees and interacts with. The software interface comprises the functions available to the user, the forms of navigation, and the level and type of interactivity, as well as the visual style, screen layout, and written communication to the user. This chapter focuses on the user interfaces encountered by the *examinee*, as this is the most critical measurement concern of computer-based testing software. However, most CBT software programs also include program modules for test development processes such as item entry and test form assembly. These program elements also have user interfaces and good design of these interfaces is of critical importance to the test developers who must use them.

A program's interface can be either easy or difficult to learn. It can be either easy or cumbersome to use and, likewise, it can be intuitive or confusing. A well-designed user interface can result not only in software that is easier to learn and use but also in software that is less prone to miskeys and other entry errors. An easy, intuitive software interface is probably always desirable, but it is particularly important for a critical application like computerized testing. If examinees must focus too much attention or learning on using the software program, the amount of their concentration available for the actual test may be lessened. Examinees' reactions to taking a test on computer are very likely to be affected by the quality of the user interface; their performance may also be affected. This would clearly lessen the validity and usefulness of their test scores.

Unlike more comprehensive software applications, the software needed for computerized test administration often has a reduced number of features available, resulting in a limited user interface. This is because, in general, there is only a small set of actions that an examinee needs to make in order to take a computerized test. For example, a simple CAT might allow an examinee to do no more than click on a response item for each multiple-choice item and then click to proceed to the next item. On the other hand, tests in which examinees are free to review and revise their responses must provide additional navigational functions, adding to the complexity of the user interface. And tests that include innovative item types often require more complex response actions on the part of the examinees, resulting in more elaborate user interfaces. Those test programs that have examinee populations with little computer experience need to exercise particular care to provide simple interfaces. Test programs that include complex multiscreen items or simulation tasks have particular challenges.

Test developers who are producing their own computerized testing software need to make decisions about the features and functions to include, as well as about the appearance of the software screens. These professionals are advised to conduct usability studies throughout the software development process in order to ensure the effectiveness of the software interface and to avoid costly mistakes. Testing professionals who are purchasing commercial software for computerized testing also need to make decisions about the kinds of computerized test features their exam programs should have. They can then evaluate existing commercial software packages to determine the program that best meets their needs.

Brief discussions of usability studies and software evaluation are provided next, followed by more details on some of the user interface design issues that are most pertinent to computerized testing software.

Usability Studies

Usability may be defined as the degree to which a computerized application is easy to learn, contains the necessary functionality to allow the user to complete the tasks for which it was designed, and is easy and pleasant to use (Gould & Lewis, 1985). Usability studies are the means by which software developers evaluate and refine their software design, particularly the user interfaces. Landauer (1997) argues that usability studies help produce software that is both more *useful*, in that it performs more helpful functions, and more *usable*, in that it is easier and more pleasant to learn and operate.

A wide variety of methods exist for examining the usability of a software program, ranging from informal reviews to full-scale, laboratory-based experiments (e.g., Kirakowski &˙ Corbett; 1990; Nielsen & Mack, 1994; Schneiderman, 1998). In informal studies, potential users of the program are asked to interact with an early version or prototype of the software and either attempt to undertake some realistic tasks or simply note problems with the software design and features. In this way, the software developers obtain information about the program's value, utility, and appeal. To be most effective, usability studies should spring from a developmental focus on users, including a thorough understanding of characteristics of the users, as well as of the nature of the tasks to be performed (Gould, Boies, & Ukelson, 1997; Landauer, 1997).

Usability studies are important because they ensure good software designs; on the other hand, making decisions without obtaining user input often leads to design flaws and operational problems. Testing successive versions of the interface on actual users and making changes based on the feedback provided lead to a program that meets users' needs and functions well in practice. This can also result in reduced user frustration, anxiety, and error rates, as well as an increased likelihood that the program will be selected for use. In fact, there is an extensive research base that documents the effectiveness of even very simple and low-cost usability methods in providing improvements so that the software is easier to learn, easier to use, and less subject to user entry errors (see, e.g., Landauer, 1995; Harrison, Henneman, & Blatt, 1994; Mayhew & Mantei, 1994; and Tullis, 1997). Furthermore, the inclusion of usability testing often results in cost savings to the software development process by prioritizing product features, reducing programming costs, and decreasing maintenance and support expenses (Bias & Mayhew, 1994; Karat, 1997; Ehrlich & Rohn, 1994).

For computerized test administration software, an important result of a well-designed user interface is that examinees have to spend less time and attention on how to take the test and more on the actual test itself. A peripheral benefit of an interface that can be quickly learned by new users is that it reduces the amount of online training that needs to be developed and administered. More critically, a poor or confusing interface is a potential source of measurement error (Bennett & Bejar, 1998; Booth, 1991; Bunderson, Inouye, & Olsen, 1989).

Usability studies may be conducted in numerous ways and a number of articles and books have described or compared methods (Gould, Boies, & Ukelson, 1997; Kirakowski & Corbett, 1990; Landauer, 1997; Nielsen, 1993; Nielsen & Mack, 1994). Users may be asked to perform specific tasks within the program and then either be directly observed or videotaped as they attempt the tasks. Questionnaires, interviews, and talk-aloud protocols or focus groups may be used to determine the interpretation users are making about the software and how it functions. The computer may store information about the actions users take, in addition to frequencies or times (through such methods as keystroke logging, etc.). Computers can even be used to track users' eye movements as they view each screen. Usability studies can be conducted using very elaborate, high-fidelity prototypes of the actual software interface, but they can also be conducted using very simple mock-ups of the interface. In fact, paper-and-pencil prototypes can be used, with human interaction imitating any program interactivity. (This approach has been referred to as the *Wizard of Oz* method of user testing.) A simple but highly effective method is that of *user testing*. In user tests, or user observation, a potential user of the software program is observed as he or she attempts to use the software to carry out realistic tasks. Nielsen (1994a, 1994b) has documented the effectiveness of low-cost, informal usability methods, including what he has termed "discount user testing." He has suggested that the greatest cost-benefit ratio actually comes from testing as few as five users, with as many iterative stages as possible (Nielsen, 2000). One set of basic steps for conducting a user test is provided in Table 4.1 (Apple, Inc., 1995).

Table 4.1 Ten Steps for Conducting a User Observation (adapted from Apple, Inc., 1995)

---

1. Introduce yourself and describe the purpose of the observation (in very general terms). Most of the time, you shouldn't mention what you'll be observing.

2. Tell the participant that it's okay to quit at any time.

3. Talk about the equipment in the room.

4. Explain how to think aloud.

5. Explain that you will not provide help.

6. Describe in general terms what the participant will be doing.

7. Ask if there are any questions before you start; then begin the observation.

8. During the observation, remember several pointers: Stay alert; ask questions or prompt the participant; be patient.

9. Conclude the observation. Explain what you were trying to find out, answer any remaining questions, and ask for suggestions on how to improve the software.

10. Use the results.

In a very restricted approach to usability analysis, a single usability study is conducted near the end of the software development cycle. At this point, any substantive redesign of the software will be very expensive or impossible to implement. As a result, only minor changes tend to be made, limiting the effectiveness of the usability analysis. A more valuable (and more cost-effective) approach is to start testing very early in development in order to get critical features addressed in an optimal way and then to continue with a process of iterative refinement. That is, the developers conduct numerous cycles of rapid prototyping, user testing, determining necessary changes, and then developing an improved prototype for retesting. Use of low-fidelity, low-tech prototypes, particularly early in the design process, make this approach inexpensive, and shorten the time between cycles. Gould, Boies, & Ukelson (1997) have provided several checklists for software developers to use to help them implement an iterative design, achieve an early (and continual) focus on users, and conduct early user testing. An adaptation of their checklist for achieving early user testing is provided in Table 4.2.

Table 4.2. Checklist for Achieving Early User Testing (adapted from Gould, Boies, & Ukelson, 1997)

_____ We made informal, preliminary sketches of a few user scenarios—specifying exactly what the user and system messages will be—and showed them to a few prospective users.

_____ We have begun writing the user manual and are using it to guide the development process.

_____ We have used simulations to try out the functions and organization of the user interface.

_____ We conducted early demonstrations.

_____ We invited as many people as possible to comment on on-going instantiations of all usability components.

_____ We had prospective users think aloud as they used simulations, mock-ups, and prototypes.

_____ We used computer conferencing to get feedback on usability.

_____ We conducted formal prototype user tests.

_____ We compared our results to established behavioral target goals.

_____ We let motivated people try to find bugs in our systems.

_____ We did field studies.

_____ We included data logging programs in our system.

_____ We did follow-up studies on people who are now using our system.

In the most general sense, usability studies help software developers ensure that all the necessary and desirable functions are present in the software and that users are easily able to tell what functions are present and how to use them. The specific nature of the necessary software features and how they might be accessed are tied to the purpose of the software program. For computerized testing software, an important consideration to keep in mind is that a typical user of the software only encounters the program once. Users of the program should be able to learn to use the program quickly as, with the exception of those examinees that can or must retest, they will not have the opportunity to learn and use the software over repeated attempts.

Software Evaluation

Software evaluation is a process through which users can, somewhat formally, consider a potential software program in terms of specific criteria (Alessi & Trollip, 1991). Test developers who intend to purchase commercial software for computerized test administration can use the software evaluation process to analyze and compare existing commercial programs. Computerized test administration software packages vary considerably in the features and functions they provide, as well as in their cost and ease of use. For example, programs vary in terms of their item banking capabilities, their ability to handle a variety of graphics formats, and the number and kinds of item types they support. They also differ in terms of test scoring and reporting functionality and in the quality of their user manuals and technical support. A thorough evaluation of competing software programs will help ensure that a testing agency selects the program that best meets its needs and the needs of its examinees. Those testing agencies that are producing their own computerized test software as part of the development process can also use software evaluation.

Testing professionals can begin the software evaluation process by developing a list of features that they would find desirable in a computerized testing software program selected for their use. While any software program is the result of compromises or tradeoffs between often-contradictory potential features, the process of evaluating multiple CBT software packages will enable the test developers to identify the software program where those tradeoffs come closest to matching the test program's most critical needs and desirable features. The list of features can be prioritized and then used to help structure and guide the test developers in evaluating the available commercial software programs. The features list can be compared to software program descriptions provided in brochures, manuals, company Web sites, and other documentation as an initial test of a given program's ability to satisfy the testing agency's needs. The software programs that appear to be at least minimally appropriate can then be evaluated further.

The full evaluation of a potential software program involves actual use of the program to carry out a variety of typical and realistic tasks. The evaluator should take a sample test, responding to on-screen instructions and prompts as carefully and correctly as possible. The evaluator should also use the software package, responding the way a careless or inattentive user might respond. This enables the evaluator to determine how the program behaves when a user keys or clicks on the wrong options, enters misspellings, or makes mistakes in navigation. The evaluator should also have representatives from the examinee population use the software to determine further whether the instructions and interface are clear to the target user group. These users can be observed as they interact with the software in a similar approach to the process of user testing discussed earlier. (A full evaluation of the program should also include a thorough examination of those software components and modules that test development staff would use.

A variety of realistic test developer tasks, such as item entry, test form assembly, and item analyses or score reporting, should also be undertaken.)

The evaluator should also look for a program that follows good software design principles and is free of errors or "bugs." The program should provide "forgiveness," or the ability to change user actions that were not intended. This does not refer to the test delivery method but rather to user actions in terms of navigation and keystrokes. Ideally, the program should provide clear instructions, intuitive navigation, feedback to user actions, and an appealing screen design. Table 4.3 displays an example of a checklist that can be used to evaluate computer-based testing software for elements such as visual clarity, clear instructions and help screens, consistency, and facility with error prevention or correction (Harmes & Parshall, 2000).

Table 4.3. CBT Software Checklist

Instructions/Help	Always	Most of the time	Some of the time	Never
Do instructions and prompts clearly indicate what to do?	4	3	2	1
Are sample items provided for each item type?	4	3	2	1
Are sample items accessible once the exam has begun?	4	3	2	1
Is it clear to the user what should be done to correct an error?	4	3	2	1
Is it clear what actions the user can take at any stage?	4	3	2	1
Does the screen change based on examinee input (e.g., doesn't register that an answer has been given)?	4	3	2	1
Is it clear what the examinee needs to do in order to answer an item?	4	3	2	1
Is the way in which items are presented appropriate for the tasks involved?	4	3	2	1
Does the screen contain all of the necessary information required to answer an item?	4	3	2	1

Comments on Instructions/Help:

Table 4.3. CBT Software Checklist (cont'd)

Visual Clarity	Always	Most of the time	Some of the time	Never
Is the information on the screen easy to see and read?	4	3	2	1
Does the use of color help make the displays clear?	4	3	2	1
Is it easy to find the required information on a screen?	4	3	2	1
Are different types of information clearly separated from one another on the screen?	4	3	2	1

Comments on Visual Clarity:

Consistency	Always	Most of the time	Some of the time	Never
Are icons, symbols, and graphics used consistently throughout the test?	4	3	2	1
Are different colors used consistently throughout the test (e.g., questions are always in the same color)?	4	3	2	1
Is the same type of information (e.g., test questions, navigation, instructions) in the same location on each screen?	4	3	2	1
Is the way the software responds to a particular user action consistent at all times?	4	3	2	1

Comments on Consistency:

Error Prevention/ Correction	Always	Most of the time	Some of the time	Never
Can the examinee look through other items within a section (forward or backward)?	4	3	2	1
Is there an easy way for the examinee to correct a mistake?	4	3	2	1
Is the examinee able to check what they have entered before the answer is evaluated?	4	3	2	1
Is there online help (in terms of using the software) available for the examinee?	4	3	2	1

Comments on Error Prevention/Correction:

A number of guidelines for software evaluation exist, and there are formal user interface design principles (e.g., Alessi & Trollip, 1991; Ravden & Johnson, 1989). One set of design principles, termed *usability heuristics,* was compiled by Nielsen and Molich (1990) and adapted by Landauer (1995); these are listed in Table 4.4. This list of usability heuristics can be used by the software evaluator as another checklist to determine whether or not the software follows good design principles.

The evaluation process should also consider the quality of supporting materials, such as examinee score reports generated by the program, and technical and users' manuals. Guidelines for evaluating software are useful for testing professionals who are selecting software for purchase, as well as for those who are developing their own test administration software. The process of software evaluation can help ensure that a testing program's most critical needs are fully satisfied.

Table 4.4. Usability Heuristics (adapted from Nielsen & Molich, 1990, in Landauer, 1995)

---

1. Use simple and natural dialogue. Tell only what is necessary, and tell it in a natural and logical order. Ask only what users can answer.
2. Speak the users' language. Use words and concepts familiar to them in their work, not jargon about the computer's innards.
3. Minimize the users' memory load by providing needed information when it's needed.
4. Be consistent in terminology and required actions.
5. Keep the user informed about what the computer is doing.
6. Provide clearly marked exits so users can escape from unintended situations.
7. Provide shortcuts for frequent actions and advanced users.
8. Give good, clear, specific, and constructive error messages in plain language, not beeps or codes.
9. Wherever possible, prevent errors from occurring by keeping choices and actions simple and easy.
10. Provide clear, concise, complete online help, instructions, and documentation. Orient them to user tasks.

Design of the User Interface

For computer-based tests, there are three user interface elements that can be considered the most critical. The first of these is *navigation*, or the means by which a user moves through the program. The next is *visual style*. This comprises all the components of the screen design, or "look" of the program. Finally, there is the aspect of *written communication*. This refers to all textual titles, instructions, and help screens through which the user is informed about the program.

These elements of the user interface are discussed in greater detail in the following sections and are considered in terms of the design principles of consistency, feedback, and forgiveness. Although there are many important design principles that should be considered in the process of software development, a few are most critical for computerized test administration software. *Consistency* in the interface design makes learning to use the software much easier and enables the user to concentrate on the content and purpose of the program rather than on how to use it. Another important design principle is that of *feedback*. When a software interface incorporates feedback, a confirmation for every user action is provided, letting the user know that each action was noted. Finally, the principle of *forgiveness* results in a software interface that guides a user to take the correct action but also enables the user to "back out" of an incorrect choice.

User interface elements are illustrated by figures provided in both this chapter and Chapter 5.

Navigation

Navigation refers to the set of methods provided in the software interface for users to move through the program. In instructional screens, for example, users are often asked to click on a button or press the **Enter** key to advance to the next screen. Sometimes, they are provided with a button or keystroke to move back to the previous screen. A program with simple but limited navigation typically is easy to learn; the tradeoff is often some reduction in user access and control.

A computerized test may have very simple navigation because very little control over movement through the program is offered to the user. A short adaptive test that consists entirely of single-screen items is likely to have very minimal navigation. A test of this type provides a single button or keystroke for an examinee to use to move forward in the test with no backward movement allowed. Very simple navigation is illustrated later, in Figure 5.3. This item screen is from an audio-based *ESL Listening* test. In this test, examinees are restricted from returning to items after moving on; thus the only navigation on this item screen is a right-arrow button, which moves the examinee forward to the next item.

A nonadaptive test (e.g., a CFT) usually provides options for both forward and backward movement through the test items. Often, this navigation is provided through buttons labeled **Next** and **Previous** or displaying right and left arrows. This type of navigation can be seen in Figure 5.1.

A test of moderate or greater length provides additional forms of navigation. For example, examinees may be able to mark an item for later review; specific keystrokes or buttons may then enable the user to page or move only through the subset of items that have been marked. Some longer computerized tests provide an item menu option. In this form of navigation, examinees can access a screen that contains a list of item numbers and perhaps some information as to whether each item has already been seen by the examinee, been answered, and/or been marked for review. The examinee is able to move directly to any given item from this screen by selecting the item number.

Figure 5.4 displays a library skills item in which examinees are asked to rank order three article titles in terms of their relevance to a search. An added navigational feature of this item is that examinees are able to click on any one of the titles to see the article's abstract. To lessen potential navigational confusion, when an abstract is displayed it appears in a pop-up window that covers only part of the item screen. In general, the most complex forms of navigation in computerized tests are those provided in simulation exams. In these tests numerous choices, or paths, may be available to the examinee for much of the exam.

In navigation, the design principle of consistency is evidenced by software that requires the same user action for the same software option throughout the program. With inconsistent navigation, users may have to select the **Enter** key at one point in the program, the right arrow key at another point, and a **Continue** button at still another point, all to accomplish the same function of advancing to the next screen. Another instance of software consistency is for buttons intended for specific purposes to have the same look and be placed in the same location on every relevant screen.

The principle of feedback is evidenced in navigation by such features as buttons that make an audible click or that appear to depress when selected. Actions that result in a noticeable delay may provide a display indicating that the computer is processing the request (e.g., the cursor may turn into a clock face or there may be a tone indicating the level of task). Feedback is also provided through such features as progress indicators. For example, a linear test can include indications such as "item 6 of 20" on each item screen. Figure 5.1 displays this type of progress indicator.

Navigational forgiveness can be implemented in a number of ways. The examinee should be able to undo actions, reverse direction in a series of instructional screens, access help throughout the program, and change item responses—unless there are good reasons to limit these actions. When reversing an action is not possible, a program designed with the principle of forgiveness in mind clearly informs the user of this fact in advance, along with any effects that may result from a given choice. This type of informative forgiveness is demonstrated in Figure 4.1. In this CBT, examinees are free to revisit items within a test section, but they may not return to those items once they have left a section. This screen clearly warns examinees before they take an action that they will not be able to reverse.

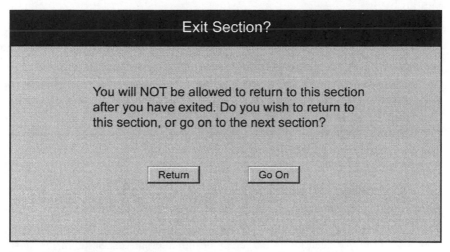

Figure 4.1. An example of informative forgiveness

An example of poor consistency in a program's interface is a test that sometimes uses the **Tab** key to move between items and at other times uses the **Tab** key to change the selected response option. An examinee could accidentally change his or her answer, for example, from b to c, when intending to move from item 6 to item 7. An example of a lack of forgiveness coupled with a lack of feedback can be seen in a program that immediately moves to the next item once an examinee has typed a letter corresponding to one of the response options. This creates a problem because the examinee's choice is not displayed on screen via checkmark, highlighting, or other means (lack of feedback), and the examinee is not given an opportunity to correct what may have been a miskey (lack of forgiveness).

Another example of forgiveness can be found in some adaptive tests that make use of a **Confirm** option. In these adaptive tests, **Previous** options are not provided, given that an examinee is typically not free to return to an item after responding to it. In some instances, however, the exams include a **Confirm** option. After an examinee selects a response option, he or she is presented with a choice, such as **Confirm** or **Cancel**. The purpose of this type of navigation is to allow an examinee to change a response or correct a miskey before going on to the next item. Although the opportunity to correct a miskey is a good implementation of forgiveness, a problem may arise. After choosing **Confirm** repeatedly, examinees can begin to respond so automatically that it loses its utility.

Visual Style

The next aspect of user-interface design is the visual style of the interface. The visual style is reflected in all the individual visual elements on the screen, from the choice of background color to the shape and labels for navigation buttons to the type and size of text fonts. One of the most basic aspects of visual style is physical layout of screen elements, including the location and relative size of all text, borders, and images. The style and detail of the screen graphics, as well as any animation or video included, also contribute to the program's visual style. Finally, the visual effect of all of these elements combined contributes to the overall visual style of the interface.

A great deal of empirical research into the effect of various screen design components has been conducted (see Tullis, 1997, for an excellent summary of some of this work). Consistent effects on proportion of user errors and search time (i.e., the amount of time it takes for a user to extract specific information from a screen) have been found for screen design alternatives. Some of the most critical visual design issues concern how much information a screen contains (or information density), how the information is grouped, and the spatial relationships among screen elements. For example, the evidence indicates that search time is clearly linked to information density, although appropriate use of grouping and layout can overcome this effect. In addition, good choice of information grouping can improve the readability of the data as well as indicate relationships between different groups of information.

In any software package, the visual style must be appropriate for the target audience and the subject matter of the program. In some user interface guidelines this is referred to as *aesthetic integrity* (e.g., Apple, Inc., 1995). It should also be designed to match the style and tone of the written communication. For computerized testing, a simple, uncluttered style is best so that examinees' attention can be focused on the test items. Clear, legible text with few screen windows open at one time is least confusing to users of the testing software, particularly novices. Soft colors, with a good level of contrast between the font and the background, are easiest on the eyes and thus help reduce potential examinee fatigue during the exam. If specific information needs to stand out, the use of an alternate color is often a better choice than use of underlining, bold text, or reverse video. The technique of flashing (turning text on and off) has been shown to be less effective than leaving the text un-differentiated, due to the increased difficulty of reading flashing text (Tullis, 1997). The item screen displayed in Figure 5.3 has a simple, clean layout. Black text on a pale yellow background makes for very readable script. Although the printed versions of the CBT screens provided in this text are all in black and white, naturally the on-screen versions use a range of text and background colors. A larger font size is used to distinguish the item instructions from the item text. The "title" information is also clearly set off—in this instance through use of underlining, although use of a different color or physical borders might have been better choices. A problem with the item in Figure 5.1 is in the use of the color red to outline an examinee's current selection. While the outline is very visible on screen, it might lead to some confusion, given that red is often associated with incorrect responses.

The layout, or physical placement of borders, instructional text, navigation buttons, item stem and response options, and other screen elements should be visually pleasing and, more critically, should lead the user to take the correct action. Size can be used to indicate priority and can guide the eye to the most important elements on a screen. For example, on an item screen the item itself should probably take up the majority of the screen space. Item instructions and navigation buttons should be available but unobtrusive. In Figure 5.2 the graphical item dominates the screen space, making it easy to see each figural component. The graphical elements that are movable are distinguished by their placement and grouping within a box labeled "Tools."

Consistency in visual style may be implemented through the use of one visual look for all item screens and a similar but distinct look for all informational and help screens. This similar-but-distinct relationship is illustrated in Figures 4.2 and 5.3, which are both from the same CBT and use the same color scheme and fonts. Certain areas of the screen can also be consistently devoted to specific purposes. For example, instructions can be displayed in a text box, separated from the item stem and response options, permanent buttons can be placed along one border of the screen, and temporary buttons can be consistently located in another area of the screen. The interface's visual style can provide feedback through such means as shadowing a button that has been clicked or displaying a checkmark next to a selected item response option. Navigation or other options that are temporarily unavailable can be "grayed out" to inform the user visually that those options cannot currently be selected. Forgiveness primarily may be reflected in a visual style that guides the user to the important information or appropriate choice on each screen. For example, in Figure 5.3 the button labeled **Play** is larger than average and is placed in line with the item options, but placed above them. This use of layout is intended to help guide the examinee to listen to the audio stem prior to attempting the item.

Figure 4.3 displays heavy use of visual elements including layout, color, fonts, borders, and size to clarify the examinee's moderately complex task in responding to the item. A weakness in this item, however, is that the use of black text on a dark blue-green background makes the instructions less legible on screen than they should be.

Writing for the Screen

This section addresses important facets of written communication with the software program users. The information presented here applies to software screens such as the introductory screens, instructional screens, practice item screens, help screens, and closing screens. As far as size, spacing, and presentation of text are concerned, it also applies to the text of the actual item stem and response options (the content of the item, of course, should be based on measurement considerations).

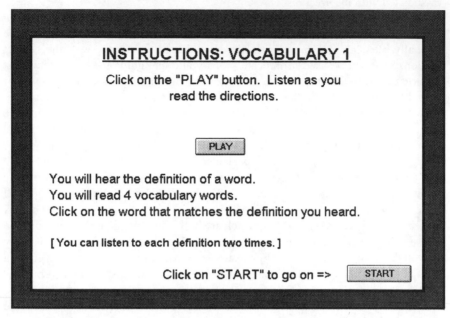

Figure 4.2.

The textual information included in a program should be well written, should communicate information clearly, and should be targeted to an appropriate reading level for the intended users. This level should be appropriate for the users' age and level of English skills. This overall goal is not different from one of producing good written communication for paper-and-pencil tests. However, writing for the screen has some additional constraints. Reading extensive information on screen is a more demanding, and slower, task than reading the same information from print (Nielsen, 1997b). Typically there is a much greater distance between a reader and a computer screen than between a reader and a printed document. Limitations on the screen resolution also result in far fewer words available per screen than per written page, along with more difficulty in scanning larger displays (such as a reading passage and all associated items).

Given these limitations and the demanding nature of reading on screen, one critical concern in writing for the screen is that the information be expressed concisely. Otherwise, it is very likely that many users simply will not read all the necessary information. Another course of action for communicating on screen is to convey information through nontextual means. For example, the use of formatting techniques such as layout, spacing, and bulleted text is a highly effective means to communicate important information with brevity. Graphics,

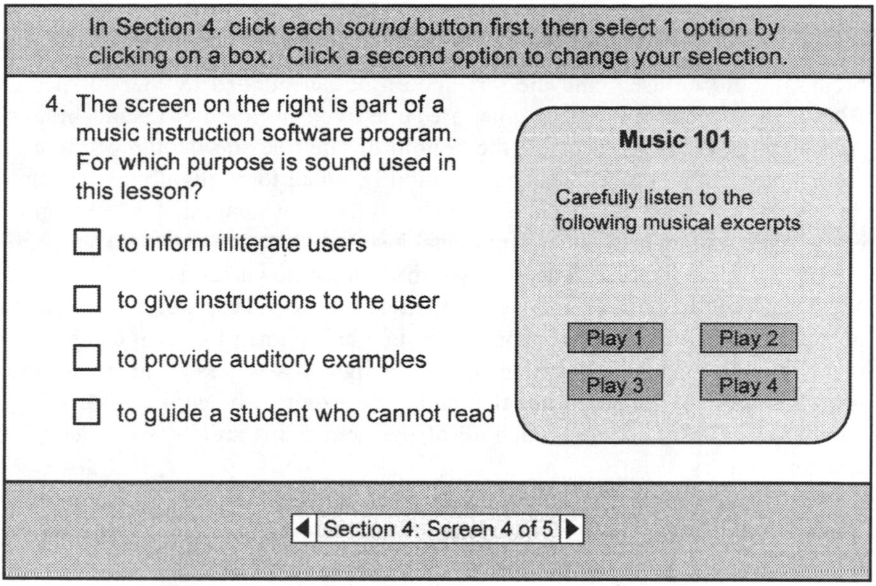

In Section 4. click each *sound* button first, then select 1 option by clicking on a box. Click a second option to change your selection.

4. The screen on the right is part of a music instruction software program. For which purpose is sound used in this lesson?

☐ to inform illiterate users

☐ to give instructions to the user

☐ to provide auditory examples

☐ to guide a student who cannot read

Music 101

Carefully listen to the following musical excerpts

Play 1   Play 2

Play 3   Play 4

◀ Section 4: Screen 4 of 5 ▶

Figure 4.3. An example of the use of visual elements

animation, and audio also can be used to help express information to the user concisely. The information should be written in a style that is pleasing to the eye, that has a good tone for the subject matter and the audience, and that flows well from one screen to the next. Appropriate word choice is also critical. In the progress indicator displayed in Figure 5.1, communication might be improved if the word "Item" were used in place of "Screen." Naturally, the text must be error-free, containing no typographical errors, grammatical mistakes, or incorrect instructions.

Many aspects of the display of textual information on computer screens have been empirically investigated. Tullis (1997) has summarized much of this research, while additional information about on-screen written communication is available in Nielsen (1997a, 1997b, 1999).

The font used for textual information should be selected carefully. It should be a font that is visually pleasing on screen (as opposed to print), large enough to be seen from a reasonable distance, and fully legible. The best font size for most on-screen reading appears to be between 9 and 12 points; fonts smaller or larger than this range tend to be less legible and to reduce reading speeds. There is also evidence that dark characters on a light background are preferred over light characters on a dark background.

The text should be carefully displayed. It should be formatted attractively and well placed on the screen. For example, text is more readable when the length of the lines is neither too short nor too long. The text should not be broken up, but neither should it extend from one edge of the screen to the other.

A recommendation is to maintain line lengths between 26 and 78 characters (Tullis, 1997).

The screen is easier to read if the text is not overly cluttered; instead, visual breaks should be used, and the text should be surrounded by "white space." Blank lines between paragraphs are one way to create visual breaks. Additionally, the space between the bottom of one line and the top of the next (sometimes referred to as "leading") should be equal to or slightly greater than the height of the text characters. In Figure 5.4 the item stem might be read more easily if the leading between the individual instructions were increased.

Use of all uppercase letters slows the reader down; however, use of an occasional word or phrase in uppercase letters can help those words to be found on screen quickly. When text is presented in a left-aligned format it can be read more quickly than fully justified text (although this is less of an issue with proportional than nonproportional fonts). One example of poor usability in a computerized test is one in which all of the item stems are displayed with the text centered.

The design principle of consistency in writing for the screen can be implemented by the use of consistent font and textual formatting choices throughout the program. All of the screens in a computer-based test may evidence the same font and formats, or one set of consistent textual choice may be used for the instructional screens and another for the item screens. For this aspect of the interface design, feedback typically is direct and verbal. All of the informational screens provide a kind of feedback to the user, but this is most evident when the user is given prompts or warnings in response to actions he or she takes. Positive verbal feedback may also be offered as the user works through the instructional screens or when taking the practice items. Forgiveness can be implemented through the use of pop-up windows or message boxes that inform the user about any software options that are currently unavailable or that address errors and miskeys.

A potentially confusing example of on-screen text can be found in the textual instruction "Click **NEXT** to continue." In a Web-based test that included this instruction, many examinees tried to click on the word "NEXT" within the statement. Although a **Next** button was prominently displayed, the fact that this was a Web-based exam and that blue lettering was used to distinguish the word "NEXT" within the instruction, led users to believe the word itself was hyper-linked to the next screen.

In Figure 4.2 the textual instructions for an ESL listening test are provided. This illustrates a particular challenge for test developers, in the conflict between concise writing optimal for computer instructions and the communication needs of nonnative speakers of English. The overall title is displayed in all uppercase letters, but the remaining instructions are given in a normal mix of upper and lowercase letters. Spacing is used to emphasize the **Play** button in the middle of the screen (whereby examinees can obtain audible instructions, in case their reading skills are inadequate). Although bullets are not used, the text is left-justified, with each instruction listed on a separate line.

Web-Based Tests

There are some additional, specific user interface issues that apply when a *Web-based* test is developed. The term *Web-based test* (WBT) is used here to refer to those computer-based tests that are administered, not only via Internet, but within Internet browser software (e.g., Netscape Navigator or Internet Explorer). Other forms of CBT software also may be transmitted or delivered over the Internet; however, their appearance and functionality will reflect the application program, rather than elements of the browser interface.

Advantages of a WBT include use of a single development platform (e.g., HTML with JavaScript) to produce an exam that can be delivered across a wide range of computer systems. However, the development and administration of a quality WBT requires specific attention to interface design, as well as many other issues.

A primary, critical aspect of interface design for WBTs is that a Web page may be rendered differently by different browsers, different hardware platforms, and different browsers on different platforms. In other words, a page may have a different appearance when accessed under Netscape Navigator on an IBM PC and on an Apple Macintosh computer or Internet Explorer on a PC. Furthermore, a given font used on the page may not be installed on an examinee's computer; or a given user may have customized his or her computer so that certain page elements are colored or displayed in ways other than what the page designer specified. This state of affairs is quite contrary to the level of control over layout and design typically required in standardized test applications. The test developer has a limited number of options available in a WBT environment to provide a truly standardized test administration, given that standardization is contrary to the underlying principles of the World Wide Web. At a minimum, the test developer can follow HTML and other Web standards in the development of the WBT and then evaluate the exam pages on multiple browser and hardware platforms, to ensure that it looks and functions appropriately. This will not provide identical pages, but it will help prevent the most serious inconsistencies or problems. In applications where standardization and consistency of design have greater importance, the test developer can constrain the WBT so that it will only run on a specified browser and hardware system. While this is not the typical approach for most Web pages, it simulates the hardware and system requirements used for most CBT development and administration.

Another critical difference between WBT interface design and other computer-based tests is related to the use of what might be termed *display space*. Some WBTs (using simple HTML coding) consist of a single, long, scrollable document, with the items displayed one below another in a single, long column. With this type of user interface, the design of the entire page must be considered, rather than a single "item screen" at a time. A page may use horizontal rulers to break up test sections or to separate instructional text from actual items. The user should not have to scroll horizontally; rather, the entire width of the WBT page should fit on the screen, even when the length does not. The WBT page should also be designed so that each discrete item can be displayed on a single screen in its entirety; an examinee should not have to scroll back and forth to view an item's stem and response options. More complex items, such as those that would typically function as multiscreen items in a typical CBT, are always challenging to display clearly and require particular care in a WBT format. The examinee should not have to struggle to access and view each item element.

An option that test developers may elect to take is to design the WBT so that it uses display space in a manner that is very similar to other computer-based tests. In this instance, a browser window is opened and displayed according to parameters that have been set by the developer (perhaps using JavaScript or other programming code), such as 640 x 480 pixels. This constrains each page of the WBT to specific elements that are somewhat comparable to the "item screens" of other computer-based tests. The layout of these item pages can be designed to include item-screen elements such as item instructions, a help option, and navigation buttons for access to the previous and next items in the exam.

This brief consideration of WBT interface design is just an introduction to some of the primary issues and options. These possible programming solutions are intended to be illustrative of the ways in which test developers can currently address the specific interface and design issues in Web-based forms of assessment. Other programming options are currently available, and no doubt more will become available in the future. Furthermore, additional interface issues will arise for any WBT that utilizes other Web elements. These may include the use of multimedia, interactivity, and navigation to other pages or resources. Given the rapid state of change on the Web, any final resolution to these issues is not likely in the near future. Attention to basic principles of interface design and measurement standards provides the best guidelines for the concerned test developer.

Quality Control

There is an additional aspect of software evaluation and testing that has not been addressed yet. That is the process of *quality control*. In many CBT applications, the quality control, or QC, phase of software development is a critical evaluation stage. In this aspect of evaluation, exam developers use and test an extensive set of software components to ensure that they are functioning as planned. This includes the correct display of items and item types on the screen. Item scoring must also be tested. For example, innovative item types that have more than one correct response may be tested to ensure that all possible correct responses are actually scored as correct. The correct functioning of psychometric components of the exam, such as an adaptive item-selection algorithm, may need to be confirmed. In other words, while each individual test and software element should have been thoroughly tested earlier in the test development process, the final QC phase evaluates the full, integrated package to ensure that all of the components are functioning together, as planned.

While QC includes many elements that are similar to software evaluation, there are distinct differences between the processes. A software evaluation can be conducted at any point in the development of the software program; earlier it was recommended as one part of the process of selecting an existing commercial package for use. QC will instead be used only on the software program in use, to ensure the final quality of the entire computerized test application.

Summary

There are many varied requirements for the development and administration of a good computerized exam program. Knowledge of the principles and process of software design is likely to be a weak point for many testing and measurement professionals. This chapter is not a comprehensive coverage of software development issues, but it has introduced many important concepts and emphasized some critical needs. Highlights of these issues are displayed in Table 4.5. Further resources on this topic are included in the References and Additional Readings.

Table 4.5. Highlights of Software Issues

Usability Studies
- Conduct them early and often
- Include user testing in which potential examinees are watched while attempting to carry out real tasks with the software

Software Evaluation
- Develop a prioritized features list
- Have experts examine the software using an evaluation checklist

Aspects of the User Interface
- Navigation
- Visual style
- Writing for the screen

Design Principles
- Consistency
- Feedback
- Forgiveness

Web-Based Tests
- Standardization concerns
- Display space

Quality Control
- Final evaluation phase

References

Alessi, S.M., & Trollip, S.R. (1991). *Computer-Based Instruction: Methods and Development*. Englewood Cliffs, NJ: Prentice-Hall.

Apple, Inc. (1995). Human Interface Design and the Development Process. In *Macintosh Human Interface Guidelines*. Reading, MA: Addison-Wesley.

Bennett, R. E., & Bejar, I. I. (1998). Validity and automated scoring: It's not only the scoring, *Educational Measurement: Issues and Practice*, 17, 9–17.

Bias, R. G., & Mayhew, E. J. (1994). *Cost-Justifying Usability*. Boston: Academic Press.

Booth, J. (1991). The key to valid computer-based testing: The user interface. *Revue Européenne de Psychologie Appliquée*, 41, 281–293.

Bunderson, V. C., Inouye, D. I., & Olsen, J. B. (1989). The four generations of computerized educational measurement. In Linn, R. (ed.) *Educational Measurement*, 3rd edition. New York: American Council on Education and Macmillan Publishing Co.

Ehrlich, K., & Rohn, J. A. (1994). Cost justification of usability engineering: A vendor's perspective. In Bias, R. G., & Mayhew, D. J. (eds.) *Cost-Justifying Usability* (pp.73–110). Boston: Academic Press.

Gould, J. D., Boies, F.J., & Ukelson, J. (1997). How to design usable systems. In Helander, M., Landauer, T. K., & Prabhu, P. (eds.). *Handbook of Human-Computer Interaction*, 2nd completely revised edition. (pp. 231–254). Amsterdam: Elsevier.

Gould, J. D. & Lewis, C. (1985). Designing for usability: Key principles and what designers think. In Baecker, R., & Buxton, (eds.), *Readings in HCI*. (pp. 528–539). Association for Computing Machinery.

Harmes, J. C., & Parshall, C. G. (2000, November). An Iterative Process For Computerized Test Development: Integrating Usability Methods. Paper presented at the annual meeting of the Florida Educational Research Association, Tallahassee.

Harrison, M. C., Henneman, R. L., & Blatt, L. A. (1994). Design of a human factors cost-justification tool. In Bias, R. G., & Mayhew, D. J. (eds.) *Cost-Justifying Usability* (pp. 203–241). Boston: Academic Press.

Helander, M., Landauer, T. K., & Prabhu, P. (eds.). (1997). *Handbook Of Human-Computer Interaction*, 2nd completely revised edition. Amsterdam: Elsevier.

Karat, C. (1997). Cost-justifying usability engineering in the software life cycle. In Helander, M., Landauer, T. K., & Prabhu, P. (eds.). *Handbook Of Human-Computer Interaction*, 2nd completely revised edition. (pp. 767–778). Amsterdam: Elsevier.

Kirakowski, J., & Corbett, M. (1990). *Effective Methodology for the Study of HCI*. New York: North-Holland.

Landauer, T. K. (1995). *The Trouble with Computers: Usefulness, Usability, and Productivity*. Cambridge, MA: MIT Press.

Landauer, T. K. (1997). Behavioral research methods in human-computer interaction. In M. G. Helander, T. K. Landauer, P. Prabhu (eds.) *Handbook of Human-Computer Interaction*, 2nd completely revised edition, (203–227). Amsterdam: Elsevier.

Mayhew, D. J., & Mantei, M. (1994). A basic framework for cost-justifying usability engineering. In Bias, R. G., & Mayhew, D. J. (eds.) *Cost-Justifying Usability* (pp. 9–43). Boston: Academic Press.

Nielsen, J. (1993). *Usability Engineering*. Boston: Academic Press.

Nielsen, J. (1994a). Guerrilla HCI: Using discount usability engineering to penetrate the intimidation barrier. In Bias, R. G. & Mayhew, D. J. (eds.) *Cost-justifying usability*. (pp. 245–272). Boston: Academic Press. [also online at: http://www.useit.com/papers/guerrilla_hci.html]

Nielsen, J. (1994b). *Heuristics for User Interface Design.* [Online at: http://www.useit.com/papers/heuristic/]

Nielsen, J. (1997a). *How Users Read on the Web.* [Online at: http://www.useit.com/alertbox/9710a.html]

Nielsen, J. (1997b). *Be succinct! (Writing for the Web).* [Online at: http://www.useit.com/alertbox/9703b.html]

Nielsen, J. (1999). *Differences Between Print Design and Web Design.* [Online] at: http://www.useit.com/alertbox/990124.html]

Nielsen, J. (2000). *Why You Only Need to Test with 5 Users.* [Online at: http://useit.com/alertbox/20000319.html]

Nielsen, J., & Mack, R. (eds.) (1994). *Usability Inspection Methods.* New York: Wiley & Sons.

Nielsen, J. & Molich, R. (1990). Heuristic evaluation of user interfaces. In *Proceedings of ACM CHI '90 Conference on Human Factors and Computing Systems* (pp. 249–256). Seattle: ACM.

Ravden, S. J., & Johnson, G .I. (1989). *Evaluating Usability of Human-Computer Interfaces: A Practical Method.* New York: Halstead Press.

Shneiderman, B. (1998). *Designing the User Interface: Strategies for Effective Human-Computer Interaction.* Reading, MA. : Addison-Wesley.

Tullis, T. S. (1997). Screen Design. In Helander, M. G., Landauer, T. K., & Prabhu P. (eds.) *Handbook of Human-Computer Interaction*, 2nd completely revised edition. (pp. 503–531), Amsterdam: Elsevier.

Additional Readings

CTB/McGraw-Hill (1997). Technical bulletin 1: *TerraNova.* Monterey, CA: Author.

CTB/McGraw-Hill. (1997). Usability: testing the test. In *Inform: A Series of Special Reports from CTB/McGraw-Hill.* (pp. 1–4). Monterey, CA: Author.

Gould, J. D. (1997). How to design usable systems. In Helander, M. G., Landauer , T. K., & Prabhu, P. (eds.) *Handbook of Human-Computer Interaction*, 2nd completely revised edition. Amsterdam: Elsevier.

Harmes, J. C., & Kemker, K. (1999, October). *Using JavaScript and Livestage to Create Online Assessments.* Paper presented at the annual meeting of the International Conference on Technology and Education, Tampa, FL.

Karat, C. (1994). A business case approach to usability cost justification. In Bias, R. G., & Mayhew, D. J. (eds.) *Cost-Justifying Usability* (pp. 45–70). Boston: Academic Press.

Nielsen, J. (1998). *Severity Ratings for Usability Problems.* [Online at: http://www.useit.com/papers/heuristic/severityrating.html]

Nielsen, J. (1995). *Technology Transfer of Heuristic Evaluation and Usability Inspection.* Keynote address at IFIP INTERACT '95, Lillehammer, Norway. [Also online at: http://www.useit.com/papers/heuristic/learning_inspection.html]

Pressman, R. S. (1992). *Software Engineering: A Practitioner's Approach.* New York: McGraw-Hill.

Rubin, J. (1994). *Handbook of Usability Testing: How to Plan, Design, and Conduct Effective Tests.* New York: Wiley & Sons.

5
Issues in Innovative Item Types

The development of innovative item types, defined as items that depart from the traditional, discrete, text-based, multiple-choice format, is perhaps the most promising area in the entire field of computer-based testing. The reason for this is the great potential that item innovations have for substantively improving measurement. Innovative item types are items that include some feature or function made available due to their administration on computer. Items may be innovative in many ways. This chapter will include a discussion of the purpose or value of innovative item types, the five dimensions in which items may be innovative, the impact of level of complexity on the development and implementation of these item types, and a view toward the future of innovative item types.

Purpose

The overarching purpose of innovative item types is to improve measurement, through either improving the quality of existing measures or expanding measurement into new areas. In other words, innovative item types enable us to measure something *better* or to measure something *more*. In general, most of the innovative item types developed to date provide measurement improvements in one or more of the following ways.

First of all, innovative item types may improve measurement by reducing guessing. While a typical four- or five-option multiple-choice item can be responded to correctly by simple guessing as much as 20–25% of the time, this guessing factor can be greatly reduced through innovative item types. One way in which they reduce the potential effect of guessing is by appropriately increasing the number of options in a selected response item type. For example, in a test of reading comprehension, the examinee can be asked to select the topic sentence in a reading passage. Thus, every sentence in the passage becomes an option rather than four or five passage sentences listed as the only response options. Examinees also can be asked to select one part of a complex graphic image. Again, the number of available responses is likely to be far greater than the usual four or five.

The potential for guessing an answer correctly can be reduced even further through the use of constructed response items. In a test of math skills, for example, examinees can be asked to type a numerical response, rather than selecting an option from a list. Short responses to verbal items also can be collected and scored in a similar manner. Acceptable misspellings, or alternative mathematical formulations, may be included as keys within the list of acceptable responses.

A second way in which innovative item types are designed to provide better measurement is by measuring some knowledge or skill more directly than traditional item types allow. These items can be designed to avoid some of the artificial constraints of traditional, multiple-choice items. One innovative item type provides for multiple-correct responses (e.g., "Select two of the following," "Select all that apply"). For example, a medical test might prompt examinees to select all of the elements listed that are symptoms of a particular illness. Another way in which innovative item types provide for a more direct measure of proficiency is in sequence items. In a history test, for example, examinees may be asked to indicate the order or sequence in which a series of events occurred. A traditional item type might provide a numbered set of events and response options that indicated various possible orderings for those numbered events (e.g., a: 2, 1, 4, 3; b: 4, 2, 1, 3). In a computerized innovative item, the examinee instead could drag the events into the desired order. More direct measurement can also be provided in graphical innovative items. Examinees may be asked to click directly on a graphic or image. Or they may be given a set of icons and tools, which they must use to *construct* a graphic as their response to the item. Innovative item types that include nontext media can provide another approach to more direct measurement. Rather than verbally describing some visual, auditory, or dynamic element, these items can directly incorporate images, sounds, animations, or videos into the item.

Innovative item types also improve measurement by expanding the content coverage of a testing program. That is, use of computer technology may enable a testing program to include areas of content that were logistically challenging, or even impossible, to assess in traditional paper-and-pencil administration. The inclusion of high-quality graphics can expand assessment in many areas. One example is the use of medical slide images in an item stem; a very different example of the same technology is the use of fine-arts graphic images.

Another use of the technology to expand content areas is the inclusion of sound. The computer's audio functions provide a fairly easy way to add assessment of listening to numerous content areas. These include content fields such as foreign languages and music as well as many others. For example, medical and scientific equipment often produce sounds that need to be interpreted and understood; tests in these areas can use innovative items that incorporate appropriate sounds. In all these examples, the innovative item types use the test administration technology to measure something more than had been feasible previously.

The final way in which innovative item types provide improved is to expand the cognitive skills measured on a test. For example, innovative item types have been designed that require examinees to construct or assemble on-screen figures. While this type of task remains completely scorable by the computer, it also provides for the measurement of productive skills not included in traditional assessments. An example of this use of innovative item types to expand the measurement of cognitive processes is seen in writing-skills assessments. Examinees are presented with an error-filled passage and then asked to identify the errors. The examinees may even be presented with the opportunity to retype sections of text or correct the errors. Both error identification and actual correction are cognitively different from traditional multiple-choice writing-skills items. Numerous other applications of innovative item types to expand the measurement of cognitive skills are possible.

Further examples of innovative item types that provide each of these measurement improvements are offered in the next sections.

Dimensions of Innovation

The phrase *innovative item types* encompasses a large number of innovations. They will be discussed here in terms of a five-dimension classification system. These five dimensions are not completely independent. However, in most cases, items are innovative in only one or two of these dimensions at a time.

The five dimensions of item innovation are item format, response action, media inclusion, level of interactivity, and scoring method. *Item format* defines the sort of response collected from the examinee; major categories of item format are selected response and constructed response. *Response action* refers to the means by which examinees provide their responses, including key presses and mouse clicks. *Media inclusion* covers the addition of nontext elements within an item, including graphics, sound, animation, and video. *Level of interactivity* describes the extent to which an item type reacts or responds to examinee input. This can range from no interactivity through complex, multistep items with branching. Finally, *scoring method* addresses how examinee responses are converted into quantitative scores. This includes completely automated dichotomous scoring along with scoring programs that need to be "trained" to model human raters who assign polytomous scores.

Further discussion of each of these dimensions is provided next, along with examples of innovative item types to illustrate the potential advantages inherent in each area. (The topic of dimensions of item type innovation is addressed more fully in Parshall, Davey, & Pashley, 2000).

Item Format

The most common item format in standardized, paper-and-pencil testing is the multiple-choice item type. Variants on this format include multiple response, ordered response, true-false, and matching items. These formats are all *selected response* instances. *Constructed response* item formats differ from these in that they require examinees to generate or construct rather than select their responses. Examples include such formats as fill-in-the-blank, short answer, and essay. All of these item types can be adapted for presentation on computer, along with many more. The most important of these are detailed in the following sections.

Selected Response Items

The most familiar selected response item format is multiple-choice, where examinees choose answers from a list of alternatives. Most often, the item consists of an item stem and a set of two to five possible responses. Computerized adaptations of this format can expand on this in order to reduce guessing or afford a more direct form of assessment. For example, items may ask examinees to click on and select the proper sentence from a reading passage or to select one part of a complex graphic image. Because the number of available options can be much greater than the usual four or five and can vary from item to item, the possibility of guessing correctly is substantially reduced.

Multiple-response items ask examinees to select more than one option, with the number to be selected either specified or left open (e.g., "Select two of the following options," "Click on all correct responses"). The test administration software may be designed so that examinees must select the specified number of options (they will not be able to proceed to the next item if they have selected more or fewer options). Or the software may be designed to allow examinees to select any number of the available options, including all options. Currently, most applications of this item type use dichotomous scoring; the response is either completely correct or incorrect. However, the use of partial-credit scoring could add to the information obtained through this item type. Like the innovations discussed earlier, this item format can provide a more direct measure or reduce the effect of guessing.

Another selected response item type is the figural response type. In figural response items, examinees respond by selecting a part of a figure or graphic. For items with visual elements, this provides a more direct measure of the examinee's response than would be offered through the use of verbal, multiple-choice descriptors of the options. An example of a selected figural response item type (with a student response) is provided in Figure 5.1 (Parshall, Stewart, & Ritter, 1996).

Ordered response items present examinees with a list of elements that they are asked to order or sequence in accord with some rule. For example, the examinees may put a series of historical events in chronological order, a series of numerical elements into size order, or even a list of alternatives into a *degree-of-correctness* order.

Another selected response item type is described in Davey, Godwin, and Mittelholtz (1997). Their test of writing skills is designed to simulate the editing stage of the writing process. Examinees are confronted with a passage that contains various grammatical and stylistic errors, but no indication is given as to the location of these errors. Examinees read the passage and use a cursor to point to sections that they think should be corrected or changed. They then are presented with a list of alternative ways of rewriting the suspect section. Examinees can select one of the alternatives or choose to leave the section as written. If an alternative is chosen, the replacement text is copied into the passage so that the changes can be reviewed in their proper context. The rationale behind the use of this item type is that the error-identification portion of the task adds to the cognitive skills assessed by the items, even though conventional multiple-choice items are used.

There are other selected-response item formats that have been used in paper-and-pencil administrations that could easily be adapted for administration in computer-based tests. One example is an item to which an examinee is able to respond multiple times, possibly with feedback regarding the correctness of each response. The final item score for the examinee is then based on *percent correct out of number attempted*, or *percent attempted until correct*.

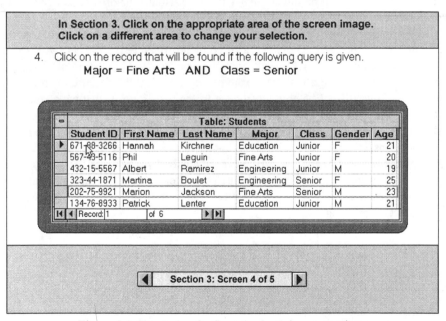

Figure 5.1. Example of a figural selected response item

Constructed Response Items

A wide range of constructed response items can be used in computer-based tests. These vary from fairly simple formats that are easy to score to far more complex formats that require the use of elaborate scoring algorithms. The simplest examples are items that require the examinee to type a short response—perhaps a numerical answer to a quantitative question or a brief verbal response to a verbal question. These responses are scored, usually dichotomously as either correct or incorrect, by comparing each response to a list of acceptable answers that may include alternate mathematical formulations or acceptable misspellings.

Another constructed response item format extends the selected figural response type described earlier. The constructed version of this type allows examinees to mark on, assemble, or interact with a figure on the screen. Examinees may be asked to do graphical tasks such as designing a building blueprint. Figure 5.2 displays a figural constructed response item in which examinees are asked to assemble an electronic circuit (French & Godwin, 1996).

Constructed response math items were presented in Bennett, Morley, and Quardt (1998). In this study, using the *generating expressions* item type, examinees respond by plotting points on a grid. In the *mathematical expressions* item type, examinees responded by typing a formula. While the correct response for this item type may take any number of forms, the automated scoring developed for these items has been designed to address this.

Breland (1998) investigated a constructed response text-editing task. This application was similar to the selected-response-editing task described by Davey, Godwin, and Mittelholz (1997) in that examinees were presented with a text passage that contained errors. However, in Breland's case sections containing errors were enclosed in brackets, and the examinees selected the bracketed text and retyped it to correct it. Automated scoring was provided by matching the examinee's response with a table of correct solutions.

Response Action

While the dimension of *item format* discussed earlier defines what examinees are asked, the dimension of *response action* defines how they are to respond. Response action refers to the physical action that an examinee makes to respond to an item. The most common response action required of examinees in conventional paper-and-pencil assessments is to use a pencil to *bubble in* an oval associated with an option.

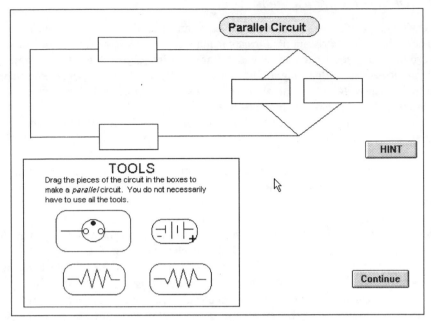

Figure 5.2. Example of a figural constructed response item

In computerized tests, response actions frequently are provided through the keyboard or mouse. Examinees respond through the keyboard by typing simple numbers and characters and by providing more extended responses. Examinees can use keyboard "command" keys (e.g., **Enter**, **PgDn**). Multiple-choice options may be chosen by using either the keyboard to type the associated letter or the mouse to click on the selected response. Examinees can use the mouse to click on a location in a text passage or on a graphic, to highlight text or images, or to drag text, numbers, or icons into some desired place or order.

The mouse may also be used for purposes other than item responses. For example, it can be used it to obtain online help or hints, to access a computerized calculator, to call up online reference materials, or to play audio or video files. In a study by Baker and O'Neil (1995), examinees used the mouse to access pull-down menus. In the study by Bennett, Goodman, et al. (1997), examinees used the mouse to identify a specific frame in an online video sequence.

Input devices beyond the keyboard and mouse are possible and, for particular applications, may be highly desirable. Other input devices that are available, relatively prevalent, and reasonably priced include touch screens, light pens, joysticks, trackballs, and microphones. Appropriate inclusion of these other input devices could offer measurement benefits. For example, very young examinees can be assessed with less error using touch screens, light pens, or enlarged and simplified keyboards. Particular skills, such as those that are highly movement-oriented, may be better measured using joysticks or trackballs. A microphone can be used, perhaps along with speech-recognition software, to collect spoken examinee responses to items.

Computer administration expands the ways in which items can be structured, creating the opportunity to obtain more meaningful samples of examinee behaviors. The structure of an item can be thought of in terms of the "task constraints" imposed on the examinees' responses (Bennett & Bejar, 1998). These task constraints focus and limit examinee response actions; they shape the ways in which examinees can respond to an item or task. They also constrain the kinds of questions that can be asked and may impact the ways in which examinees think about these questions. Item types that have been developed with task constraints that aptly reflect the construct of interest and that use the most appropriate input devices and response actions can improve measurement by reducing error, offering a more direct form of assessment, and expanding coverage of content and cognitive skills.

It will be important for the design of items that use alternative response actions, and possibly alternative input devices, that their inclusion be substantively appropriate. While articulated use of these devices and actions may offer improvements over collecting responses via paper and pencil or the keyboard, it will also be important to ensure that the task does not become inappropriately more difficult or unnecessarily confusing. Many of these considerations relate to the quality of the software interface. Further discussion on that topic is included in Chapter 4.

Media Inclusion

Another dimension of item innovation is that of media inclusion. Perhaps the primary measurement benefit provided by this dimension is the opportunity to expand a test's coverage of content areas and cognitive skills. The addition of nontext media can enhance the validity and task congruence of a test and reduce inappropriate dependence on reading skills.

The computer's built-in functions provide the capacity for adding nontext media to computer-based examinations. The computer can be used to display graphics, play sounds, or run animations and videos. Innovative item types that include these nontext media frequently include them in the item stem. Often, this richer item stem is then used in conjunction with a traditional multiple-choice set of response options, although other possibilities exist.

Graphics can be included easily in computerized tests, in both the item stem and the response options. In the simplest case, a graphic image may be presented along with the item stem, in a manner similar to that of some paper-and-pencil exams. The comparative ease with which images can be stored and displayed on computer may facilitate their inclusion in additional appropriate content areas. In other cases, the innovative item type using a graphic may be designed so that examinees can manipulate the image by rotating or resizing it. In still other cases, examinees can respond by selecting one of a set of figures, clicking directly on some part of a graphic, or dragging icons to assemble a relevant image.

Audio files, or sounds, also may be included in computerized items and can be used to assess listening skills. An exam that includes audio items typically will be administered with the use of headphones. The volume of the sound files, the timing over when they are played, and possibly even the number of times they are played can all be placed under the examinee's control. Primary examples of the use of audio in computerized innovative items include language testing (ACT, Inc., 1999; ETS, 1998) and music tests (Vispoel, Wang, & Bleiler, 1997). The assessment of listening to speech forms of audio has also been considered in assessing the general skill of listening comprehension (ACT, Inc., 1998) and listening in the fields of history and medicine (Bennett, Goodman, et al., 1997). Further applications of appropriate assessment of listening, including nonspeech sounds, are easy to imagine. One example is a mechanics' exam that includes an item that played the sound of an engine misfiring; a second example is a medical item that includes sounds that might be heard through a stethoscope. Figure 5.3 displays an example of an item from an ESL Listening test (Balizet, Treder, & Parshall, 1999). (Audio can also be included in computerized tests for other purposes. For further discussion about potential uses of audio, see Parshall [1999].)

Animation and video are additional media elements that can be included in computer-based innovative items. Animation and video provide a marked difference from most other prompt material in that they are dynamic, rather than static in nature. That is, they can display motion and changes over time. Animation has the advantage of being far less memory-intensive than video. Due to its greater simplicity, it may also be better able to focus examinee attention on essential visual elements, just as a line drawing may have advantages over a photograph. Video can provide better "real-world" congruence than animation and is preferred for some applications. Animation has been used in investigations of innovative science assessments (French & Godwin, 1996; Shavelson, Baxter, & Pine, 1992). The potential utility of animation was also considered by Bennett, Goodman, et al., (1997), who developed an item in which a series of static maps of a given region was displayed in quick succession to show the changes in nation boundaries over time. (The correct response to this item consisted of one of these static maps.) These researchers also developed prototype items that used video. A physical education item included video clips of students demonstrating athletic skills. A history test item included video of recent historical events. More extensive use of video was provided in an interactive video assessment developed and validated by Olson-Buchanan, Drasgow, et al. (1998). This test of conflict-resolution skills shows scenes of people interacting in the workplace. After an instance of workplace conflict is presented, the scene ends and examinees are presented with a multiple-choice question that asks them to select the best action for resolving the conflict. (The interactive component of this exam will be discussed in the next section.)

In addition to the single use of each of these forms of nontext media, innovative items can appropriately include multiple forms of these media. An item in a language listening skills test can display a still photo or video of two people holding a dialogue while the sound file containing their conversation is played. Bennett, Goodman, et al. (1997) developed a sample multimedia item that included an image of a static electrocardiogram strip, an animation of a heart monitor trace, and the sound of a heartbeat. Many more applications of media-based innovative item types are likely to be developed in the near future.

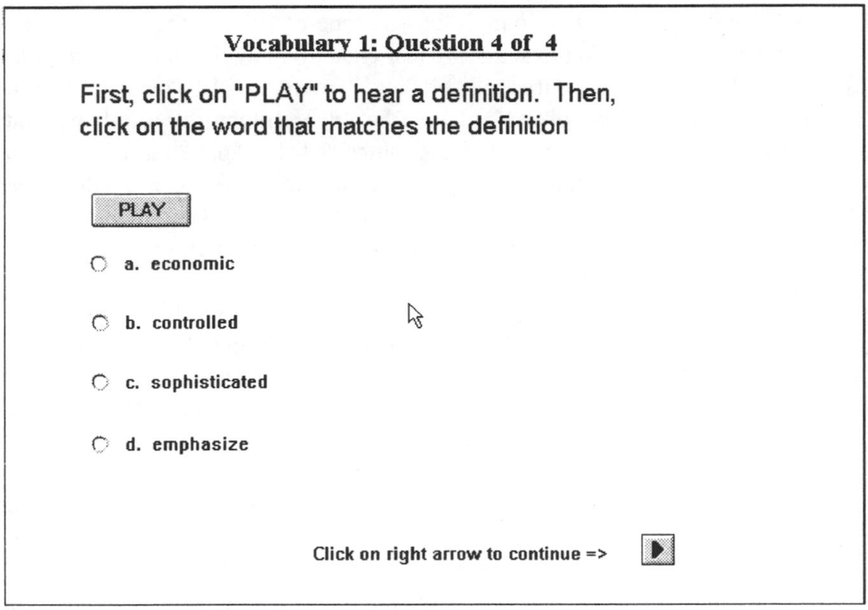

Vocabulary 1: Question 4 of 4

First, click on "PLAY" to hear a definition. Then, click on the word that matches the definition

PLAY

○ a. economic

○ b. controlled

○ c. sophisticated

○ d. emphasize

Click on right arrow to continue =>   ▶

Figure 5.3 Example of an audio item

Level of Interactivity

Most computerized items, including most current innovative items, are completely noninteractive. The examinee takes an action (e.g., makes a selection), and the item is complete. However, there are a few computer-based items that use a limited type of interactivity and a very few that are more highly interactive. Several distinct types or levels of interactivity can be distinguished.

A few item types use a limited kind of feedback, increasing item-examinee interaction slightly. With these, the examinee acts and then the computer responds with some sort of reaction. For example, in an item where examinees edit text, the new text can be displayed within the original passage, letting the examinees reread the passage with the change reflected. In sequencing items, once examinees have indicated their sequence or ordering for a set of elements, they can see the elements rearranged in the new order. And when examinees click on a histogram, scale, or dial they may see the bar or gauge move to reflect their action. While the examinees are not being given feedback about the correctness of their responses, this limited form of interactivity can be used to help them decide whether a response should be changed. It allows them to consider the item and the response within a particular context

In another level of interactivity, an innovative item provides a set of online tools for the examinee's use within the response. This application may be regarded as a "passive" form of interactivity; the computer interacts with, or responds to, the examinee's actions by displaying the results on screen in an integrated way. An elaborate example of this type of item interactivity can be seen in the computer-based credentialing test created by the National Council of Architectural Registration Boards (NCARB; see Braun, 1994). This test offers a computerized simulation of performance-based architectural problems and assignments. The examinee must use computerized drawing tools to design a solution to the problem "vignette" within specified criteria. The computer does not directly react to or interact with the examinee, but it does provides a forum for an extensive set of the examinee's actions to be made and displayed in an integrated, contextual manner.

A number of certification exams in the information technology (IT) field display this type of passive interactivity. These exams are often designed to simulate or model the use of a given software program, and the examinees are provided with software-use tasks to undertake. The tests may be designed so that examinees are basically free to select any software command or option that would be available in actual use of the program, or they may be constrained so that a more limited subset of software features are "live." In either case, far more options are likely to be available throughout the exam than would be typical of noninnovative forms of testing. The examinees may be able to complete an assigned task in a number of different ways, and scoring of the task may not even distinguish between inefficient or optimal means of accomplishing the end goal. An example of this type of interactivity is provided in Figure 5.4. A Web-based library skills item provides the functionality of library search software and displays additional information in a pop-up window upon examinee request (Harmes & Parshall, 2000).

A further type or level of interactivity incorporates a two- or multistep branching function within the item. In this type of innovative item, simple branched structures are built into the item's response options, and the examinee selection determines which branch is followed. An example of this type of interactivity is provided in the interactive video assessment of conflict resolution skills discussed earlier (Drasgow, Olson-Buchanan, & Moberg, 1999; Olson-Buchanan, Drasgow, et al. 1998). In this application, an item begins with a video-based scene of workplace conflict, followed by a multiple-choice question relating to the best way to resolve the conflict. Once the examinee selects a response, a second video scene is displayed, followed by another multiple-

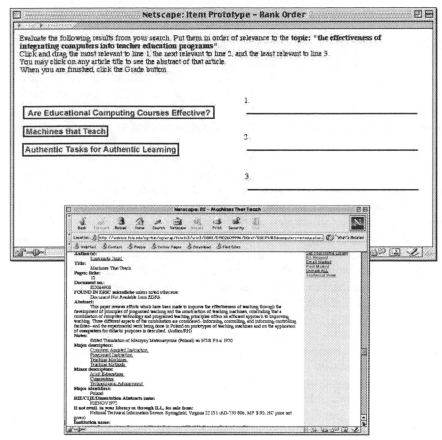

Figure 5.4. Example of a "passive" interactive item

choice item. The particular second scene displayed is based on the examinee's selected action, and the action or conflict within the scenario moves forward based on that choice. This assessment uses a two-stage branching level of interactivity (although the sense of interactivity is probably enhanced further through the use of the video prompts in which the characters interact with one another).

In yet another level of interactivity, an online problem situation may be accompanied by an extensive set of options or choices made available to the examinee. In this case, the examinee may be able to select multiple options or actions at any given time. The computer will then react to these choices, updating and revising the on-screen problem. The number of steps to completion of this type of innovative item may be variable, depending on the actions an examinee takes and the computer reactions they engender. An example of this type of interactivity can be seen in a test of physicians' skills in patient management (Clauser, Margolis, Clyman, and Ross, 1997). In this computerized performance test, an examinee is presented with an interactive patient "case." The examinee must diagnose and treat the on-screen patient through a series of interactions. The examinee can order medical tests, interpret the results of those tests, prescribe medications, and monitor changes in the patient in response to the condition and treatment. All the steps taken by the examinee are recorded, along with the simulation-based time in which each action occurred. The result is a list of "transactions" undertaken by the examinee during the interactive treatment.

The limited development of interactivity, compared to some of the other innovation dimensions, is probably related to the challenges inherent in developing interactive assessments. Drasgow, Olson-Buchanan, and Moberg (1999) point out that while the application they have developed consists of only two stages of interaction, even this limited level of interactivity results in numerous test paths that are taken by few if any examinees. Test developers are thus required to produce much more content than will be seen by any given examinee. Godwin (personal communication) noted a related potential difficulty with development of branching item types. Without care, test developers can produce interactive tests in which a great number of entire paths and all of their associated options are incorrect. Examinees may drift further and further away from correct choices or from providing any useful assessment information. Finally, Braun (1994) and Clauser, Margolis, Clyman, and Ross (1997) describe some of the difficulties inherent in developing appropriate scoring for interactive simulation-based assessments. The scoring methods used by complex interactive items must consider many factors, including the optimal weight of various components of the task and the dependency of the examinees' various responses to the task, among other things.

Despite these difficulties, it is also clear from the limited development of interactive assessments to date that this innovation has the potential to contribute substantively to new forms of assessment and to enable measurement in additional valuable arenas.

Scoring Method

Automated scoring is expected in traditional standardized paper-and-pencil testing and for traditional item types in CBT administrations. Automated scoring may also exist for many innovative item types. When the item includes no interactivity, is selected response, and produces a dichotomous score, then automated scoring is a simple matter. Automated scoring can be accomplished for other innovative item types as well, but it is a more complex matter in these cases.

Scoring for multistep items must address response dependency, the tendency for an examinee's response on one step to clue or aid his or her response to subsequent steps. Also, for any multipart item in which an examinee is prompted to provide more than a single response, scoring needs to address how the individual parts should be weighted and how they should be combined into a polytomous item score.

Typically, scoring is more complex for constructed-response item types. For example, simple open-ended items may be scored by comparing the examinee's response to a keylist, which includes alternate formations or acceptable misspellings. For selected figural response items, scoring is based on the position of the examinee's mouse click on the graphic image.

The more complex constructed-response items require even more complex scoring algorithms. The scoring solutions for these item types are often rule-based. The item types and their scoring algorithms are developed jointly for use in computer-based tests. The item and component scores initially are developed by human raters, even though the automated scoring may later be conducted by computer.

A somewhat different approach to automated scoring can be taken with essay items. Several distinct programs have been written to score essay responses (e.g., PEG, E-rater, Intellimetric Engineer, Intelligent Essay Assessor, InQuizit). The criteria for these programs vary greatly, from a consideration of surface features, such as overall length, to the use of advanced computational linguistics. Despite these differences, research on many of these programs has shown that they are capable of producing a score that is as similar to one from a human rater as a second human rater's score would be (Burstein et al., 1998; Landauer, Laham, Rehder, & Schreiner, 1997; Page & Petersen, 1995). All of the various automated-scoring programs require some number of human scores to "train" the computer program and to handle any difficult responses.

There are a number of issues related to automated essay-scoring that remain unresolved at the present time. For example, it is unclear how robust these essay scoring programs may be to "cheating" (i.e., examinee responses that are tailored to the computer program's criteria rather than to the prompt or question) or how accepting the public may be of computerized scoring. For these reasons, the most likely application of an automated essay-scoring program is as a replacement for a second human rater in those testing programs where essay responses are scored by two raters. Currently, operational use of these programs is relatively limited, but that is likely to change dramatically in the next few years.

Task Complexity

Innovative item types span a very wide range of *task complexity,* as can be seen through the examples of innovative items presented in this chapter. This level of task complexity has implications for item and item-type development as well as for implementation with a test delivery method.

Items with low task complexity can be seen to have the greatest similarity to traditional text-based multiple-choice items. They require a similar amount of examinee response time and provide a similar amount of measurement information. Also, like traditional items, these low-complexity innovative item types typically are scored dichotomously. In general, the modest differences between these innovative item types and more traditional items imply that item-writing efforts can incorporate the new item types without difficulty, producing the new items with a comparable development effort.

Because of their similarities to traditional items, items with low task complexity can be incorporated into an existing test structure fairly easily. They can be used along with, or in place of, traditional items. At most, only minor adjustments to the overall test length, test administration time, and score scale should be needed. It is also possible to use these low task complexity items, either alone or with traditional items, within any of the test-delivery methods presented in this volume. An example of an item type with low task complexity is a mathematics item in which the examinees are required to type their answers rather than select a response option.

Innovative item types with high task complexity, however, are a very different matter. Items with high task complexity tend to require greater examinee response time, whether the items consist of a computerized simulation of a performance-based task, an online essay prompt, or other extended assignment. A single "item" or task of this type also is expected to provide a great deal more information than would be available from a single, discrete, multiple-choice item. Thus, items with high task complexity typically produce a polytomous score. Due in part to the greater time requirement for high-complexity items, an exam must be comprised of far fewer of these items or tasks. An example of high-task-complexity items can be seen in the test of physician skills through diagnosing and treating an on-screen patient (Clauser, Margolis, Clyman, & Ross, 1997).

The limitation on the number of items in a given test form can result in problems of limited task specificity and poor generalizability for the assessment as a whole, as it may for extended high-complexity paper-and-pencil tasks. Tests in which only a few extensive tasks are given may be especially subject to memorability and item exposure. However, the related advantages for extensive, complex, and integrated tasks also hold, in that they can provide a more contextualized assessment and better real-world congruence.

Typically, assessments of high task complexity are developed for a specific testing program, to satisfy particular needs for coverage of content knowledge and cognitive skills within the domain of interest. Due to the complexity of these tasks, considerable effort must be devoted to the development of the item types themselves and to the development and validation of the scoring methods.

Innovative items of high task complexity are usually not incorporated into an existing test program or administered as part of a combined test-delivery model. Rather, they are administered in a "stand-alone" fashion, and any traditional or low-complexity tasks are administered in a separate section of the exam. One or only a very few high-complexity items typically would be administered to a given examinee, usually in some kind of fixed-form test-delivery approach.

The majority of the research and development of innovative item types has been conducted at these two extremes of task complexity. Relatively little work has been accomplished in terms of developing item types of *moderate* task complexity. Items or tasks at this level of complexity could be expected to take a moderate amount of examinee response time, compared to the very low- and very high-complexity item types. They would also utilize some form of partial-credit or polytomous scoring, although the weighting of any single item with moderate task complexity would probably be less than that of a single high-complexity item. A relatively simple example of an item with moderate task complexity is the circuit assembly item displayed in Figure 5.2. This item would take more time and would require an examinee to provide more than the single response of a multiple-choice item, but with the careful application of partial-credit scoring it could also yield greater information about the examinee's knowledge of circuitry.

Depending on where along the complexity continuum the items might fall (and thus, the amount of examinee-response time required by these innovative items), they might not be easily used in conjunction with traditional, multiple-choice items. If they cannot, an exam could be developed to consist solely of moderately complex innovative items.

Such an exam would include a moderate number of these tasks—fewer than would be feasible for a traditional multiple-choice exam but more than might be reasonable for performance-based simulations. Due to this factor, exams composed of moderate task complexity could offer a compromise between the two extremes. Ideally, these moderately complex tasks could provide measurement improvements over more traditional multiple-choice items. At the same time, an exam of this sort might be better able to provide adequate content coverage than the more time-consuming high-task-complexity exams, thus avoiding mitigating problems of task specificity and limited generalizability. A test composed of moderately complex item types could be designed to use any of the test-delivery methods presented in the chapters to follow.

Summary

This chapter has included a discussion of the benefits of innovative item types along with a description of various dimensions of innovation. The foundational purpose of item innovations was seen to be improved measurement, either by measuring something *better* or by measuring something *more*. Innovative item types that measure in better ways may reduce the effect of guessing, or they may enable a more direct measure of the skill or attribute of interest. Innovative item types that measure more may provide for the assessment of additional content areas or for the assessment of additional cognitive processes. The dimensions in which items may be innovative include item format, response action, media inclusion, level of interactivity, and scoring method. The task complexity of innovative item types was also discussed, while it was noted that most developmental work has been conducted at the two extremes of low- and high-task complexity. Some of the ways in which these elements of innovation can be integrated are illustrated in Table 5.1. This table provides a few examples of innovative item types taken from this chapter, categorized by the measurement purpose of the innovation, one or more dimensions in which the item type is innovative, and the level of task complexity that might be typical for that item type.

The majority of the innovative item types presented in this chapter have been used in either research or operational settings. They are all within the realm of the possible for current development and implementation. Far more extensive innovations are on the assessment horizon. One promising possibility concerns assessment tasks that are embedded within instruction. Greater use of interactivity can also be imagined. Fuller use of media, moving toward immersed testing environments, can be envisioned. And, the development of items or tasks that call for examinees to use online resources, perhaps including the World Wide Web, may be a rich testing application.

An important point to recognize is that for many innovative item types, special test administration software may be necessary. Existing CBT software may be able to administer some of the low-task-complexity item types, but in most other cases, a customized effort is needed. It is also important to acknowledge that as great as the potential for these further innovative item types may be, the need to do the foundational psychometric work is even greater. The items and tasks should be developed in congruence with a testing area's construct definition and test design. It is likely that a variety of innovative item types need to be investigated to find those that are truly useful. Even then, research will be needed to establish the validity of the item types and of their associated scoring rubrics.

Table 5.1 Examples of Innovative Item Types by Measurement Purpose, Innovative Dimension, and Task Complexity

Innovative Item Type	Measurement Purpose	Innovative Dimension	Task Complexity
Numerical constructed response	To reduce guessing	Item format	Low
Click on an area of a graphical image	To reduce guessing	Item format Response action Media inclusion	Low to moderate
Select all that apply	To measure more directly	Item format Scoring method	Low
Audio in stem	To expand content coverage	Media inclusion	Low to moderate
Figural constructed response	To expand cognitive skills measured	Item format Response action Interactivity	Low, moderate, or high
Two-stage branching	To expand cognitive skills measured	Interactivity	Moderate to high
Simulation of software use	To measure more directly To expand content coverage	Interactivity Response action Scoring method	Moderate to high

References

ACT, Inc. (1998). Assessing listening comprehension: A Review of Recent Literature Relevant to an LSAT Listening Component. Unpublished manuscript, LSAC, Newton, PA.

ACT, Inc. (1999). *Technical Manual for the ESL Exam.* Iowa City: Author.

Baker, E. L., & O'Neil, H. F. Jr. (1995). Computer technology futures for the improvement of assessment. *Journal of Science Education and Technology, 4,* 37–45.

Balizet, S., Treder, D. W., & Parshall, C. G. (1999, April). The development of an audio computer-based classroom test of ESL listening skills. Paper presented at the annual meeting of the American Educational Research Association, Montreal.

Bennett, R. E., & Bejar, I. I. (1998). Validity and automated scoring: It's not only the scoring. *Educational Measurement: Issues & Practices, 17,* 9–17.

Bennett, R. E., Goodman, M., Hessinger, J., Ligget, J., Marshall, G., Kahn, H., & Zack, J. (1997). *Using Multimedia in Large-Scale Computer-Based Testing Programs* (Research Rep. No. RR-97-3). Princeton, NJ: Educational Testing Service.

Bennett, R. E., Morley, M., & Quardt, D. (1998, April). Three Response Types for Broadening the Conception of Mathematical Problem Solving in Computerized-Adaptive Tests. Paper presented at the annual meeting of the National Council of Measurement in Education, San Diego.

Braun, H. (1994). Assessing technology in assessment. In Baker, E. A., & O'Neil, H. F. (eds.), *Technology Assessment in Education and Training* (pp. 231–246). Hillsdale, NJ: Lawrence Erlbaum Associates.

Breland, H. M. (1998, April). Writing Assessment Through Automated Editing. Paper presented at the annual meeting of the National Council on Measurement in Education, San Diego.

Burstein, J., Kukich, K., Wolff, S., Lu, C., & Chodorow, M. (1998, April). Computer Analysis of Essays. Paper presented at the annual meeting of the National Council on Measurement in Education, San Diego.

Clauser, B. E., Margolis, M. J., Clyman, S. G., & Ross, L P. (1997). Development of automated scoring algorithms for complex performance assessments: A comparison of two approaches. *Journal of Educational Measurement, 34,* 141–161.

Davey, T., Godwin, J., & Mittelholtz, D. (1997). Developing and scoring an innovative computerized writing assessment. *Journal of Educational Measurement, 34,* 21–41.

Drasgow, F., Olson-Buchanan, J. B., & Moberg, P. J. (1999). Development of an interactive video assessment: Trials and tribulations. In Drasgow, F., & Olson-Buchanan, J. B, (eds.), *Innovations in Computerized Assessment.* (pp. 177–196). Mahwah, NJ: Lawrence Erlbaum Associates.

Educational Testing Service (ETS). (1998). *Computer-Based TOEFL Score User Guide.* Princeton, NJ: Author.

French, A., & Godwin, J. (1996, April). Using Multimedia Technology to Create Innovative Items. Paper presented at the annual meeting of the National Council on Measurement in Education, New York.

Harmes, J. C., & Parshall, C. G. (2000, November). An Iterative Process for Computerized Test Development: Integrating Usability Methods. Paper presented at the annual meeting of the Florida Educational Research Association, Tallahassee.

Landauer, T. K., Laham, D., Rehder, B., & Schreiner, M. E. (1997). How well can passage meaning be derived without using word order? A comparison of latent semantic analysis and humans. In Shafto, G., & Langley, P. (eds.), *Proceedings of the 19th Annual Meeting of the Cognitive Science Society* (pp. 412–417). Mahwah, NJ: Erlbaum.

Olson-Buchanan, J. B., Drasgow, F., Moberg, P. J., Mead, A. D., Keenan, P.A., & Donovan, M.A. (1998). Interactive video assessment of conflict resolution skills. *Personnel Psychology*, 51, 1–24.

Page, E. B. & Petersen N. S. (1995, March). The computer moves into essay grading: Updating the ancient test. *Phi Delta Kappen*, 76, 561–565.

Parshall, C. G. (1999, February). Audio CBTs: Measuring More through the use of Speech and Nonspeech Sound. Paper presented at the annual meeting of the National Council on Measurement in Education, Montreal.

Parshall, C. G., Davey, T., & Pashley, P. J. (2000). Innovative item types for computerized testing. In Van der Linden, W. J., & Glas, C. A. W. (eds.), *Computerized Adaptive Testing: Theory and Practice.* (pp. 129–148). Norwell, MA: Kluwer Academic Publisher.

Parshall, C. G., Stewart, R, & Ritter, J. (1996, April). Innovations: Sound, Graphics, and Alternative Response Modes. Paper presented at the annual meeting of the National Council on Measurement in Education, New York.

Shavelson, R. J., Baxter, G. P., & Pine, J. (1992). Performance assessments: Political rhetoric and measurement reality. *Educational Researcher,* 21, 22–27.

Vispoel, W. P., Wang, T., & Bleiler, T. (1997). Computerized adaptive and fixed-item testing of music listening skill: A comparison of efficiency, precision, and concurrent validity. *Journal of Educational Measurement,* 34, 43–63.

Additional Readings

ACT, Inc. (1995). *Work Keys.* Iowa City: Author.

Bejar, I. I. (1991). A methodology for scoring open-ended architectural design problems. *Journal of Applied Psychology,* 76, 522–532.

Bennett, R.E. (1998). *Reinventing Assessment.* Princeton, NJ: Educational Testing Service.

Bennett, R. E., & Sebrechts, M. M. (1997). A computer-based task for measuring the representational component of quantitative proficiency. *Journal of Educational Measurement,* 34, 64–77.

Bennett, R. E., Steffen, M., Singley, M. K., Morley, M., & Jacquemin, D. (1997). Evaluating an automatically scorable, open-ended response type for measuring mathematical reasoning in computer-adaptive tests. *Journal of Educational Measurement,* 34, 162–176.

Booth, J. (1991). The key to valid computer-based testing: The user interface. *Revue Européenne de Psychologie Appliquée*, 41, 281–293.

Bosman, F., Hoogenboom, J., & Walpot, G. (1994). An interactive video test for pharmaceutical chemist's assistants. *Computers in Human Behavior,* 10, 51–62.

Braun, H. I., Bennett, R. E., Frye, D., & Soloway, E. (1990). Scoring constructed responses using expert systems. *Journal of Educational Measurement,* 27, 93–108.

Breland, H.M. (1998, April). Writing Assessment through Automated Editing. Paper presented at the annual meeting of the National Council on Measurement in Education, San Diego.

Bugbee, A. C. Jr., & Bernt, F. M. (1990). Testing by computer: Findings in six years of use. *Journal of Research on Computing in Education, 23*, 87–100.

Buxton, W. (1987). There's more to interaction than meets the eye: Some issues in manual input. In Baecker, R. M. & Buxton, W. A. S. (eds.) *Readings in Human-Computer Interaction: A Multidisciplinary Approach* (pp. 366–375). San Mateo, CA: Morgan Kaufmann.

Clauser, B. E., Ross, L. P., Clyman, S. G., Rose, K. M., Margolis, M. J., Nungester, R. N., Piemme, T. E., Chang, L., El-Bayoumi, G., Malakoff, G. L., & Pincetl, P. S. (1997). Development of a scoring algorithm to replace expert rating for scoring a complex performance-based assessment. *Applied Measurement in Education*, 10, 345–358.

Dodd, B. G., & Fitzpatrick, S.J. (1998). Alternatives for scoring computer-based tests. Paper presented at the ETS Colloquium, Computer-Based Testing: Building The Foundation For Future Assessments, Philadelphia.

Fitch, W. T., & Kramer, G. (1994). Sonifying the body electric: Superiority of an auditory over a visual display in a complex, multivariate system. In Kramer, G. (ed.), *Auditory Display*, (pp. 307–325). Reading, MA: Addison-Wesley.

Gaver, W. W. (1989). The SonicFinder: An interface that uses auditory icons. *Human-Computer Interaction, 4*, 67–94.

Godwin, J. (1999, April). Designing the ACT ESL listening test. Paper presented at the annual meeting of the National Council on Measurement in Education, Montreal.

Gruber, J. S. (1998, October). [Interview with James Kramer, head of Virtual Technologies, Inc.] Gropethink. *Wired*, pp. 168–169.

Koch, D. A. (1993). Testing goes graphical. *Journal of Interactive Instruction Development, 5*, 14–21.

Luecht, R. M., & Clauser, B. E. (1998, September). Test methods for complex computer-based testing. Paper presented at the ETS Colloquium, Computer-Based Testing: Building The Foundation For Future Assessments, Philadelphia.

Martinez, M. E. (1991). A comparison of multiple-choice and constructed figural response items. *Journal of Educational Measurement, 28*, 131–145.

Martinez, M. E. (1993). Item formats and mental abilities in biology assessment. *Journal of Computers in Mathematics and Science Teaching, 12*, 289–301.

Martinez, M. E. & Bennett, R. E. (1992). A review of automatically scorable constructed-response item types for large-scale assessment. *Applied Measurement in Education, 5*, 151–169.

Nissan, S. (1999, April). Incorporating Sound, Visuals, and Text for TOEFL on Computer. Paper presented at the annual meeting of the National Council on Measurement in Education, Montreal.

O'Neill, K., & Folk, V. (1996, April). Innovative CBT Item Formats in a Teacher Licensing Program. Paper presented at the annual meeting of the National Council on Measurement in Education, New York, NY.

Perlman, M., Berger, K., & Tyler, L. (1993). *An Application of Multimedia Software to Standardized Testing in Music.* (Research Rep. No. 93–36) Princeton, NJ: Educational Testing Service.

Shea, J. A., Norcini, J. J., Baranowski, R. A., Langdon, L. O., & Popp, R. L. (1992). A comparison of video and print formats in the assessment of skill in interpreting cardiovascular motion studies. *Evaluation and the Health Professions*, 15, 325–340.

Stone, B. (1998, March). Focus on technology: Are you talking to me? *Newsweek*, pp. 85–86.

Taggart, W. R. (1995). Certifying pilots: Implications for medicine and for the future. In. Mancall, E. L. & Bashook, P. G. (eds.), *Assessing Clinical Reasoning: The Oral Examination and Alternative Methods* (pp. 175–182). Evanston, IL: American Board of Medical Specialties.

Vicino, F. L., & Moreno, K. E. (1997). Human factors in the CAT system: A pilot study. In Sands, W. A., Waters, B. K, & McBride, J. R. (eds.), *Computerized Adaptive Testing: From Inquiry To Operation* (pp. 157–160). Washington, DC: APA.

Vispoel, W. P., & Coffman, D. (1992). Computerized adaptive testing of music-related skills. *Bulletin of the Council for Research in Music Education,* 112, 29–49.

Vispoel, W. P., Wang, T., & Bleiler, T. (1997). Computerized adaptive and fixed-item testing of music listening skill: A comparison of efficiency, precision, and concurrent validity. *Journal of Educational Measurement,* 34, 43–63.

Williams, V. S. L., Sweeny, S. F., & Bethke, A. D. (1999). The Development and Cognitive Laboratory Evaluation of an Audio-Assisted Computer-Adaptive Test for Eighth-Grade Mathematics. Paper presented at the annual meeting of the National Council on Measurement in Education, Montreal.

6
Computerized Fixed Tests

Overview of the CFT Method

The computerized fixed test (CFT) method is the test-delivery method that provides the most direct analogue to paper-and-pencil testing. This method administers a fixed-length, fixed-form computerized exam without any type of adaptive item selection. In some earlier literature, this test-delivery method is referred to as computer-based testing, or CBT. However, that term has gradually come to refer to *any* computer-administered exam. For this reason, and to emphasize the fixed nature of the exam, we will use CFT to identify this delivery method.

The CFT delivery method provides many of the basic benefits of computerized test administration. The items are presented on computer, and a computer can score the test. Item innovations, such as audio or video prompts, can be included. In a CFT, examinees are allowed to review and revise their item responses; this flexibility usually is not provided on most adaptive tests. Further, the CFT method has the advantage of ease of development. Because fixed computerized tests are administered without adaptive item selection or automated forms assembly, their development and implementation are simpler than most other delivery methods. CFTs are usually developed using methods from classical test theory (CTT) rather than item response theory (IRT) methods necessitated in adaptive delivery models. Given that CFTs do not need to use IRT, some test development complexity can be avoided. Furthermore, the examinee sample sizes necessary for pretesting and calibrating items can be smaller for CFT programs based on classical statistics than for IRT-based programs. Finally, it is easier to explain to testing boards, examinees, and the general public the psychometric logic of test programs that are not adaptive and that do not use IRT.

The CFT is not, however, a suitable choice for many testing applications. This delivery method provides no efficiency advantage, given that fixed forms are administered. The CFT also offers limited provisions for test security in a continuous testing environment, due to its lack of adaptivity and limited number of exam forms. The testing programs that are most amenable to CFT delivery include short exams, where the efficiency advantages of adaptive tests are relatively unimportant, and low-stakes exams, in which security is of minor concern. CFTs are suitable for exam programs with small numbers of examinees or with rapidly changing content. The small sample size makes the adaptive test use of IRT more difficult and reduces some security concerns. Exam programs that have content that quickly becomes dated (e.g., many technology-related exams) may also find the CFT method to be suitable. Given the need to replace items frequently, it may be desirable to avoid the psychometric efforts involved in the extensive item pretesting and calibrating required in adaptive exams. Finally, the CFT method may be appealing to exam programs with limited funds, due to its lower development costs. Of course, that motivation should not lead test developers or boards to choose the CFT if it results in poorer measurement for a given exam program.

Typical applications of the CFT include low-stakes educational assessments such as placement tests and assessments in distance education applications. CFTs are used for a number of voluntary certification programs and for many low-volume certification and licensure exams. The information technology (IT) field is making use of CFTs for a large variety of certification applications (e.g., Adair & Berkowitz, 1999). These IT exams are characterized by extensive innovations in terms of simulating software functionality, very simple scoring algorithms, and rapidly changing content, making the CFT a suitable delivery method.

Test Procedures

Each test-delivery method can be considered in terms of the test procedures involved in implementing the method. These procedures include the processes followed for test assembly and scoring and the requirements or needs for the item pool characteristics. These elements and testing procedures are discussed next.

Test Assembly

Test assembly for the CFT delivery method is most frequently conducted using classical test theory methods. In classical test theory, exam forms are constructed according to test specifications, or test blueprints. A *test blueprint* is a set of rules that specifies attributes of a test form, such as the overall length of the form, content representation, and statistical characteristics. For example, test specifications may require that all test forms for a given exam program be 100 items in length, with 25, 35, and 40 items each coming from three content areas. The test specifications could include further requirements regarding the statistical characteristics of the test form. For example, all of the item p-values (i.e., difficulty indices) could be constrained to be greater than .3 and less than .8, while no item biserial correlation could have a value less than .2. Further discussion of test form assembly is provided later in this chapter.

Clearly, this approach to test assembly can be used whether the test forms are to be administered in paper-and-pencil or computer mode. Many CFTs are assembled using the same procedures that have long been applied in paper-and-pencil testing. At other times, CFTs are developed simply by importing an existing paper-and-pencil exam into a computerized test administration software program. (The issue of comparability of test scores obtained across the two test administration modes is addressed in Chapter 2.)

While it is a less common approach, the test forms for the CFT also can be constructed and scored using IRT methods. One IRT-based approach to test construction is to specify a target Test Information Function (TIF) along with the exam's content requirements. The specified target TIF should be related to the test purpose. For example, a classification exam might have a target TIF that is highly peaked around the cutoff or passing score, while a proficiency exam might have a relatively flat target TIF across the full score range. Items are then selected from the pool based on their individual item information functions (IIFs). Because information is additive, it is a relatively straightforward matter to select items that satisfy the content requirements and produce an actual TIF that is closely related to the target TIF. (In any test assembly method, successful forms construction is related, of course, to the availability of a sufficient quantity of good-quality items.)

Scoring

As indicated earlier, the test forms in a CFT usually are constructed using classical item statistics. Given the classical test theory methods of test construction, the exams are scored based on the number or proportion of items answered correctly. The examinee score may be reported as a scaled number-correct score. If there are multiple test forms, the scores can be equated using such methods as linear or equipercentile equating. And if necessary, cutoff scores for each test form can be established by standard-setting committees.

IRT methods also can be used, for both constructing the test form and scoring the examinee responses. The IRT item parameter estimates are not used in a CFT during the actual exam for either item selection or scoring purposes. At the conclusion of the fixed exam, however, the test can be scored based on an IRT estimate of examinee ability, using the IRT item parameters and the examinee's responses to the fixed set of items. This scoring procedure results in an estimated ability score, which usually is converted to some type of scaled score for reporting purposes. If parallel (i.e., equivalent) tests are constructed in this manner, no equating is necessary. Cutoff or passing scores can still be set by standard-setting committees.

Whether they use classical or IRT methods, CFTs can be designed to provide an immediate score. An official score may be offered at the conclusion of testing, or a provisional score may be provided, with an official score to follow by mail some weeks later. Provisional scores at the time of the exam are offered when a testing agency or board wants the opportunity to confirm the examinee's registration information, to conduct key validation, and to check for possible problems such as test anomalies or test-center irregularities before providing an official score. In these instances, the official score is released after the other considerations have been addressed.

Item Pool Characteristics

In any testing program, a considerable effort needs to be devoted to the development and maintenance of the item pool. A good item pool should have a sufficient supply of well-written items in each content category, at all appropriate difficulty levels. The total size of the required pool is based on a number of aspects of the testing program. These include the test purpose and stakes (i.e., the critical nature of the test scores), the total volume of test-takers, and the frequency of examination dates. It also includes the average test length, the number of test forms or the desired level of test overlap across administrations (or the percentage of items shared between test forms), and the test delivery method. For example, a high-stakes exam tends to require many more items in the pool than a low-stakes exam. An exam offered with high frequency to a large number of examinees is likely to need a much larger pool than an exam offered less frequently or to fewer examinees.

The overall quality of any item pool is based on more than size. An item pool needs to provide a breadth of content coverage, as well as a depth (or sufficient numbers) of items in each important content area. The item pool should be designed to satisfy the test purpose, whether that purpose is proficiency estimation, classification, or diagnostic assessment (e.g., a classification test will often be designed to have many highly informative items in the vicinity of the cutoff score). The items also need to meet appropriate statistical criteria, for either classical or IRT measurement.

Given these pool requirements, CFTs tend to be less demanding than other test-delivery methods in terms of pool preparation and maintenance. In the simplest case, a low-stakes CFT program may have no more items in the "pool" than the items on a single, computerized exam form.

Measurement Characteristics

Each test-delivery method has certain measurement characteristics. These measurement characteristics consider how each method addresses test length, content constraints, test reliability estimation, test security considerations, and set-based items. These measurement characteristics of the CFT are addressed separately in the following sections. However, in practice, most of these elements serve as competing pressures on test-form construction, and so these considerations must be addressed in concert.

Test Length

When a testing program is developed, a decision must be made about the overall length of the exams, considering the intended use of the test score and reasonable limits on examinee time. The various test-delivery methods establish test length and address the competing measurement concerns noted earlier in different ways. For CFTs, as for paper-and-pencil exam administrations, the test length is fixed, defined as the total number of items in the fixed form. Content coverage, reliability, and security must be designed to be satisfied within that test specification.

For other test-delivery methods, test length may be defined as a range; that is, in a variable-length adaptive test, a given exam may be constrained to have at least a required minimum number of items and no more than a specified maximum number of items. However, for any adaptive delivery method, even the maximum number of items is likely to be less than the number of items in a CFT or other fixed-form method. CFTs do not have any of the test efficiency advantage of adaptive exams.

Content Constraints

The test specifications for most exam programs typically include requirements for the content levels to be included in a test form, as well as the number or proportion of items from each content level. For a fixed-form test-delivery method like the CFT, these content constraints are addressed and satisfied during the test-form assembly process within the requirement for test length. If multiple forms are developed, each form is constructed to satisfy the content rules specified in the test blueprint (while also meeting test length and reliability requirements).

Other test-delivery methods may address content constraints in other ways. For example, a CAT or CCT program may be designed to administer a minimum number or proportion of items from each of the test's content categories (Kingsbury & Zara, 1991). Alternatively, an adaptive test may be designed to satisfy target information functions for each content level (Davey & Thomas, 1996).

Reliability

In fixed-form exam programs, there is a direct relationship between test length and reliability. All other things being equal, longer tests are more reliable. Different means of computing reliability estimates are appropriate for different test-delivery methods. For the CFT, which is usually assembled according to classical test-construction methods, a classical measure of reliability is appropriate. Often, the reliability estimate of choice is a measure of the internal consistency of the exam form (e.g., KR-20). Depending on the test purpose and the particular inferences to be drawn from the test scores, reliability also might be addressed in terms of parallel test forms or the test-retest reliability of a single form across two administration times (Crocker & Algina, 1986). If a particular CFT program elects to use IRT methods for form construction, then an appropriate measure of reliability, or test score precision, is the standard error of measurement (SEM) at a given score level. Alternatively, a marginal reliability estimate can be reported (Thissen, 1990).

Item/Test Security

Test security in the CBT environment potentially includes two new concerns not typically present in standardized paper-and-pencil test administrations. First, the more frequent administrations available in any CBT (i.e., continuous testing) result in a new type of security concern: that items will become known over time. (Actually, a paper-and-pencil exam program that continued to use a given test form over multiple administration dates rather than regularly replacing used test forms with new ones, also could have this problem. But the problem may be exacerbated by continuous testing environments typical of CBT programs, where an examinee could pass on item information to another examinee who would test the next day or next week, rather than three or four months later.)

For adaptive exams, an additional security issue is that individual items are administered or exposed at different rates; some items are administered very frequently and can become exposed quickly. This second factor is not an issue for the fixed delivery methods. CFTs, like standardized paper-and-pencil tests, administer items at a constant and predictable rate. Every item on a form is exposed every time the form is administered. The overall exposure of an item is easily predicted, based simply on the number of forms, the number of administration dates, and the number of test-takers. If the item exposure is regarded as too high, then additional test forms must be developed. In order to keep exposure from becoming a security problem, multiple forms can be used, and forms can be retired and replaced after a given number of uses. Item exposure is far more complex for adaptive test-delivery methods. This problem often is addressed statistically in adaptive delivery methods through the use of item exposure control parameters. (The concept of an item exposure control parameter will be detailed further in Chapter 8). Some operational exam programs have begun to rotate entire item pools or to construct pools from larger "vats" in order to limit item exposure and to ensure adequate security (Way, 1998).

There is one additional type of test security that is available to CFTs and not to adaptive exams. The correct answers can be omitted from the test administration software. This approach is only possible for fixed exams like the CFT, as adaptive item selection procedures are dependent on interactive computations of item scores and examinee ability estimates. However, a limitation of test programs that do not store the correct answers is that they will not be able to provide immediate scoring of the exams. Because of this, few testing programs elect to address test security in this manner. In fact, it may not be necessary as long as other security measures are taken. Restricted access to the test software or to the machines on which the software has been installed, password protection, and data encryption methods have proven to be effective test security measures (Rosen, 2000; Shermis & Averitt, 2000; Way, 1998).

Set-Based Items

The CFT delivery method is fully able to incorporate set-based items. These sets of items may be associated with a reading passage, graph, or other stimulus, or for some other reason may have been designed to be administered together. Although adaptive exams must modify their item selection procedures when test material is set-based (see Chapter 8), fixed exams using classical test assembly methods have no such difficulty. An exam can include one or more sets of items, which can be scored using classical test scoring methods.

Practical Characteristics

There are a number of important considerations beyond those discussed thus far that must be addressed when any exam is delivered through the computer mode. These practical characteristics include the examinee volume, the initial development effort required by a test-delivery method, the ease with which an exam can be maintained across dual platforms, pretest accommodations, examinee reactions, and the probable cost of the CBT. Each of these factors is discussed next for the CFT.

Examinee Volume

Test-delivery methods differ somewhat in terms of the examinee volume they require and support. For the CFT method using classical item statistics, much smaller numbers of examinees are needed to provide item pretest data than the sample sizes required for IRT-based methods. Another aspect of examinee volume is the effect of numbers of examinees on test security. With larger numbers of examinees and exam programs that have greater security concerns (e.g., high-stakes exams), the CFT method could result in a gradual exposure of the entire item pool due to the continuous test administrations.

Initial Development

The CFT method is usually the simplest approach to developing and administering a computerized exam, and it requires the least initial development of any of the approaches. Whether a new exam program is being developed or an existing paper-and-pencil test program is being moved to the CBT environment, an exam usually can be put online using the CFT method with less time or effort than any other test-delivery method.

Dual Platform

An advantage of the CFT delivery method is the relative ease in maintaining an exam on dual platforms. CFTs often are developed directly from existing paper-and-pencil exam forms and administered concurrently with paper-and-pencil test administrations. It is an easier and more direct matter to establish the comparability of a paper-and-pencil test to a CFT than to an exam administered adaptively.

Pretest Items

Each delivery method must accommodate the need for pretest items in some fashion. Ideally, items for any computerized exam are pretested online. Over time the items, test forms, and even the entire pool need to be retired and additional items need to be developed. In order to support the pool replenishment or replacement, continual item pretesting needs to be conducted. In a CFT, the pretest items can be administered in several fashions. The non-operational (and nonscored) items can be interspersed randomly within the operational items, or they can be given as a set at either the beginning or the end of the exam. After the items have been administered to a sufficient number of examinees, item statistics are computed and the quality of the items is evaluated. Those items that are found to be satisfactory can then be used to supplement the pool and eventually replace used items. (Issues in item development and pretesting are further discussed in Chapter 2.)

Examinee Reactions

While examinee reactions to computerized testing are discussed at greater length in Chapter 3, there are some typical reactions specific to features in the CFT method. One advantage of the CFT method is that examinees are free to omit items, to review and revise items, and even to preview upcoming items on their fixed test form (in order to evaluate the difficulty and time demands of the remainder of the test). However, this advantage of the CFT over many adaptive approaches may be offset by the longer test necessitated by a fixed delivery method.

Cost to the Examinee

The cost of developing and administering any CBT is often higher than typical costs for paper-and-pencil exams. Some portion of that cost is usually passed on to examinees in the form of higher examination fees. The amount charged an examinee for any test is related to the developmental effort and expenses incurred by the testing company or certification/licensure board. The amount charged for a CBT is also related to the administrative expenses such as "seat time." CFTs typically require a more modest developmental effort than other test-delivery methods, but they do not have the efficiency advantage of adaptive programs. The overall cost, and the cost borne by the examinee, will reflect these and other specific expenses.

Summary

A summary of the test procedures, measurement characteristics, and practical characteristics of the CFT delivery method is provided in Table 6.1. These features highlight the method's strengths and weaknesses. Overall, a CFT program is relatively easy to develop and maintain but cannot address security well. In spite of this drawback, the CFT approach is the test-delivery method of choice for many testing programs, particularly those that comprise low-volume, low-stakes tests without any particular need for measurement efficiency. For exam programs that have greater security concerns or a need for testing efficiency, however, it is a relatively poor choice.

An Example of the CFT Method

In order to demonstrate each test-delivery model, an illustrative example is provided. For the CFT, this practical example emphasizes the elements of classical test form assembly, as applied to a computerized exam program. For the example CFT application, the test blueprint provided in Table 6.2 is used to guide the development of a 10-item test.

Table 6.1. Summary Features of the CFT Delivery Method

Test Procedures	Feature
Test assembly	Classical or methods
Scoring	Number correct or proportion correct
Item pool size	Typically small size
Measurement Characteristics	
Test length	Fixed
Reliability	Usually internal consistency
Item/test security	Minimal provisions
Set-based items	Easily addressed
Practical Characteristics	
Examinee volume	Typically modest
Initial development	Modest effort
Dual platform	Easily handled
Pretest items	Easily handled
Examinee reactions	Relatively positive
Cost to examinee	Modest for CBT

Because this exam will be administered on computer, an important additional step will be to conduct an evaluation of the level of computer experience present in the target test population. This information will be useful in planning for elements of the test administration software such as instruction screens and practice items. It will also be important when item format decisions are made. For example, a test program might take a conservative approach and restrict items to traditional, discrete, selected-response item types that fit on a single screen. Alternatively, usability studies can be conducted as the interface for more complex, innovative item types (e.g., multiscreen, interactive items) is developed.

Table 6.2. Example Test Blueprint

Content Area	Number of Items
A	3
B	4
C	3
Total	10

After the test blueprint for the exam program has been developed, items are written to the specifications. Typically, it is a good idea to have many more items written than are desired, as not all items produced will prove adequate. Once a number of items have been generated, they can be reviewed by additional subject matter experts, a fairness review panel, and test development staff, to ensure that they appropriately address the subject matter, meet criteria of cultural and ethnic group sensitivity, are clearly and correctly written, and are consistent with the item format specifications for the exam. At this point, a test form can be assembled and the items can be pretested or field-tested on examinees.

Ideally, items are pretested on examinees similar in every characteristic to the target test population, under motivated conditions, and in the mode in which the items are to be delivered. For CBT programs, this means that it is best to pretest items on computer, using the actual test-delivery software that will be used during operational testing. Although this is the best-case scenario, many CBT programs have had reasonable success using item statistics that were obtained through paper-and-pencil administrations.

Once the items have been administered to a sufficient number of examinees, item statistics can be computed. Table 6.3 displays the item statistics obtained on a set of 15 pretest items for the sample application.

In addition to satisfying the content specifications detailed in the test blueprint, the testing program may have statistical criteria. For example, no item may be accepted for inclusion if the discrimination index is less than .20 (i.e., $r_{(pbis)} < .20$) and each item difficulty measure must fall between .30 and .80 (i.e., $.30 \leq p\text{-value} \leq .80$).

Given these requirements, several of the items in Table 6.3 have been flagged with an asterisk (*). These items would be examined and, where possible, revised to improve their performance. Typically, items that have been revised must then be pretested again to verify that the revision was effective and to obtain new item statistics. In the example, for illustrative purposes, three of the flagged items (items 2, 8, and 9) were revised and new, satisfactory item statistics were obtained. Upon examination, however, two of the items were simply deleted from the pool (items 3 and 15). Table 6.4 displays the final item pool (of 13 items) resulting from these changes.

In this test-development example, the final pool does not contain many more items than are needed for a single (10-item) exam form. However, the items available do allow full satisfaction of the test specifications for a single form. As a final step, items are selected for inclusion in the computerized exam. These are items 1, 2, and 4 for the three items required in the test blueprint (Table 6.2) for content area A; items 6, 7, 9, and 10 for the four items needed from content area B; and items 12, 13, and 14 as the three content area C items. These 10 items will comprise the CFT. The highlighted rows in Table 6.4 indicate the final test form.

Table 6.3 Sample Pretest Items

Item	Content	p-value	$r_{(pbis)}$	
1	A	.50	.55	
2	A	.40	.15	*
3	A	.90	.05	*
4	A	.80	.45	
5	A	.50	.40	
6	B	.70	.40	
7	B	.40	.35	
8	B	.20	.05	*
9	B	.90	.40	*
10	B	.70	.50	
11	B	.60	.60	
12	C	.30	.30	
13	C	.40	.35	
14	C	.50	.40	
15	C	.20	.15	*

Table 6.4 Sample Item Pool Items

Item	Content	p-value	$r_{(pbis)}$
1	A	.50	.55
2	A	.40	.25
4	A	.80	.45
5	A	.50	.40
6	B	.70	.40
7	B	.40	.35
8	B	.30	.30
9	B	.80	.40
10	B	.70	.50
11	B	.60	.60
12	C	.30	.30
13	C	.40	.35
14	C	.50	.40

If a second exam form was desired, only minor changes between the two forms could be obtained using the available items. A single item could be changed in content area A and two items in content area B, but no item changes could be made for content area C, given that the number of items available in the pool exactly equals the number of items required in the test specifications. Due to the constraints on content and the small pool, the overlap between test forms would be very high. Within content area C, the overlap rate across two exam forms would be 100%. Even though two exam forms were constructed, the exposure rate for each item in content area C would also be 100%. It is important to note that the item exposure rate is the rate at which an item is administered; for fixed exam forms, an item is exposed once each time a form on which it is present is administered.

In order to provide better test security by lowering item exposure and test overlap rates, it would be necessary to develop a larger item pool. If a greater number of items were written, reviewed, and pretested, then multiple forms could be assembled. An additional goal in assembling multiple forms is to ensure that the forms are equivalent in some sense. Ideally, it is desirable for the average test form difficulty and variance to be identical across multiple forms. This requirement can necessitate the availability of many more items in order to satisfy it exactly.

Given a large enough item pool and a set of test specifications, one or more test forms can be assembled manually. However, if more than a very few forms are needed, a much better option would be to use the automated methods discussed in Chapter 7.

Summary of Example

This example illustrated the test-delivery process for the CFT delivery method. It is a fairly straightforward approach, having a great deal in common with the test-delivery process used in most standardized, paper-and-pencil exam programs. Additional considerations include preparing for examinee reactions, addressing software issues, and managing administrative elements such as the effects of continuous testing on test security.

The CFT method provides all of the advantages of computer-based test administration, including more frequent exam administrations and the potential to improve measurement through the use of innovative items. However, the CFT model provides no advantage of adaptive testing in that tests are not tailored to the examinee and cannot be shortened. Furthermore, given that one or only a few fixed forms are usually available and that they are offered on a more frequent basis, no security advantage is typically present. Test-delivery methods that provide greater security and/or efficiency advantages are covered in the next chapters.

References

Adair, J. H., & Berkowitz, N. F. (1999, April). Live application testing: Performance assessment with computer-based delivery. Paper presented at the annual meeting of the American Educational Research Association, Montreal.

Crocker, L., & Algina, J. (1986). *Introduction to Classical And Modern Test Theory*. Fort Worth: Holt, Rinehart & Winston.

Davey, T., & Thomas, L. (1996, April). Constructing adaptive tests to parallel conventional program. Paper presented at the annual meeting of the American Educational Research Association, New York.

Kingsbury, G. G., & Zara, A. R. (1991). A comparison of procedures for content-sensitive item selection in computerized adaptive tests. *Applied Measurement in Education,* 4, 241–261.

Rosen, G. A. (2000, April). Computer-based testing: Test site security. Paper presented at the annual meeting of the National Council on Measurement in Education, New Orleans.

Shermis, M., & Averitt, J. (2000, April). Where did all the data go? Internet security for Web-based assessments. Paper presented at the annual meeting of the National Council on Measurement in Education, New Orleans.

Thissen, D. (1990). Reliability and measurement precision. In H. Wainer (ed.), *Computer Adaptive Testing: A Primer*. (pp. 161–186). Hillsdale, NJ: Lawrence Erlbaum.

Way, W. D. (1998). Protecting the integrity of computerized testing item pools. *Educational Measurement: Issues and Practice,* 17, 17–27.

7
Automated Test Assembly for Online Administration

Overview of the ATA Method

So far, we have discussed computerized tests that are usually fixed in terms of length and items and are constructed offline to be administered at a later time. When testing volumes are moderately high, several such forms may have to be administered randomly to examinees for security purposes. However, multiple test forms require that each one be psychometrically equivalent to every other. This results in either a delay in score reporting so that the test scores can be equated after administration or separate studies to establish passing scores for each form prior to administration. If examinee volumes are fairly high, there may need to be many such equivalent fixed forms constructed in advance. If delays in score reporting are unacceptable, another solution must be found to construct equivalent test forms prior to test administration.

This chapter presents a discussion of what is commonly referred to as *automated test assembly (ATA) or automated test design.* The methods discussed basically have the same goal: to produce tests of a fixed length that satisfy a number of constraints or conditions. These constraints often include test length, test content outline or content restrictions, a desirable percentage of non-overlapping test items, and certain psychometric properties. Under certain situations, such tests constructed prior to test administration can be assumed to be parallel in terms of equitable form difficulty and content.

Test Procedures

Test Assembly

In general there are two types of ATA that can be used to build tests automatically. The first is based on a mathematical concept often referred to as *linear programming* (LP). A linear programming approach to ATA is an attempt to solve an optimization problem, such as finding the set of test items that provide maximum reliability at the passing score, subject to many limitations or constraints. The solution to such a problem produces a simultaneously selected set of items from an item pool. Prior to major advances in current computer technology, this approach used to take a very long time to accomplish and often could be used only to produce fairly short tests, especially if the number of test constraints was large. Obviously, computing capabilities have increased and implementation of the methodology is no longer limited. It does, however, require a reasonably sophisticated understanding of mathematics, and its complex algorithms may not yield better tests (in terms of their parallelism) or tests with fewer numbers of nonoverlapping items, especially if the item pool is small.

The second general ATA method often is referred to as a heuristic approach. Here, the term *heuristic* generally refers to an item selection rule that requires items to be selected sequentially, one at a time, rather than all at once as with the LP approach. Van der Linden (1998) has described this general class of procedures as *greedy heuristics* and presents an excellent overview of the methods.[1] In this respect, the resulting test or tests selected are not necessarily optimal in the sense that all constraints are satisfied exactly, but they may be *close enough* in terms of being ideal test forms.

Often what is required of ATA is to produce a set of test forms prior to administration with minimum test overlap, each of which satisfies the same test blueprint or content outline and is equitable for examinees in terms of test difficulty and reliability. Test overlap, or test overlap *rate*, is defined as the percentage of shared items between any two test forms. We will present a popular heuristic approach to ATA in this chapter, one developed at ETS by Swanson and Stocking (1993) based on the *weighted deviations method* or WDM. This method is extremely flexible in its implementation and allows for either classical equivalent test construction based on a reference form or IRT test construction (resulting in weakly parallel tests) based on a target test information function or TTIF.

Scoring

A fixed-length test constructed by ATA methods can be scored using standard number correct procedures if each form of the test is assumed to be strictly parallel. For example, a score of 75% correct on one ATA form would be equivalent to a score of 75% correct on another, provided that the forms were parallel. This is an advantage over other forms of computer-based tests, such as

---

[1] The 1998 Van der Linden reference also contains an excellent reference list of many of the most recent methods and procedures for ATA or optimal test assembly.

the CAT or CCT, in which variability in test length, item selection, and item difficulty make traditional scoring methods inappropriate in many situations. The ATA number-correct score is easy to understand and requires no score adjustment between forms. It also doesn't have to be converted into a scaled score; the number correct metric is readily interpretable.

As we have mentioned, by ensuring that the tests are constructed using the ATA approach described, there is no guarantee that the tests will be strictly parallel for each examinee. Parallel tests are defined as having the same mean difficulty and variability for each individual examinee within the population. For the classical construction problem (given by example later in this chapter), the constructed tests can only claim a general equivalence in terms of average test difficulty and observed score variability.

In IRT construction, the use of a TTIF does not guarantee parallel tests in the classical sense, but it does produce tests that are nominally or weakly parallel (Samejima, 1977).

Item Pool Characteristics

The only real requirement in terms of item pool size for ATA tests is that the pool be large enough to support the construction of at least one test form. Obviously, test overlap is a function of pool size. In general the larger the pool, the smaller the test overlap rate. However, not every testing program has the luxury of developing and maintaining a large item pool, so that many programs must tolerate fairly small pools, even when there are many test content specifications that must be met.

Similarly, pool quality isn't always a major consideration for some testing programs. Many programs simply construct multiple forms that follow a reference test of a previously administered test form, even though that form is less than ideal. However, if the multiple test forms were constructed to meet a specific psychometric goal, such as to provide maximum accuracy and precision at the passing score or pass point, then the item pool should consist of items that discriminate well at that score or point.

Measurement Characteristics

Test Length and Reliability

All test forms constructed to meet the specifications of a given reference form should have the same test length and overall reliability as that reference form. In some instances, test reliability and length can be used as construction constraints in the ATA process. The type of test reliability reported or used in the ATA process depends on whether a classical or IRT approach is used. In the classical construction of equivalent test forms, internal reliability, as measured by such indices as KR-20 or coefficient alpha, is appropriate. In an IRT setting, the target test information function or target TIF can be used to construct a test with a certain precision at various points along the ability continuum.

Item/Test Security

In general, item or test security for ATA can be controlled by limiting the number of times an item is included on multiple test forms. Ideally, each item would be limited to a single form, thereby minimizing each item's exposure. This would also ensure that the test overlap rate would be an optimal minimum, in this case zero.

While an item exposure rate that results in a zero test-overlap rate is ideal, it is rarely obtainable. Usually, item pool size is small relative to desired test length, and some overlap between test forms is inevitable. In addition because of content requirements, items may be shared across test forms simply because there are so few items available for inclusion in a particular content category.

There are two approaches to controlling item inclusion on test forms. The first is to simply limit or restrict item usage on test forms or to use item inclusion (or exclusion) as a constraint in the ATA process itself. For example, in addition to the usual content classification and psychometric properties, an item can have associated with it an inclusion number designating the maximum percentage of times that the item can appear across multiple test forms. The second approach is to allow each item to have an item exposure parameter or rate to be associated with it. This parameter is an estimate of a conditional probability, the probability that the item will be included on a test form given that it has been selected to be included on the form, or $P(I|S)$. This probability can be estimated and stored with the item's other parameters (e.g., content classification, psychometric properties, etc.) and used during the test assembly process to limit the number of times any one item can be included across forms. More discussion on this topic follows the ATA example later in this chapter.

Set-Based Items

Items in an ATA pool can either be discrete items or occur as a member of a *set*, where an *item set* is defined as a collection of items that usually refer to the same stimulus. In many applications of test construction, general rules apply whereby items enter the test individually or in some combination. For example, a three-item set can be considered for test inclusion as (1) three individual items, (2) one out of three, (3) two out of three, or (4) a complete set. Other constraints can be used to exclude certain items from appearing with other items in the pool. These antagonistic items are sometimes referred to as item *enemies*.

Practical Characteristics

Examinee Volume

Multiple equivalent test forms allow for increased testing volumes and/or increased testing frequency and therefore are ideal for large numbers of examinees. However, once the test forms have been constructed, large numbers of examinees are not necessary to maintain the program unless new items are to be added to the ATA item pools. In this case new item statistics must be fairly stable, which usually implies that they be based on large numbers of examinees per item.

Initial Development

Because tests can be constructed using classical item statistics, the development of multiple forms can be accomplished quickly. Once the test forms are delivered online, item responses can be collected and the pool eventually can be calibrated using IRT methods. An IRT calibrated pool may be more stable across different examinee populations because the item statistics can be scaled to the same metric. Once put on the same scale, IRT item parameter estimates are considered invariant across different examinee populations (i.e., they are considered to be the same for all examinees regardless of their ability levels).

Dual Platform

ATA methods offer the best option for constructing multiple test forms that can be delivered online on a computer platform and offline by traditional paper-and-pencil methods. It is relatively easy to construct several test forms and designate some for online administration and others for a paper-and-pencil format.

Pretest Items

Pretest or tryout items can be included on multiple test forms constructed to be parallel to a reference form. As with most pretest items, they usually are not scored (i.e., they do not contribute in any way to the test score of the examinee). Item statistics are collected on these items and, if the items perform reasonably well, they can be added to the item pool for future use as scored or operational items.

Examinee Reactions

Examinees are not aware that they are taking test forms that have been constructed to be equivalent to other forms. Therefore, their test-taking behavior or patterns should not change from those they experience in the traditional paper-and-pencil format. Thus, the examinees are allowed to review items previously answered and even to change their answers.

The examinees may experience a sense that each test form administered is somewhat unique because there will be multiple forms and each form may be administered in a *scrambled* format (i.e., one in which item order is determined randomly by the computer). Following the testing sessions, examinees that tend to discuss the test with others may sense that they received different forms. Thus, the perception of unique test forms can improve overall test security.

Cost to Examinee

Because ATA tests are fixed in terms of their length, examinee costs for online computerized administration are easy to estimate. However, because the forms are constructed to parallel the fixed length of a reference form, ATA tests normally do not offer any savings in testing time to examinees.

Summary

A summary of the test procedures, measurement characteristics, and practical characteristics of the ATA method is provided in Table 7.1. These features highlight the method's strengths and weaknesses. Overall, an ATA program is relatively easy to develop and maintain, and it addresses security issues well by constructing multiple test forms. It also handles both classical and IRT construction methods.

An Example of the ATA Method

As mentioned previously, we have chosen to use a heuristic procedure to illustrate the ATA method. The heuristic procedure selected uses a weighted deviations model or WDM and was developed by Len Swanson and Martha Stocking (1993). This procedure has several advantages over more complicated and complex linear programming methods. First, it does not require a high degree of mathematical knowledge or computer programming to implement. Second, it will always provide a solution (i.e., it will always produce a constructed test), even if the constructed test does not satisfy all of the constraints of the construction problem.

Table 7.1 Summary Features of the ATA Method

Test Procedures	Feature
Test assembly	Classical or IRT methods
Scoring	Number correct or proportion correct
Item pool size	Handles small and large pools
Measurement Characteristics	
Test length	Fixed
Reliability	Usually internal consistency
Item/test security	Creates multiple forms to minimize test overlap
Set-based items	Easily addressed
Practical Characteristics	
Examinee volume	Any size
Initial development	Minimal effort unless item pool is to be calibrated
Dual platform	Easily handled
Pretest items	Easily handled
Examinee reactions	Relatively positive
Cost to examinee	Modest but test lengths usually are not reduced

The WDM heuristic is illustrated with a simple, classical ATA problem.[2] Table 7.2 provides a sample item pool consisting of 10 test items, or $N_{(pool)} = 10$. Each item has a classical difficulty index or p-value and a classical discrimination index, the *point-biserial correlation coefficient* or r_{pbis}. We will assume that these indices were calculated on large samples of examinees and that the examinee populations did not change over time. In addition to the statistical characteristics, each item has been classified into one of two content categories, A or B.

---

[2] For an example of an ATA problem using an IRT approach, see the reference by Stocking, Swanson, and Pearlman, 1993.

Table 7.2. Sample Item Pool			
Item	**Content**	**_p_-value**	**$r_{(pbis)}$**
1	A	.50	.30
2	A	.40	.15
3	A	.90	.05
4	A	.80	.45
5	A	.70	.40
6	B	.50	.40
7	B	.40	.35
8	B	.20	.05
9	B	.90	.40
10	B	.70	.40

Constructing a Test: An Example

The test construction task is defined in terms of a set of conditions that must be met for each test form selected. Earlier, these conditions were referred to as test *constraints*. There are really two different types of constraints: (1) content constraints and (2) statistical or psychometric constraints. A third condition, test length or n, is sometimes referred to as a constraint, but in the current context, it is really only a constant. It is assumed that the test length is fixed rather than variable.

A simple content outline for this test might consist of the following:

Content	Percentage of Items
A	40%
B	60%

This content outline dictates that $.4n$ items should be from content area A and the remaining $.6n$ items should come from content area B. These would be the content constraints for this test construction problem.

In terms of the statistical or psychometric properties of the test, suppose that it is desirable to have the overall test difficulty be defined as the sum of the p-value across the n items. For example, we might state that we want the average item difficulty of the test to be between .60 and .70. Or, stated another way, we want the expected observed test score or first moment of the observed score distribution to be between $.60n$ and $.70n$. Another psychometric constraint might involve the variability of this distribution. We might stipulate that tests must be constructed in such a way that the standard deviation of observed test scores or S_X is greater than some value but less than another.

Usually these upper (U) and lower (L) bounds of the psychometric constraints are taken from previously administered test forms. A form that is used as the basis for constructing other forms is sometimes referred to as the *target form, reference form,* or *domain-referenced item set.* Again, referring to our example from Table 7.2, suppose the following constraints have been proposed:

Constraints

0. Test length, $n = 5$ items
1. 40% A items, or A = 2, or $2 \leq A \leq 2$
2. 60% B items, or B = 3, or $3 \leq B \leq 3$
3. $3.00 \leq \Sigma p \leq 3.50$ (test difficulty for a 5-item test)
4. $.50 \leq S_x \leq .60$ (standard deviation of observed test scores)

Constraints 1 and 2 are content constraints, while constraints 3 and 4 are psychometric constraints. As mentioned previously, test length is not considered an actual test constraint in this context, but it does have to be defined before any tests can be constructed. Note that the upper and lower bounds of the content constraints, 1 and 2, are equal.

If there were no psychometric constraints, it would be possible to draw (5-choose-2) times (5-choose-3) or 100 tests that would meet content requirements. However, the added restrictions concerning the tests' overall difficulty level and variability will tend to favor some item combinations over others, and some item combinations probably won't satisfy the psychometric requirements at all. The problem thus becomes one of trying to find a set of *best tests* that satisfy all of the constraints (or nearly so). The set of best tests might be one that minimizes individual item exposure and/or test overlap rate. Individual item exposure is the percentage of time that any item appears on a test. An item with *attractive* statistical properties might appear on all test forms, for example, and therefore would have an item exposure percentage or rate of 1.0, meaning that it was always selected. Recall that test overlap rate is the percentage of items that any two tests have in common. Both individual item exposure and test overlap are important considerations in maintaining a high level of test security in any computer based testing program. This concept will be discussed in more detail later in this chapter.

Steps in Test Construction

Step 1: Select the First Item

If only one test is to be constructed, the first item selected should be the best item in the pool, in terms of its ability to satisfy all of the constraints. On the other hand, if many constructed tests are required, the first item to be selected should be drawn at random from the item pool because a random draw of the first item guarantees that the same test form won't be constructed repeatedly. This is why the ATA procedure is not accurately described by the phrase *domain sampling*. Except for the first item, selection from the item pool is not the result of any statistical sampling process. For our example, we will assume that item 2 has been selected at random to begin the process.

Step 2: Determine Which Item Should Enter the Test Next

The item that should enter the test next must be selected from the remaining nine items that make up the pool. The general idea behind the WDM heuristic is that each item not already in the test can be evaluated in terms of its (positive) deviations from each constraint. When these deviations are summed over all of the constraints, we then will consider adding the item that has the smallest overall sum of these deviations from the constraints.

Of course, it is possible that some of the constraints have more influence than others in reaching the decision to add an item. Therefore, Swanson and Stocking (1993) proposed the application of a weight to each of the positive deviations. In this example, because there are four constraints, there are four weights, $w_1, w_2, w_3,$ and w_4. The primary purpose of the weights is to influence one set of constraints more heavily than another. For example, we might wish to have the psychometric constraints be weighted more heavily than the content constraints, so that $w_1 = w_2 < w_3 = w_4$. A second reason for making the deviation weights unequal is presented later in the chapter. The value of the weights is purely arbitrary. It frequently makes the most sense to begin with equal weights on all constraints and then make adjustments once some of the tests have been drawn and evaluated. For this example, we will assume that all weights are equal and that $w_1 = w_2 = w_3 = w_4 = 1.0$.

In our example, there are now nine items that could be selected to fill the remaining four slots for this five-item test. As each additional item is considered for inclusion in the test, we will calculate its suitability in terms of how well it meets all of the constraints. This is accomplished by evaluating each item's sum total of its positive deviations from each of the constraints. And, because each of the constraint deviations can be weighted, this sum is referred to as a *weighted sum of (positive) deviations* from the constraints. We abbreviate this sum as S_t, where $t = 1, 3, 4, 5, 6, 7, 8, 9,$ and 10, the items that have not yet been included in the test. Then we define $S_t = \Sigma w_j d_{Lj} + \Sigma w_j d_{Uj}$ for $j = 1, 2, 3, 4$ constraints, with the summation over the four constraints.

The deviations, d_{Lj} and d_{Uj}, represent lower and upper deviations of the jth constraint, respectively. They are computed by considering three types of items: (1) those items that are already in the test; (2) the item under consideration to be added to the test; and (3) those items that might be added to the test in the future. We can think of these types of items in terms of temporal events: (1) **past** (items previously selected to be in the test), (2) **current** (the current item being considered for the test, item t), and (3) **future** (items that may appear in the test).

Characteristics of Past Items

For each constraint, j, $j = 1, 2, 3, 4$, we compute or count the number of items already in the test that have that constraint characteristics. We can write the past as $\Sigma a_{ij}x_i$ (Swanson & Stocking, 1993) where the sum is over all items in the pool, or $i = 1, 2, \ldots, 10$. The first two constraints, $j = 1, 2$, are content constraints, and a_{ij} is an indicator variable that equals 1 when item i has the characteristic of content j; otherwise it equals 0. The variable, x_i, is also an indicator variable. It equals 1 when item i is in the test; otherwise, it equals 0. Therefore, for each content constraint, $j = 1, 2$, the term $\Sigma a_{ij}x_i$ will simply be a count of those items already in the test that have content classification A (for $j = 1$) versus those already in the test with classification B ($j = 2$).

For the psychometric constraint, $j = 3$, a_{ij} is the p-value of item i, $i = 1, 2, \ldots, 10$, and the indicator variable, x_i, is defined as before. For $j = 3$, $\Sigma a_{ij}x_i$ is the sum of the p-values of those items already selected for the test. For the last constraint, $j = 4$, a_{ij} is the quantity $\{[p_i(1-p_i)]^{1/2} r_{i(pbis)}\}$ for item i. It is the contribution made by the item to the standard deviation of the observed test score or S_x, given by the relationship $S_x = \{\Sigma [p_i(1-p_i)]^{1/2} r_{i(pbis)}\}$ (Gulliksen, 1961).

Characteristics of the *Current* Item

We define a_{tj} as an indicator variable for item t, the current item being considered for inclusion. For $j = 1$, a_t is equal to 1 if item t has content classification A, 0 otherwise. For $j = 2$, a_t is equal to 1 if item t has content classification B, 0 otherwise. The values of a_{tj} for $j = 3$ and $j = 4$ are defined as before.

Characteristics of *Future* Items

Swanson and Stocking (1993) suggested that the simplest way to predict what will happen to future item selections is to assume that they will be drawn at random "and will therefore contribute to the satisfaction of bounds in proportion to the distribution of item properties in the pool" (p. 159). They further stated that the assumption that "the remaining items are randomly selected implies that the expected value of the sum of the constraint properties is equal to the number of items remaining to be selected times the average of the constraint values taken over the remaining items in the pool" (p. 159). If k items have been selected to be entered into the n-item test, then $(n-k)$ items remain to be selected. If v_j is the average of the jth constraint values taken over the remaining items in the pool, then $(n-k) v_j$ is a term that can be used to predict the contribution to the jth constraint for those items that remain to be selected.

Characteristics of the Entire Test

According to the notation used by Swanson and Stocking (1993), the characteristics of all of the items that could make up a test for constraint j can be represented by q_j where q_j = past + current + future or $q_j = \Sigma a_{ij}x_i + a_{tj} + (n-k)v_j$.

Relationship between q_j and Boundaries, U_j and L_j

We can now define the positive deviation values d_{Lj} and d_{Uj} in the equation for $S_t = \Sigma w_j d_{Lj} + \Sigma w_j d_{Uj}$ for j = constraints 1, 2, 3, 4, again with the summation over the four constraints. If $q_j < L_j$, the lower bound for the jth constraint, set $d_{Lj} = L_j - q_j$ (i.e., the positive deviation from the lower bound); otherwise $d_{Lj} = 0$. If $q_j > U_j$, the upper bound for the jth constraint, set $d_{Uj} = q_j - U_j$ (i.e., the positive deviation from the upper bound); otherwise $d_{Uj} = 0$. The term $S_t = \Sigma w_j d_{Lj} + \Sigma w_j d_{Uj}$ is the weighted sum of positive deviations over J constraints when considering whether to add item t to the test. After considering all remaining items, the item with the smallest value of S_t will be added next. The process repeats until all n items have been selected.

Tables 7.3–7.6 provide the values of q_j and S_t for the items in Table 7.2 for $k = 2, 3, 4$, and 5, respectively. Recall that the value of k provides the next item to enter the test (i.e., second, third, fourth, fifth). At each stage, the values of S_t are considered; the item associated with the smallest value of S_t is written in bold in the table and is added to the test next.

Evaluation of Tables 7.3–7.6 show that the five-item test consists of items 2, 3, 7, 9, and 10. The order of entry into the test was actually 2, 9, 10, 7, and 3.

Table 7.3. Values of q_j and S_t for $k = 2$

Item	q_j: Constraint j				S_t
	1	2	3	4	
1	3.125	1.875	2.812	.626	2.464
3	3.125	1.875	3.062	.542	2.250
4	3.125	1.875	3.000	.645	2.295
5	3.125	1.875	2.937	.647	2.360
6	2.500	2.500	2.812	.657	1.245
7	2.500	2.500	2.750	.639	1.289
8	2.500	2.500	2.625	.545	1.375
9	2.500	2.500	3.062	.607	**1.007**
10	2.500	2.500	2.937	.647	1.110

Table 7.4. Values of q_j and S_t for $k = 3$

	q_j: Constraint j				
Item	**1**	**2**	**3**	**4**	S_t
1	2.857	2.143	3.000	.616	1.730
3	2.857	2.143	3.286	.519	1.714
4	2.857	2.143	3.214	.637	1.751
5	2.857	2.143	3.143	.640	1.754
6	2.143	2.857	3.000	.652	0.338
7	2.143	2.857	2.929	.631	0.388
8	2.143	2.857	2.786	.523	0.500
10	2.143	2.857	3.143	.640	**0.326**

Table 7.5. Values of q_j and S_t for $k = 4$

	q_j: Constraint j				
Item	**1**	**2**	**3**	**4**	S_t
1	2.500	2.500	3.083	.655	1.055
3	2.500	2.500	3.417	.543	1.000
4	2.500	2.500	3.333	.680	1.080
5	2.500	2.500	3.250	.683	1.083
6	1.667	3.333	3.083	.697	0.763
7	1.667	3.333	3.000	.673	**0.739**
8	1.667	3.333	2.833	.547	0.833

Table 7.6. Values of q_j and S_t for $k = 5$

	q_j: Constraint j				
Item	**1**	**2**	**3**	**4**	S_t
1	2.000	3.000	2.900	.698	0.198
3	2.000	3.000	3.300	.563	**0.000**
4	2.000	3.000	3.200	.728	0.128
5	2.000	3.000	3.100	.732	0.132
6	1.000	4.000	2.900	.748	2.248
8	1.000	4.000	2.600	.568	2.400

Step 3: Improving the Test

The problem with all heuristics of this nature is that, because they select items on a one-by-one basis sequentially, there is no guarantee that the test ultimately selected is optimal in any sense. Once a test has been assembled, it is possible to implement a replacement process by evaluating the items that did not enter the test. In the preceding example, the five-item test consists of items 2, 3, 7, 9, and 10. These five items therefore form a test that satisfies all four constraints, in that:

1. There are two items from content A (2 and 3).
2. There are three items from content B (7, 9, and 10).
3. The difficulty of the test is $\Sigma p = 3.30$.
4. The observed score standard deviation $= \Sigma[p(1-p)]^{1/2}$ $r = .563$.

If this were the only test that had to be drawn, we might question if this particular test was the best one that could have been constructed. Swanson and Stocking (1993) suggested that a *replacement phase* could be implemented where we could consider adding one of the remaining five items, $t = 1, 4, 5, 6$, and 8, by first evaluating their sums of weighted deviations, as computed by q_j and S_t. The only difference is that in the formula for q_j, the **future** term is ignored because all n items are already in the test. Therefore, $q_j = \Sigma a_{ij}x_i + a_{ij}$ and the summation is over the items in the pool as before. When S_t is evaluated for the five remaining items, item 8 yields the smallest weighted sum of positive deviations when it is added to the five-item test, so it will be the item considered for addition to the test next, provided that another one can be removed (see Table 7.7).

Table 7.7. S_t for the Replacement Phase

Item	S_t
1	1.413
4	1.743
5	1.647
6	1.463
8	**1.000**

When item 8 is entered into the test, the length of the test is now (tentatively) $n + 1$. We next compute $q_j = \Sigma a_{ij}x_i + a_{ij}$ and S_t for the items provisionally in the test, or for items 2, 3, 7, 8, 9, and 10. However, we will evaluate S_t as each of these items is removed from the test in order to find the item whose removal will most reduce the weighted sum of positive deviations.

When each item is removed from the calculation of S_t, $t = 2, 3, 7, 8, 9$, and 10, in Table 7.8, we find that item 8 shows the smallest weighted sum of positive deviations. Thus, item 8 would be the most logical item to remove from the test, and the test would still consist of the original items selected, 2, 3, 7, 9, and 10.

Table 7.8. Values of q_j and S_t for $(n + 1)$ Provisional Items

Item	q_j: Constraint j				S_t
	1	2	3	4	
2	1.000	4.000	3.100	.810	2.000
3	1.000	4.000	2.600	.568	2.400
7	2.000	3.000	3.100	.412	0.088
8	**2.000**	**3.000**	**3.300**	**.563**	**0.000**
9	2.000	3.000	2.600	.463	0.437

We might ask if it is possible to repeat the replacement phase and find another item that would lower the value of S_t. As Swanson and Stocking (1993) stated "the replacement phase will monotonically improve the weighted sum of positive deviations. If it is not possible to find a pair of items whose replacement in the test would result in a smaller weighted sum of positive deviations, then the process stops" (pp.161–162). In this example, the removal of item 8 caused the weighted sum to be zero and the process was stopped.

Selection of the Weights

We might wonder if the initial selection of items could have been better, in terms of meeting the constraints, if other weight values had been used. We mentioned previously that one reason for making the deviation weights unequal is to emphasize one or more constraints over the others. In addition, Van der Linden (1998) pointed out that another reason to make the weights unequal is to balance the effect of the weights if the constraint metrics are unequal. In the previous example, we note that the first three constraints have lower and upper bounds that are approximately the same magnitude. However, the fourth constraint, that of the standard deviation of the observed test score, is about one-fifth the magnitude of the others. If we let $w_1 = w_2 = w_3 = 1.0$ and $w_4 = 5.0$, we will ensure that all four constraint deviations will contribute to S_t in approximately the same proportion. If the weights in the previous example are changed accordingly, the reader can verify that the test selected would change so that the items selected would have been 2, 9, 10, 8, and 4. The new test would have the following specifications:

1.   There are two items from content A (2 and 4).
2.   There are three items from content B (8, 9, and 10).
3.   The test's difficulty is $\Sigma p = 3.00$.

    4.   The test's observed score standard deviation $= \Sigma[p(1-p)]^{1/2}$ $r = .577$.

Compared to the original item selection of items 2, 9, 10, 7, and 3, this test is slightly more difficult and has a larger standard deviation of observed test scores. However, both tests satisfy the constraints. After implementing the replacement phase, the test would remain as originally constructed.

As mentioned previously, by making a weight or weights considerably large relative to the remaining weights, the test constructionist also can emphasize one or more test characteristics over the others. A word of caution is required, however. If the goal is to construct many equivalent tests with minimal test overlap (i.e., percentage of shared items), the emphasis of one or more constraints may yield tests with many repeated items across test forms.

IRT Test Construction

In our example, we showed how the Swanson and Stocking WDM heuristic could be used to construct a test using classical item characteristics. The WDM approach also can be used to construct a test using IRT characteristics. Here, the goal is to achieve weak parallelism by constructing tests whose test information function approximates a target test information function or TTIF (Samejima, 1977) while also meeting all of the other constraints (e.g., content specifications). The IRT procedure differs from the classical procedure only by the way in which the psychometric constraints are defined.

A number of points are defined on the unidimensional ability scale, θ. For example, if 13 such points are defined, we might choose them to span [−3.0, +3.0] in increments of .5, (i.e., $\theta = -3.0, -2.5, -2.0, -1.5, -1.0, -0.5, 0.0, 0.5,$ 1.0, 1.5, 2.0, 2.5, and 3.0.) Then there would be 13 psychometric constraints and these would be lower and upper bounds of the TTIF at these values of θ. The magnitude of the vertical distance between boundaries of the TTIF need not be equal. Table 7.9 contains values of a sample TTIF along with arbitrary lower and upper bounds of the TTIF at 13 values of θ.

Once these psychometric characteristics and bounds have been defined, the test can be constructed using steps 1, 2 and 3 as described previously.

Test Overlap Rate

We have already discussed the fact that for our sample item pool in Table 7.2, it is possible to create or construct (5-choose-2) x(5-choose-3) tests that would meet content specifications (i.e., that would contain two items from content area A and three items from content area B) regardless of the psychometric properties of the items. We might be interested to know what the *test overlap rate* would be (1) between any pair of tests and (2) on average over the entire set of 100 tests. The test overlap rate is defined as the percentage of

Table 7.9. Sample TTIF and Bounds

θ	TTIF	Lower Bound	Upper Bound
−3.0	.008	.000	.010
−2.5	.016	.005	.020
−2.0	.033	.010	.040
−1.5	.077	.050	.080
−1.0	.170	.100	.200
−0.5	.302	.250	.350
0.0	.405	.350	.450
0.5	.446	.400	.500
1.0	.406	.350	.450
1.5	.278	.250	.300
2.0	.151	.100	.200
2.5	.072	.050	.100
3.0	.034	.010	.050

shared items that occur between tests of a fixed length (i.e., in this case, $n = 5$). In an ideal situation, we would like to minimize this rate between any two tests that we construct. However, we must keep in mind that there exists this *baseline rate* that we can estimate and use as a point of reference to achieving this goal as we begin to apply the other constraints. Obviously, the overlap rate will increase as we begin to consider other constraints because some items will be selected at a higher rate. The rate at which an item is selected and then appears on an ATA form is called the item's *exposure rate*; it is discussed later.

The expected value of the baseline overlap rate, or E [BOR], of a set of fixed-length tests can be computed as follows:

Let J = the number of content constraints.
Let $N_{(pool)}$ = the number of total items in the item pool.
Define the number of items in the pool with each content constraint, C_j, $j = 1, 2, ..., J$. Therefore, $\Sigma\, C_j = N_{(pool)}$.
Let m_j = the number of items required to be on the test from content j.
Let n = the length of the test, and $n = \Sigma m_j$.

Then E [BOR] = $\Sigma\, \{(m_j)^2 \div (C_j)\} \div n$. A formal proof of this definition appears in the appendix for this chapter and stems from work done by Chen, Ankenmann, and Spray (1999).

In our example, $J = 2$; $N_{(pool)} = 10$; $C_1 = 5$; $C_2 = 5$; $m_1 = 2$; $m_2 = 3$; and $n = 5$. The E [BOR] = $\{(2^2 \div 5) + (3^2 \div 5)\} \div 5$ or $(.80 + 1.80) \div 5 = .52$. This means that, on average, any two automated tests will share 52% of their items when psychometric constraints are *not* considered. By including psychometric constraints such as constraints 3 and 4 (i.e., the mean and variance of the observed scores), the average test overlap rate will probably increase.

The 52% figure may be a bit misleading because it is only a mean or expected value and does not provide any information about the distribution of all possible overlap rates. Still, it is a helpful figure to know because once you compute this value, you will at least have a relative figure from which to assess the observed overlap rates of all the tests that are constructed with psychometric or other constraints in effect.

Individual Item Exposure Rate

As mentioned earlier, the rate at which an item is selected and administered is called that item's *exposure rate*. Individual items that appear on almost every form constructed will have exposure rates near 1.0. It should be obvious that the exposure rate of an item and test overlap rate are related. If tests are constructed using items with high exposure rates, the overall overlap between any pair of tests will also be high. Sometimes this is unavoidable. For example, if certain content areas are underrepresented within the pool, there may only be enough items to satisfy the blueprint demands exactly. When this occurs, all items within that content area will have exposure rates of 1.0, and test overlap rates will increase.

If the pool is large enough, individual exposure rate maximums can be formulated as constraints. For example, we could provide an estimate of each item's maximum exposure rate in our sample pool in Table 7.2 by selecting many tests and tallying the number of times each item is selected for a form. This would provide an unconstrained exposure rate per item. Then, using these estimates, we could apply exposure boundaries to each item; the upper bound would be some number less than the unconstrained value (assuming that this value was unacceptably high) and the lower bound would be zero. An internal, uniform random-number generator (U: [0,1]) could then be used to determine if the item, once selected, actually should be added to the test (i.e., it would only be added if the random number, U, was less than the upper bound). This process would be expected to reduce test overlap rates but would also most likely weaken the desired statistical properties of the tests. Readers interested in more work on the topic of the relationship between item exposure rates and test overlap rates for fixed-length tests should consult the reference by Chen, Ankenmann, and Spray (1999) and Davey and Parshall (1995).

Summary of Example

This example illustrated the major steps in the process of automated test assembly or construction of a test form from a sample item pool. In practice many such forms may be assembled so that they can be assumed to be equivalent in some sense. Under certain conditions, the forms may even be assumed to be parallel and have the same passing score or standard. The construction of multiple equivalent test forms makes the dual platform format (i.e., simultaneous paper-and-pencil administration plus computer-based administration) much easier to implement.

Chapter 7 Appendix

Each content area, $j, j = 1, 2, \ldots, J$, is independent of the other content areas. We will show the expected value of the baseline overlap rate or E [BOR] for one content area first and then show that E [BOR] for the entire test of length n is just the sum of these expected values. We define the random variable Y to be the number of identical items between any two (paired) tests and $Y \div n$ is the observed overlap rate for those tests. Possible values for the random variable Y or y could be 0, 1, $\ldots$, n, where $y = 0$ would imply no shared items between any two forms, while $y = n$ would be complete overlap or identical test forms. We desire the value of E [Y] and ultimately, $1/n$ E [Y].

There are C_j items in each content area, and we wish to draw m_j items at random from each content area. We abbreviate these values (for a fixed j) as simply C and m and recognize that within each content area j there are X_j overlapping items (or simply X for abbreviation). Each X is distributed as a hypergeometric random variable. For any content area, there are $\binom{C}{M}$ possible combinations of the m items selected from the C items in that content area. Repeated draws will produce X items that are identical. Therefore,

$$\text{Prob}(X = x) = \frac{\binom{m}{x}\binom{C-m}{m-x}}{\binom{C}{m}}$$

is the probability that X, the number of shared items in content area j, will be equal to $x = 0, 1, \ldots, m$. The expected value of X (Ross, 1976) is

$$E(X) = \sum_{x=0}^{m} \frac{\binom{m}{x}\binom{C-m}{m-x}}{\binom{C}{m}} x = \frac{m^2}{C}$$

where E(X) is actually equal to E(X_j) and E(X_j) = $(m_j)^2/C_j$ for the jth content area. The expected value of Y over all J content areas is $E(Y) = \Sigma \{E(X_j)\} = \Sigma \{(m_j)^2/C_j\}$, while the expected value of the baseline overlap rate, Y/n, is $E(Y/n) = 1/n$ or $E(Y) = \Sigma \{(m_j)^2/C_j\} \div n$.

References

Chen, S., Ankenmann, R., & Spray, J. (1999). *Exploring the Relationship between Item Exposure Rate and Test Overlap Rate in Computerized Adaptive Testing.* (ACT Research Report Series No. 99-5). Iowa City: ACT, Inc.

Davey, T., & Parshall, C. G. (1995, April). New Algorithms for Item Selection and Exposure Control with Computerized Adaptive Testing. Paper presented at the annual meeting of the American Educational Research Association, San Francisco.

Gulliksen, H. (1950). *Theory of Mental Tests.* New York: Wiley.

Ross, S. (1976). *A First Course in Probability.* New York: Macmillan Publishing Co., Inc.

Samejima, F. (1977). Weakly parallel tests in latent trait theory with some criticisms of classical test theory. *Psychometrika, 42,* 193198.

Stocking, M. L., Swanson, L., & Pearlman, M. (1993). Application of an automated item selection method to real data. *Applied Psychological Measurement, 17,* 167–176.

Swanson, L., & Stocking, M. L. (1993). A method and heuristic for solving very large item selection problems. *Applied Psychological Measurement, 17,* 151–166.

Van der Linden, W. (1998). Optimal assembly of psychological and educational tests. *Applied Psychological Measurement, 22,* 195–211.

8
Computerized Adaptive Tests

Overview of the CAT Method

A traditional computerized adaptive test (CAT) selects items individually for each examinee based on the examinee's responses to previous items in order to obtain a precise and accurate estimate of that examinee's latent ability on some underlying scale. The specific items, the number of items, and the order of item presentation are all likely to vary from one examinee to another. Forms are drawn adaptively and scored in real time, and unique tests are constructed for each examinee. Scores are *equated* through reliance on item response theory (IRT)[1] ability estimates.

A traditional CAT differs from the computerized classification test or CCT delivery method, discussed in Chapter 9, primarily in the goal of the test. The CCT is optimal when a decision regarding the examinee's performance is required. When this decision is dichotomous (e.g., pass/fail) and there is only one passing criterion, items usually are selected for administration because they are optimal in distinguishing between the two classification categories. In a CAT, however, the interest is in obtaining the most precise and accurate estimate of each examinee's ability level. Therefore, items that measure best at an examinee's **current ability estimate** are selected for administration for that examinee and are somewhat *tailored* to that examinee. A CAT is generally the most efficient test-delivery method available. Under ideal conditions, it can produce an equally reliable score with about half the items of a fixed-form, non-adaptive test.

Every item pool contains some fixed amount of information at each ability level, a quantity computed by summing the item information functions[2] across the items in the pool. These functions fix the upper bound of how precise any adaptive test can be at each ability level. An effective CAT quickly identifies and administers items that are most informative at an estimate of the examinee's true ability, efficiently extracting the information that the item pool has available at that true ability level.

---

[1] See the appendix for a discussion of the basic principles of IRT.

[2] Also see the Appendix for a discussion of item information functions.

Test Procedures

Test Assembly

Item Selection Algorithms And Stopping Rules

The item selection algorithm for a CAT implements rules that govern (1) which item should be used to begin testing, (2) which item should be used to continue testing, and (3) when to stop testing. These steps are then followed by computation of a final ability estimate or score.

Initial Item Selection

The starting point for a CAT refers to the difficulty level of the initial item or items administered to an examinee. There are three approaches that may be used to select these initial items. The *best guess* approach administers an item of medium difficulty on the grounds that, "if we know nothing about an examinee, our best guess is that he or she is like most other examinees." In the *use what you've got* method, other test scores or information can be used to refine the initial estimate of examinee ability and thus the most appropriate level of item difficulty. Finally, the *start easy* method begins the test with relatively easy items in order to give the examinee time to "warm up."

Continued Item Selection

The goal of unconstrained, optimal CAT item selection is to maximize efficiency and produce a short, informative test for each examinee. While adaptive tests achieve their efficiency by successively selecting items that provide optimal measurement at each examinee's estimated level of ability, operational testing programs typically must consider additional factors in item selection. Generally, items are selected with regard to at least three, often conflicting goals: (1) to maximize test efficiency by measuring examinees as quickly and as accurately as possible; (2) to assure that the test measures the appropriate balance of content categories; and (3) to protect the security of the item pool by controlling the rates at which optimal items are administered. This section addresses the first of these concerns; the other two are considered later in this chapter. Items may be selected for maximal test efficiency through three different approaches. These are maximum information (MI), maximum posterior precision (MPP), and weighted information (WI).

Maximum Information. Item or Fisher information is the usual standard by which an item's contribution to the measurement of an examinee's ability level is gauged. Because information is inversely related to the sampling variance of an ability estimate, the goal of most item selection procedures is to accumulate as much information as possible as quickly as possible. For the 3-PL or 3-parameter logistic IRT model, the information value for each item at each ability level is closely related to the value of the a-parameter for that item at that ability level. Under the simplest of the CAT item-selection procedures, maximum information, the item that has the largest information value at the examinee's current ability estimate is selected for administration (Brown & Weiss, 1977). Maximum information item selection computationally is very simple during testing because the heavier calculation of information functions can be done before any examinees are tested. The results are tabled on a discrete grid of ability values. Items then are usually rank-ordered by the amount of information they provide at each of the gridded ability values and listed in the columns of an information table. Items are selected simply by finding the column of the information table that brackets the provisional ability estimate and pulling the top-ranked item in that column *off the stack*.

Unfortunately, estimation error often leads to items being selected from columns that do not cover the true ability value. This is particularly true early in the test when few items have been administered. This problem is exacerbated when items are highly discriminating and are near the top of the information table. Such items generally are tightly focused, discriminating well over a narrow ability range and often poorly outside this range. Therefore, an item measuring well at a provisional ability estimate may measure poorly at the true ability value.

Maximum Posterior Precision. The maximum posterior precision (MPP) selection procedure selects the item that leads to the largest decrease in the variance of the posterior ability distribution. This method was developed from the recognition that provisional ability estimates contain error. Thus, items are selected based on the entire posterior distribution of ability rather than a single point estimate. The item selected may not be the most informative at the particular provisional ability level, or at any other ability level for that matter. Instead, the selected item is a compromise that measures well on average across the high-density region of the posterior distribution. This approach is more conservative in nature and often yields superior results. However, the MPP approach cannot be based on information tables and therefore is much more computationally intensive than MI. The procedure must continually search the entire bank of unpresented items to find the one that leads to maximal reduction of the posterior variance, a process that can be extremely time-consuming for even moderately large item pools.

Weighted Information. The *weighted information* (WI) method is an item selection procedure in which weights from the examinee's current posterior ability distribution are applied to the columns of an information table. During item selection, the information values provided by each item at each ability level are multiplied by these weights and summed. The item with the largest weighted, summed information is then chosen for administration. (The maximum information criterion can be viewed as a special case under which all weight is massed on the single column of the table that contains the provisional ability estimate.) The WI is similar to the MPP in acknowledging that provisional ability estimates are subject to error. However, while WI is not as computationally simple as MI, it is much simpler than MPP. This is because Owen's (1969, 1975) approximation to the posterior ability distribution can be used efficiently to compute the weights.

Stopping Rules

Current CAT test administration methods fall into two basic categories. These two types of CATs are defined by their stopping rules; they are fixed-length and variable-length tests. A fixed-length CAT administers the same number of items to each examinee. Different examinees therefore may be tested to different levels of precision, just as they would be by a conventional nonadaptive test. Examinees who are more easily "targeted" by their selected test, either because they respond more predictably or because their ability falls where the CAT item pool is strong, are measured more precisely than poorly targeted examinees. In contrast, a variable-length CAT tests each examinee to a fixed level of precision even if this requires administering different numbers of items to different examinees. Well-targeted examinees generally receive shorter tests than poorly targeted examinees.

Scoring or Ability Estimation

Almost all computerized adaptive tests are scored by estimating an examinee's unidimensional latent ability, θ, or some function of θ. Because this facet of a CAT is so important to item selection, test length, measurement precision, and test outcome, it is presented in some depth.

Most computerized testing situations that rely on IRT item parameter estimates assume that the estimates are actually known values (i.e., they exist without error as known values that describe each item in the pool). The only parameter that has to be estimated during the computerized test is the examinee's latent ability, θ.

Ability estimates are updated following each item response to provide the current *best estimate* of an examinee's true ability. The sequential estimates obtained as the test proceeds are commonly termed *provisional*, reflecting the fact that each estimate is based only on what is known about the examinee at that point in the testing process. Several methods for computing provisional estimates have been proposed; each has its own advantages and disadvantages.

Three popular ability estimation methods are maximum likelihood estimation (MLE), expected a posteriori (EAP), and maximum a posteriori (MAP). These last two are Bayesian methods and can be referred to as the Bayes mean and Bayes mode approaches, respectively.

Characteristics of Latent Ability Estimates

The three ability estimation methods can be compared in terms of their relative bias and stability. *Bias* is defined as the tendency of a method to commit or avoid consistent estimation errors. For example, consider administering a test to a number of examinees with the same "true" latent ability[3]. Because of measurement error, observed scores do not always faithfully track true latent ability. Scores therefore differ across examinees even though their true abilities are identical. It is how these differences are arranged that determines whether an estimation procedure is biased. With a less biased procedure, observed scores are about as likely to overestimate true latent ability as to underestimate it. Furthermore, the average score across examinees is roughly equal to the true latent ability. In contrast, a more biased procedure returns scores that consistently over- or underestimate true latent ability. Therefore, the average score across examinees is likely to be less than or greater than the true value.

In addition to *bias*, the estimation characteristic most important to a discussion of ability estimation is *stability*. *Stability* measures the extent to which an estimation method is affected by adding new and different data to what has already been collected. For example, a stable method would not dramatically increase an established low latent ability estimate because a single response was changed from incorrect to correct.

Bias and stability often conflict with one another, with stable estimation procedures tending to be more biased and less stable procedures tending to be less biased. MLE methods have the advantage of being relatively unbiased, at least when compared to Bayesian procedures (Lord, 1980). However, MLEs can be very unstable for very short tests, often to the point of being undefined or taking on infinite values. In contrast, Bayesian estimates are always bounded, but can be significantly biased. Further details about these three estimation methods are provided next.

Maximum Likelihood

The maximum likelihood estimate of ability is determined by finding the modal or maximum value of the likelihood function. (Further details about likelihood functions can be found in the IRT appendix.) The MLE is unstable for short tests and even is often unbounded (e.g., it may take on values of $\pm\infty$). It has a relatively minor centripetal bias (i.e., the MLE tends to be slightly overestimated for high abilities and slightly underestimated for low abilities), and multiple modes are occasionally a problem. It also requires a lengthier computation than Bayesian methods, although this is of minimal importance with fast computers.

---

[3] "True" latent ability can be defined as the score an examinee would attain on a test much longer than that actually being administered.

Bayes Estimates

An arguably more proper approach to determining estimates of an examinee's ability in the likelihood function is to make use of *Bayes theorem*. This states that in general

$$\text{Prob}(B \mid A) = \frac{\text{Prob}(A \mid B)\,\text{Prob}(B)}{\text{Prob}(A)},$$

so that for the CAT application

$$\text{Prob}(\theta \mid \underline{U}) = \frac{L(\underline{U} \mid \theta)\,\text{Prob}(\theta)}{\text{Prob}(\underline{U})}.$$

The (unconditional) probability $\text{Prob}(\theta)$ is called the *prior* distribution of latent ability. The prior distribution expresses what is known before the test is administered about how latent ability is distributed in the tested population. The effect of using a prior distribution for θ is that some values of θ are thought to occur more frequently than others; hence those values receive a higher weight in all subsequent calculations involving the ability distribution or density function.

Although it may seem odd to assume this distribution before testing, there usually is some basis for doing so. Earlier experience with the same population may lend some guidance. A generic or *noninformative* prior is also a common choice. A noninformative prior is one that assigns equal probability to all possible occurrences. In this respect it is not necessarily very helpful. Usually assuming a noninformative prior is equivalent to assuming no prior distribution at all.

The second unconditional probability, $\text{Prob}(\underline{U})$ in the denominator, is the probability of the observed response pattern, $\underline{U}$, appearing. Because this probability does not depend on any particular latent ability value, it can safely (and conveniently) be ignored when the posterior probability, $\text{Prob}(\theta|\underline{U})$, is used to make inferences regarding θ.

The posterior distribution, like the likelihood function, defines the range of values into which an examinee's true latent ability is likely to fall after a certain number of test items have been answered and the responses observed. Generally, this range must be reduced to a single value for reporting purposes. The task here is to determine the single value that best summarizes or characterizes the full distribution. The field of statistics has long dealt with this problem and has produced a number of common solutions, called measures of *central tendency*. The average or mean is the most common of these measures. The mode or maximum value that a distribution achieves is another popular measure. Both are also estimators, the *Bayes mean* and *Bayes mode,* when applied to the posterior distribution, $\text{Prob}(\theta|\underline{U})$. These estimators usually are abbreviated as the EAP (mean or *expected a posteriori*) and the MAP (*mode or maximum a posteriori*).

In the EAP, or Bayes mean approach, the mean of the posterior distribution is computed as the point estimate of ability. In the MAP, or Bayes mode approach, the mode or maximum value taken on by the posterior is used. The EAP, unlike the MLE approach, is quite stable for short tests and is always bounded but it does have some centrifugal bias. In other words, for high abilities it produces underestimates, and for low abilities it produces overestimates. While an unbiased method would be best, this bias is at least in the "right" direction (i.e., it pulls the estimates back from being too extreme and more toward the center of the distribution of θ). However, computation for the EAP is quite lengthy. The MAP, like the EAP, is relatively stable for short tests and is always bounded. It also has a moderate centrifugal bias and multiple modes are infrequent. An advantage of the MAP over the EAP is that a quick computational approximation, called Owen's Bayes method, is available (Owen, 1969, 1975).

Provisional vs. Final Ability Estimation

Any of the procedures discussed earlier for use in provisional estimation may also be used to obtain final ability estimates. However, use of Owen's Bayes is not recommended for final ability estimation because of its order dependence (e.g., two examinees that answered the same items in the same ways may receive different estimates if the order of presentation was different). Final ability estimates may remain on the ability metric, or they may be transformed to the expected number-correct score or some other scale-score format.

Item Pool Characteristics

A CAT testing program is often very demanding in terms of the size of the item pool required. This is due most directly to the uneven item exposure typical of CAT item selection algorithms. It is also the result of the fact that CATs are frequently used for high-stakes exam programs and are offered in a continuous or on-demand test setting. The high-stakes characteristic of an exam program means that item exposure is a serious test security concern, while continuous testing results in the continuous exposure of items. Stocking (1994) recommends that the item pool for an exam program contain 12 times the number of items in an average CAT. For licensure and certification testing, Way (1998) suggests, for a number of reasons, that a pool size of six to eight times the average CAT length might be adequate.

A large item writing and pretesting effort is needed to support the test security needs of most CATs. Over time, exposed items need to be retired and new items added to the pool. In some current exam programs, entire item pools are rotated or retired. Elaborate methods are being developed for assembling parallel item pools and for rotating, replenishing, and redistributing items across these pools (Way, 1998).

For a latent ability estimation exam, such as a CAT, it is necessary for the item pool to contain not merely a large number of items, but items that span a wide range of difficulty and provide adequate content coverage. The quality of the items is always important. And in testing programs that use the 3-PL model, the distribution of an item's a-parameter is also important.

Measurement Characteristics

Test Length and Reliability

In adaptive tests, the concepts of test length and the reliability or precision of the estimated score are closely linked. Therefore, these two concepts are presented together in this chapter. The relative advantages and disadvantages of fixed- and variable-length adaptive tests have been debated elsewhere. Arguments favoring fixed-length tests cite the method's simplicity and its avoidance of a particular type of measurement bias (Stocking, 1987). Proponents of variable-length tests contend that such tests are more efficient and allow test measurement properties to be precisely specified (Davey & Thomas, 1996; Thompson, Davey & Nering, 1998). Both views are briefly summarized herein.

As its label suggests, a fixed-length adaptive test administers the same number of items to each examinee. The number of items administered is determined by weighing such factors as content coverage, measurement precision, and the time available for testing. Measurement precision is usually specified in the aggregate, or averaged across examinees at different latent ability levels (Thissen, 1990). However, the measurement models that underlie adaptive tests recognize that precision varies across examinees. Examinees whose latent ability levels are identified quickly and accurately can be repeatedly targeted with items of an appropriate difficulty and consequently measured very efficiently and reliably. Examinees whose performance levels are located in a range where an item pool is particularly strong are also likely to be well measured. Conversely, examinees that are difficult to target or whose latent ability levels fall where the item pool is weak are measured more poorly.

The function traced by measurement precision over latent ability level can be manipulated in limited ways by test developers. Item pools can be bolstered where they are weak and weakened where they are unnecessarily strong. Test length can be shortened or lengthened. Item selection and exposure control procedures can be finessed. However, the level of control is far short of complete, leaving conditional measurement precision more a function of chance than of design.

Variable-length tests allow measurement precision to be addressed directly by using it as the criterion to determine when a test ends. Rather than administering a specified number of items to each examinee, variable-length tests administer items until a specified level of precision is met. Examinees, who are measured efficiently because they are well targeted, for example, reach the criterion quickly and take shorter tests. Examinees in other circumstances take longer tests. However, regardless of test length, all examinees are measured with the precision specified so that test precision is dictated rather than left to fate.

Being able to specify exactly the precision of a test is a crucial advantage in test development. However, it does not come without cost, as variable-length tests have two faults, one relatively trivial and the second potentially important. The first problem is that the rule by which tests are stopped is necessarily a function of estimated examinee latent ability. Properly, it should be a function of true latent ability, which is unavailable. The result is that bias in latent ability estimates influences, and in turn is influenced by, test length. Low-ability examinees that are administered shorter tests generally are underestimated, as are high-ability examinees that receive longer tests.

Conversely, longer tests administered to low-ability examinees and shorter tests administered to high-ability examinees generally produce higher-than-expected ability estimates. However, the effect is subtle and disappears almost entirely as test length and reliability increase. The larger problem with variable-length tests becomes apparent when they are administered under time limits. Equity concerns abound unless these limits are generous enough to allow all examinees to finish even the longest test they might be administered. Short of this, examinees that receive longer tests are put at a disadvantage. This situation must be addressed before variable-length tests, with their attendant benefits, can be a viable option for most high-stakes testing programs. One solution is to vary test time with test length. This option is also open to criticism, in that examinees taking longer tests are subject to increased fatigue.

Item/Test Security

The security of items and tests in a CAT is related to exposure control, or restrictions placed on the frequency of an item's administration across exams. As with the previous discussion of test length and reliability, the concept of controlling item exposure is linked to the concept of meeting or satisfying content constraints.

Balancing Test Content

Conventional tests usually are constructed with respect to a "blueprint" that specifies how many items of each content type are to be included. The best item to administer to an examinee during either a conventional test or a CAT is not always the one that contributes the most information to an ability estimate. The content measured by an item often is equally important.

Balancing item content through a test blueprint serves two general purposes. First, it helps assure that the test shows content or construct validity evidence. For example, test developers may decide that a geometry test simply must include an item that uses the Pythagorean theorem. The required content is such an important component of the domain from which the test is drawn that reasonable judgment dictates its inclusion. A content blueprint also serves to ensure that alternate forms of the same test are as nearly parallel as possible. Balancing item content across forms increases the likelihood that each form measures the same composite of skills and knowledge.

Blueprints developed for conventional tests often are applied directly to the CAT delivery method in hopes of deriving the same benefits. However, care should be taken to see that the conventional blueprint is either necessary or sufficient to control item content during a CAT. For example, if the CAT item pools are truly unidimensional, content balance is more a matter of "face validity" than anything else is. Absolute unidimensionality results from responses being driven solely by the examinee's ability, whatever an item's content. Thus, distinctions drawn between items on content grounds are wholly artificial, existing in theory but not in the response data. Balancing item content would result only in lowered test efficiency.

Truly unidimensional item pools are rarely, if ever, encountered in practice. Most pools cover a range of item content and, as a result, are no more unidimensional than conventional tests. Balancing the content of the tests drawn from typical pools, therefore, can provide the same advantages to a CAT as it provides to conventional tests. For example, suppose an item pool included two content domains, with the first consisting of primarily easy items and the second more difficult items. If item content were not balanced, lower-ability examinees would be tested almost exclusively with items from the easier domain. The converse would be true for high-ability examinees. Scores for these two groups of examinees subsequently would have different meanings and interpretations, reflecting the differences in content between the two domains. Balancing item content makes it more likely that the tests selected for different examinees are parallel and will produce comparable scores. This is directly analogous to constructing parallel alternate forms of a conventional test by following the same content blueprint.

Consider, for example, the test specifications presented in Table 8.1. With a conventional test scored by number correct, 20% of every examinee's score is determined by the examinee's performance on trigonometry items. However, in a CAT, because these items tend to be difficult, they may never be selected for low-ability examinees, while able examinees would see little else. To ensure that each examinee is measured on the same ability composite, we need to force the selection of what are often inappropriately easy or difficult items.

Table 8.1 Sample Test Specifications

Content	% of Test	Average *p*-Value
Arithmetic	50%	.72
Algebra	30%	.56
Trigonometry	20%	.41

There are several possible approaches to content balancing. In the *split pool* approach, the item pool can be divided into more unidimensional subpools and separate CATs administered from each. In the *menu* approach, separate information tables can be maintained and alternated in their use according to some plan. In the *optimal selection* method, a penalty function or integer-programming algorithm can be used to select an optimal test that balances both statistical and content concerns.

With the most common form of CAT content balancing, the numbers or relative proportions of items of each content type are constrained to certain ranges (Stocking & Swanson, 1993). However, balancing the proportions of items administered during a CAT does not necessarily balance the influence that each content domain has in determining the final ability estimate. Ability estimates are not influenced so much by the *number* of items selected from a content domain but rather by the *amount of information* that those items provide toward estimation. While the test administered to a high-ability examinee might have half of its items drawn from the easy content domain, those items may make a negligible contribution to the total information accumulated at the final ability estimate. Because noninformative items exert very little influence on an ability estimate, the easy content domain would be effectively excluded from the test score.

Because balancing numbers or proportions of items administered can be ineffective, Segall and Davey (1995) developed and evaluated algorithms that balance the amount of information provided by each content type. The proportions of information provided by each content domain are not fixed but rather are allowed to vary across ability levels in the same way they do on conventional forms. As a result, low-ability examinees may take tests dominated by one domain while tests administered to high-scoring examinees have a different emphasis. While this means that interpretation of the obtained scores changes across ability ranges, it does so in the same way with a CAT as it does on a conventional test.

Controlling Item Exposure Rates

When items are selected solely with regard to their measurement properties, it is commonly found that certain items are administered to nearly every examinee. Furthermore, a small number of the available items account for a large proportion of the item administrations. This presents a clear security risk for testing programs that are available on more than a few scheduled test dates distributed throughout the year. The concern is that items administered frequently become compromised quickly and no longer provide valid measurement. Some general approaches for addressing this concern include the following:

1. the use of enormous item pools containing more than 5000 items. Such pools also could be organized into subpools used on a revolving schedule to minimize the possibility of the same items reappearing in the same time period or geographical area.
2. restriction of testing to certain time "windows." This approach stops short of full testing on demand but offers examinees greater flexibility in scheduling test dates than could be provided with most conventional tests.
3. direct control of item exposure rates through a statistical algorithm incorporated in the item selection procedures.

The use of either the "big pool" or restricted testing windows approach is largely dictated by practical and policy issues. However, in any case, some means of directly controlling item exposure likely is necessary. Neither large item pools nor restricted testing windows alone are sufficient to ensure integrity of the item pool. Accordingly, a number of statistical procedures for controlling item exposure rates have been devised.

One simple method recommended early in the history of computerized testing is the so-called 4-3-2-1 procedure. This simple procedure requires that an item-selection algorithm identify not only the best (e.g., most informative) item for administration at a given point but also the second-, third-, and fourth-best items. Item exposure then is limited by allowing the best item to actually be administered only 40% of the time it is selected. The second-, third-, and fourth-best items are presented 30%, 20%, and 10% of the time, respectively. This method is reasonably easy to implement but provides limited protection against overexposure of those items that are more "popular," or most likely to be selected for administration.

Another approach, the Sympson-Hetter method (Sympson & Hetter, 1985), was developed to provide more specific exposure control through the use of *exposure parameters*. The *exposure control parameter* for each item is a probability value between zero and one. Selected items actually are administered only with these probabilities. Items that are selected but not administered are set aside until the pool is empty. These exposure parameters are obtained through simulations conducted in advance of operational testing.

Even under Sympson-Hetter, we find that sets or clusters of items appear together with unwelcomed frequency and drive overlap rates upward. The problem is that exposure probabilities are treated *unconditionally*; the probability of an item being administered does not depend on which items have appeared already. Conditional approaches *factor in* the other items that have already appeared. Thus, they are useful because the real goal of exposure control is not merely to limit the rates of item use. It is also to limit the extent of overlap across tests administered. Recall that the *item overlap rate* is the percentage of shared items that occurs between pairs of tests of a fixed length. More specifically, there are two distinct test conditions in which overlap needs to be considered. In test-retest overlap, the concern relates to examinees that retest without intervening treatment to change their ability level (or examinees of highly similar ability). In peer-to-peer overlap, the concern is related to tests given to examinees of randomly dissimilar ability.

Procedures have also been developed that build on the general Sympson-Hetter framework but are conditional. One type of conditional exposure control conditions on examinee ability (Stocking & Lewis, 1995; Thomasson, 1995). In this conditional Sympson-Hetter approach, a matrix of item exposure parameters is produced, with differing exposure parameters for each item, at each of a number of discrete ability levels. The Davey-Parshall method (Davey & Parshall, 1995; Parshall, Davey, & Nering, 1998) conditions on the items that have already appeared during a given CAT on the grounds that item-pool security may be protected best by directly limiting the extent that tests overlap across examinees. The "hybrid," or Tri-Conditional method (Nering, Davey, & Thompson, 1998; Parshall, Hogarty, & Kromrey, 1999), combines these approaches and conditions on the individual item, examinee ability, and the context of testing of those items that have already been administered.

Set-Based Items

The procedures outlined earlier extend readily to either set-based item units or item bundles. The former are natural groups of items that each draw on the same common stimulus. The most frequent example is a unit that asks examinees to read a text passage and then answer a series of questions about that passage.

Item bundles are sets of discrete items that have no direct association with one another but that are always presented collectively. Bundles may either be formed as arbitrary collections of items or carefully defined in accord with substantive and statistical considerations (see Wainer (1990) for a discussion of the benefits of these bundles, also called *testlets*).

CAT administration procedures accommodate set-based units and item bundles in a variety of ways. The simplest is to consider them as indistinguishable from discrete items. A unit or bundle may provide more information or have more complicated substantive properties, but it would be selected and administered according to the same process. That is, the most informative unit at the examinee's current ability estimate would be selected for administration; provisional ability estimates would be computed after the examinee answered all items in the unit, and units would be collectively assigned a single parameter for protection against overexposure.

More sophisticated uses of item units are also possible. For example, the items attached to a unit may themselves be adaptively selected from among a small pool available when the unit is chosen. The item selection process here would mirror that of the units themselves in best suiting the current ability estimate. The more difficult items attached to a unit would then be presented whenever that unit was administered to able examinee. The same unit would take on a different easier set of items when administered to a poorly performing examinee.

Practical Characteristics

CAT may not be the best choice for every testing program or in every situation. A number of practical issues must be considered to determine where and when adaptive testing is best applied. These include the examinee volume, the ease with which an exam can be maintained both on computer and conventionally, initial development costs and effort, accommodation of pretest items, examinee reactions, and the probable cost to the examinee of the computerized exam. Each of these factors is discussed herein.

Examinee Volume

CAT is best applied to high-volume testing programs. The principal reason is the requirement that item pools contain the equivalent of five to ten conventional test forms. High-volume programs are much more likely to have sufficient items on hand to comprise an acceptable pool. Furthermore, each item in these pools must have been calibrated via IRT. The examinee samples needed to perform these calibrations typically are available only with large-scale programs. Comparably large samples also must be obtained routinely during a program's operational life to pretest and calibrate the new items. This again is practical only when large numbers of examinees are tested.

Initial Development

CAT is not a test-delivery method that can be reasonably "eased into" over time. Calibrated item pools of substantial size must be available from the onset of a testing program. As such, considerable work must be done to establish an item pool before any tests are administered. A number of important test development decisions are also required. These decisions determine the size of the item pool, whether the test is of fixed or variable length, how long the test will be, how items will be selected, including whether content balancing will be imposed and how items are protected from overexposure, how ability will be estimated, and whether and how reported scores will be determined from ability estimates. The usual way of informing these decisions is through a series of simulations designed to predict how an adaptive test might perform once operational. Conducting and interpreting the results of these simulations are time-consuming and require some psychometric expertise.

Dual Platform

It is possible but difficult to simultaneously maintain both CAT and conventional versions of a testing program. First, it is uncertain whether scores obtained under the two modes of test delivery are comparable. Test items displayed on the computer may perform differently from those printed on paper. Furthermore, an adaptive test varies the order, context, and composition of the items and tests administered. These differences make it possible that CAT and conventional tests will measure slightly different abilities in slightly different ways even if the two tests share the same items or item formats.

The ways in which conventional and CAT tests are developed, managed, and delivered also tend to work against the two types of programs operating smoothly in parallel. Conventional programs generally are managed following a "batch" process, with test development, administration, and analysis taking place in distinct cycles. In contrast, CATs are often developed, administered, and analyzed through a continuous process during which most or all of the activities are taking place simultaneously most or all of the time. These different schedules and procedures do not lend themselves to convenient coordination with tests administered in both formats.

Pretest Items

Computerized tests generally, and CATs in particular, are well suited for accommodating pretesting. Pretest items are new questions being evaluated to determine whether they are suitable for future inclusion in a test form or item pool. Because their properties are unknown, pretest items generally are not allowed to contribute to examinee scoring. This is especially true of adaptive tests, where newly administered pretest items would lack the IRT parameter estimates needed to allow them to be included in an ability estimate. In fact, for a CAT, the very reason items are pretested is to obtain the data needed for IRT calibration.

A CAT allows for pretest items to be included either isolated from or combined with the scored or operational items. An example of the former approach would be to administer a distinct separately timed test section that consists exclusively of pretest items. Alternatively, pretest items can be appended to or embedded within a test section that also includes operational items.

Pretesting in a separate section offers the advantage of ensuring that experimental or poorly constructed items in no way influence or affect an examinee's performance on the "real" or operational test items. Embedding or appending pretest items within or to an operational test offers the benefit of concealment. The concern is that if it is too apparent to examinees that certain test sections do not "count," the examinees will not bother to respond appropriately or to the best of their ability. The resulting data may not allow the quality of pretest items to be judged accurately. More important, it may not allow IRT parameters to be properly estimated. These poor parameter estimates would then follow an item into operational use and distort the scores of future examinees.

The choice of embedding or appending pretest items is based on the same conflicting considerations of concealment versus potential negative influence. Pretest items embedded in or interspersed among operational items may be very difficult for examinees to spot and therefore are treated as unimportant. Even examinees who thought a particular item odd or out of place would be unlikely to be so secure in their judgment as to skip it or respond to it randomly. However, embedded pretest items do run the risk of disturbing examinees or otherwise wasting time that could be better applied to operational items.

Appending pretest items to the end of an operational test lessens the chances of their exerting a negative influence. By the time examinees reach these items, they have completed their operational test and their score is secure. Even so, it remains the case that examinees may hurry through operational items in order to finish the test, not knowing that the items they hurried to reach did not apply to their score. Appended items are also somewhat less concealed than embedded items. Reliably spotting a whole set of pretest items is somewhat easier than identifying a single pretest question surrounded by operational items.

A CAT can be "self-sustaining" if it is able to support the pretesting and calibration needed to prepare enough new items to replace older operational ones that have been retired from use due to overexposure or dated content. The calculations for determining whether a given testing program can become self-sustaining are as follows:

1. Begin by assuming that no more than about one-quarter of any examinee's testing can be devoted to pretesting. To use more of an examinee's time on unscored items imposes an unfair burden.

2. Next, determine what proportion of the item pool an examinee is administered. As noted earlier, the pool should be at least five and ideally ten or more times larger than average test length. Third, determine how many responses are needed to effectively calibrate each pretest item. This depends on the IRT model employed, ranging from 100 to 300 responses for the Rasch or one-parameter model to 700 to 1000 under the 3-PL.

3. Finally, assume that anywhere from 5% to 50% of the items pretested will be discovered to be unfit for operational use.

These assumptions, combined with the number of examinees tested each year, yield the number of new items that can be successfully pretested, calibrated, and judged fit for operational duty. This, in turn, fixes the number of operational items that can be retired or otherwise taken out of use. Whether or not this meets operational requirements depends on the degree to which test content is required to remain secure and the speed with which that content ages. If it is decided that circumstances prevent items being replaced as fast as they must be taken out of service, either supplemental pretesting and calibration efforts must be undertaken or a different test administration model considered.

Examinee Reactions

Examinees have sometimes been found to enjoy computerized testing and even to prefer it to conventional paper-and-pencil-based administration. Whether this is due to the novelty of CBT or something deeper is as yet unclear. There are some specific advantages to adaptive test-delivery methods such as the CAT. Clearly, the prospect of shortened tests is viewed favorably. That the test is geared to an examinee's level of ability is also appreciated, particularly by low-performing examinees whose CATs appear easier than the conventional tests they are used to encountering.

However, there are features of CATs that have been identified as objectionable. Foremost among these is the usual policy applied to CATs that prohibit examinees from returning to previously answered questions to review or revise their responses. The concern is that this may offer some examinees an opportunity to "game" the system and unfairly boost their scores. For example, an examinee may recognize a newly presented item as easier than one just answered. The inference would then be that the answer just given was incorrect and should be revised. Other strategies include intentionally responding incorrectly to most or all of items as they are initially presented. This generally results in successively easier items being administered. Once all items have been administered, the examinee would return to revise the responses to each, ideally answering most or all correctly. Depending on the sort of final ability estimate employed, this can result in dramatically inflated scores. In any case, this strategy would produce exceptionally unreliable or imprecise tests being administered. Of course, the examinee would have to possess knowledge of the adaptive item selection algorithm to use this strategy effectively.

Other negatives, related to any CBT, include difficulty in reading long text passages from a computer monitor or graphics that are difficult to view due to inadequate screen resolution. Some examinees also miss being able to make notations or calculations in the test booklet. This is a particular problem when figures need to be copied onto scratch paper or otherwise manipulated.

Cost to Examinee

Although computer hardware is becoming cheaper, it remains the case that it is more expensive to provide examinees with a computer than it is to give them a number 2 pencil. This will continue to be the case whenever a CBT in general or a CAT specifically is administered at sites dedicated to that purpose. Even when tests are delivered on computers and at sites that are normally used for other purposes, the incremental costs of adding examinees to an existing administration will remain high relative to conventional tests. Again, it is easier to accommodate an extra examinee by moving a desk into a room than it is to find an extra computer station. Administration of conventional tests will always possess an economy of scale that eludes computerized testing. The costs per examinee decrease with increased volume under both modes, but do so faster with conventional tests.

The cost of initial development and making a CAT program operational also exceeds what is required for a conventional test (or fixed-form CBT) because the initial development of a CAT simply involves more work and more specialized knowledge. Development costs for CAT will decline, as procedures become better known and more routine. However, they will likely not reach the level of conventional tests.

Distribution is one area in which CBTs achieve greater efficiency than paper-and-pencil tests. Conventional tests need to be printed, shipped to examinees for administration, and then shipped again for scoring. Computerized tests, in contrast, can be immediately and cheaply transmitted electronically all over the world. Printing and shipping are not required.

Despite advantages in distribution, the overall costs associated with CATs and other CBTs far outstrip the expense of conventional testing, with the added cost generally passed on to examinees. As a tradeoff, examinees are sometimes offered the advantages of more flexible scheduling of exams and immediate score reporting. Whether these benefits outweigh the costs is a decision that needs to be made by both testing programs and examinees.

Summary

A summary of the test procedures, measurement characteristics, and practical characteristics of the CAT delivery method is shown in Table 8.2. This highlights the method's strengths and weaknesses. Overall, CAT is a good choice for testing programs that meet some or all of the following conditions:

1. Large numbers of examinees are tested each year.
2. Examinees naturally distribute themselves evenly across the year. For example, a program certifying individuals who have completed a home-study course at their own pace would thus enjoy a relatively steady examinee volume and would be a good candidate for a CAT

Table 8.2 Summary Features of the CAT Method

Test Procedures	Feature
Test assembly	Usually depends on IRT methods; tests are assembled in real time
Scoring	IRT ability estimates that may be transformed to another scale for reporting simplicity
Item pool size	Large item pools (i.e., 5 to 10 times the number of items administered to the average examinee)
Measurement Characteristics	
Test length	Fixed or variable, usually shorter than conventional tests
Reliability	Measured by the standard error of the ability estimates or their transformed values
Item/test security	Goal is to minimize the extent to which tests overlap across examinees
Set-based items	Easily implemented, but use of set-based items degrades test efficiency
Practical Characteristics	
Examinee volume	Large
Initial development	Substantial effort
Dual platform	Possible but difficult and expensive
Pretest items	Easily handled
Examinee reactions	Generally positive
Cost to examinee	High relative to conventional tests

while a program that certifies students that complete a more traditional semester-based course of study would not. Steady and continuous examinee volume continues to be an important requirement whenever CATs are administered in a network of fixed sites dedicated to testing.

3. Test security requirements are moderate. Nothing can be done to make a continuously administered CAT as secure as a conventional testing program that administers a new test form on each of a limited number of occasions throughout the year.

4. Maximum test efficiency is important. If examinees need to be tested in a variety of domains in a very limited period of time, CAT is an excellent choice.

5. Examinees must receive precise scores on each measure administered. A CAT is ideal for effectively distinguishing between examinees regardless of their level of ability. Conventional tests usually fail to discriminate well in the upper and lower extremes of the score distribution. Classification tests generally discriminate well only in the region of the cut score.

An Example of the CAT Method

The operation of an actual CAT is quite complex. Item selection and administration algorithms, item exposure control and content balancing, and ability estimation and scoring all interact to maintain a balance between the construction and administration of a reliable test for each examinee while simultaneously controlling for item exposure and content distribution. Presenting a complex, realistic example under these conditions is difficult. However, a simple example can illustrate the essence or philosophy of the CAT method. One such simple example is presented herein.

Consider a 10-item pool with the following item parameter estimates from a 3-PL model, as produced from an IRT item calibration computer program, such as *BILOG*. The parameters of these ten items are given in the second, third, and fourth columns of Table 8.3.

Before the test is administered to any examinee, another table must be constructed that provides the item information, $I(\theta)$, for each item in the pool for values of θ that are listed in increments across the entire ability range, usually from $(-4.0, +4.0)$. For example, a table might list 33 values of θ from -4.0 to $+4.0$ in increments of .25. Thus, the columns of the table would be labeled as these 33 values of θ, and the row headings would be the item numbers. The body of the table would then contain the values of $I(\theta)$ at each of these 33 values of θ.

During a CAT, whenever a new item must be selected for administration or even just considered for administration, the table is used in a *look-up* fashion to find the item in the pool that has maximum information at a value of θ that is closest to the current estimate of θ. This assumes that maximum information is the criterion for item selection. Other options are discussed under the *test assembly* section of this chapter. Basically, this is how most CAT algorithms locate, select, and administer items in a CAT. The major idea behind the creation of such a table is to make the increments small enough so that they represent the continuous information function, $I(\theta)$, but large enough so that the table is still manageable. In an actual CAT, it is not necessary to create the information table; rather, at each incremental value of θ, the item information is ranked and a list of item numbers is reported so that the look-up table contains a 10-by-33 table of item numbers.

Table 8.3. Sample CAT Item Pool

Item	$\hat{a}$	$\hat{b}$	$\hat{c}$
1	.397	−2.237	.139
2	.537	−1.116	.139
3	1.261	−.469	.023
4	.857	−.103	.066
5	1.471	.067	.093
6	.920	.241	.061
7	1.382	.495	.190
8	.940	.801	.111
9	1.290	1.170	.147
10	1.440	1.496	.310

However, even for a fairly small pool, this table can become quite large. In the 10-item example presented here, there would have to be 330 values of $I(\theta)$ computed and then listed in the table. Following each item response, an updated estimate of the examinee's ability is determined (see the explanation that follows) and the *next* item to be administered to this examinee is located from the table. It is the item that has the most information at a value of θ that is closest to the newly updated estimate of θ for that examinee.

To simplify the example, the 10-by-33 table has been reduced to a 10-by-17 table with the values of θ incremented by .5 from −4.0 to +4.0. In an actual CAT, this table would be insufficient, in terms of the increments of θ, to be useful. However, it does simplify the example that follows. Table 8.4 gives the information at these values of θ for each of the ten items in the pool.

The steps taken for the administration of this sample CAT are as follows:

Step 1.   The easiest item in the pool is administered to a sample examinee. This is the *start easy* method that begins the test with relatively easy items in order to give the examinee time to "warm up."

Step 2.   The examinee provides a correct answer to the easiest item, item 1, or the examinee's response to item 1 is 1.

Step 3.   The likelihood function (LF1) for the different values of θ for item 1 is given in Table 8.5. The value of θ that gives the maximum probability or likelihood of a single correct response or $P_1(\theta)$, in terms of the θ values given in the table, is $\theta = 4.0$.

Table 8.4. Item Information Look-up Table for Determining Item Selection

Item	θ																
	-4.0	-3.5	-3.0	-2.5	-2.0	-1.5	-1.0	-0.5	0.0	0.5	1.0	1.5	2.0	2.5	3.0	3.5	4.0
1	.048	.062	.075	.084	.087	.085	.078	.068	.056	.045	.035	.027	.020	.015	.011	.008	.006
2	.015	.029	.052	.083	.117	.146	.159	.154	.133	.106	.078	.055	.037	.024	.016	.010	.007
3	.000	.000	.003	.020	.097	.332	.772	1.098	.876	.444	.177	.064	.022	.008	.003	.001	.000
4	.000	.001	.005	.018	.054	.135	.268	.410	.468	.401	.273	.159	.084	.043	.021	.010	.005
5	.000	.000	.000	.000	.002	.019	.147	.644	1.272	1.041	.453	.148	.044	.013	.004	.001	.000
6	.000	.000	.001	.006	.021	.069	.177	.351	.511	.531	.405	.245	.129	.063	.030	.014	.006
7	.000	.000	.000	.000	.000	.002	.017	.121	.505	.942	.758	.346	.122	.039	.012	.004	.001
8	.000	.000	.001	.001	.002	.010	.039	.119	.277	.456	.513	.408	.250	.131	.063	.030	.013
9	.000	.000	.000	.000	.000	.000	.002	.015	.093	.381	.819	.844	.481	.198	.071	.024	.008
10	.000	.000	.000	.000	.000	.000	.000	.001	.008	.067	.358	.792	.662	.292	.098	.030	.009

Step 4.   Based on the look-up table presented in Table 8.4, the next item that should be administered to this examinee is item 8 because this item has the largest amount of information for examinees with $\theta = 4.0$.

Step 5.   Assume that this examinee misses item 8 so that the response *vector* now contains the correct response to the initial item and an incorrect response or 0 to item 8. The examinee's responses (i.e., the response vector) are now (1 0).

Step 6.   Based on the updated likelihood function (LF2), which is now the product of a successful response to item 1 followed by an incorrect response to item 8, or $P_1(\theta) \, Q_2(\theta)$, the maximum of this likelihood occurs for an ability estimate of $\hat{\theta} = -.5$; see Table 8.5.

Step 7.   For an individual with $\hat{\theta} = -.5$, the next item that should be administered (i.e., the item with the largest amount of information at $\theta = -.5$) is item 3; see Table 8.4.

Step 8.   Assume that this item is answered correctly so that the examinee's responses are (1 0 1). The likelihood function after three items (LF3) is $P_1(\theta) \, Q_2(\theta) \, P_3(\theta)$. The maximum of this likelihood occurs at $\hat{\theta} = 0.0$. This is the next update of the examinee's ability; see Table 8.5.

Step 9.   The item with the most information for values of $\theta = 0.0$, is item 5; see Table 8.4. Assume that the examinee correctly answers item 5 so that the responses thus far are (1 0 1 1). The likelihood function after four items (LF4) is $P_1(\theta) \, Q_2(\theta) \, P_3(\theta) \, P_4(\theta)$. The maximum of this likelihood occurs for a value of $\hat{\theta} = .5$. This is the next ability update for this examinee; see Table 8.5

Step 10.   The item with the most information at $\theta = .5$ is also item 5. Because this item has already been administered to this examinee, we administer the item with the next largest likelihood, or item 7; see Table 8.4.

Step 11.   Assume that the examinee answers this item incorrectly so that the responses are (1 0 1 1 0). The likelihood function after five items (LF5) is $P_1(\theta) \, Q_2(\theta) \, P_3(\theta) \, P_4(\theta) \, Q_5(\theta)$. The maximum of this likelihood occurs for a value of $\hat{\theta} = 0.0$. The sequence of ability estimates for this examinee has been (4.0, −.5, .0, .5, .0).

The initial item (item # 1) was selected because it was the easiest item and no ability estimate was required to select this item.

Step 12:   For this small example, assume that the stopping rule of the test is as follows: The test is stopped whenever the standard error of the estimate of θ falls at or below .70;[4] see Table 8.6 for the standard error of each updated ability estimate, $\hat{\theta}$. This criterion value falls below the .70 criterion or standard only after the fifth (and final) item has been administered. Recall that the standard error of $\hat{\theta}$ is simply the square root of the reciprocal of the test information function of the test up to and including the latest updated value of $\hat{\theta}$.

The final ability estimate for this examinee using this procedure is $\hat{\theta}$ = 0.0, with a standard error of .58. In an actual CAT administration, the final estimate of ability most likely would be refined using a computational procedure such as the Newton-Raphson algorithm (Lord, 1980, pp. 180–181).

Summary of Example

This example illustrated the steps in the CAT delivery method. This is a complex approach, requiring a fairly extensive test development and psychometric effort to develop and maintain. However, this complexity results in very quick efficient testing, and will be worth the effort for some exam programs. In addition to the developmental effort needed, the CAT method is best suited to exam programs that have large item pools available, test large numbers of examinees year-round, require only a moderate level of test security, benefit from test efficiency, and need proficiency estimates (rather than classification decisions). For exam programs that do not fit this description, other test-delivery methods may have advantages that outweigh those of the CAT.

---

[4] This criterion value is arbitrary.

Table 8.5. Likelihood Functions of θ

θ	LF 1	LF 2	LF 3	LF 4	LF 5
−4.0	.340	.302	.007	.001	.001
−3.5	.396	.352	.008	.001	.001
−3.0	.461	.409	.011	.001	.001
−2.5	.531	.470	.016	.002	.001
−2.0	.604	.531	.031	.003	.002
−1.5	.674	.585	.070	.008	.006
−1.0	.739	.623	.161	.024	.019
−0.5	.796	**.630**	.312	.084	.062
0.0	.844	.588	**.434**	.221	**.136**
0.5	.883	.486	.432	**.333**	.134
1.0	.913	.342	.328	.302	.057
1.5	.936	.205	.202	.197	.014
2.0	.953	.109	.108	.107	.003
2.5	.966	.053	.053	.053	.002
3.0	.976	.025	.025	.025	.000
3.5	.982	.012	.012	.012	.000
4.0	**.987**	.005	.005	.005	.000

Table 8.6. CAT Item Administration

Item Order	Item	Item Response	$\hat{\theta}$	$SE(\hat{\theta})$
1	1	1	4.0	13.32
2	8	0	−0.5	2.31
3	3	1	0.0	0.91
4	5	1	0.5	0.71
5	7	0	0.0	0.58

References

Brown, J. M., & Weiss, D. J. (1977). *An Adaptive Testing Strategy for Achievement Test Batteries.* (Research Report 77-6). Minneapolis: University of Minnesota, Psychometric Methods Program.

Davey, T., & Parshall, C. G. (1995, April). New algorithms for item selection and exposure control with computerized adaptive testing. Paper presented at the annual meeting of the American Educational Research Association, San Francisco.

Davey, T., & Thomas, L. (1996, April). Constructing adaptive tests to parallel conventional programs. Paper presented at the annual meeting of the American Educational Research Association, New York.

Lord, F. M. (1980). *Applications of Item Response Theory to Testing Problems.* Hillsdale, NJ: Lawrence Erlbaum.

Owen, R. J. (1969). *A Bayesian Approach to Tailored Testing.* (Research Report 69-92). Princeton, NJ: Educational Testing Service.

Owen, R. J. (1975). A Bayesian sequential procedure for quantal response in the context of adaptive mental testing. *Journal of the American Statistical Association, 70,* 351–356.

Nering, M. L., Davey, T., & Thompson, T. (1998). A hybrid method for controlling item exposure in computerized adaptive testing. Paper presented at the annual meeting of the Psychometric Society, Champaign-Urbana.

Parshall, C. G., Davey, T., & Nering, M. L. (1998, April). Test development exposure control for adaptive testing. Paper presented at the annual meeting of the National Council on Measurement in Education, San Diego.

Parshall, C. G., Hogarty, K. Y., & Kromrey, J. D. (1999, June). Item exposure in adaptive tests: An empirical investigation of control strategies. Paper presented at the annual meeting of the Psychometric Society, Lawrence, KS.

Segall, D. O., & Davey, T. C. (1995). Some new methods for content balancing adaptive tests. Presented at the annual meeting of the Psychometric Society, Minneapolis.

Stocking, M. L. (1987). Two simulated feasibility studies in computerized testing. *Applied Psychology: An International Review, 36*(3), 263–277.

Stocking, M. L. (1994). *Three Practical Issues for Modern Adaptive Testing Item Pools.* (Report No. ETS-RR-94-5). Princeton, NJ: ETS.

Stocking, M. L., & Lewis, C. (1995). *Controlling Item Exposure Conditional on Ability in Computerized Adaptive Testing.* (Research Report 95-24). Princeton, NJ: Educational Testing Service.

Stocking, M., & Swanson, L. (1993). A method for severely constrained item selection in adaptive testing. *Applied Psychological Measurement, 17,* 277–292.

Sympson, J. B., & Hetter, R. D. (1985). Controlling item-exposure rates in computerized adaptive testing. *Proceedings of the 27th annual meeting of the Military Testing Association* (pp. 973–977). San Diego: Navy Personnel Research and Development Center.

Thissen, D. (1990). Ability and measurement precision. In Wainer, H. (ed.), *Computer Adaptive Testing: A Primer* (chap. 7, pp. 161–186), Hillsdale, NJ: Lawrence Erlbaum.

Thomasson, G. L. (1995). New item exposure control algorithms for computerized adaptive testing. Paper presented at the annual meeting of the Psychometric Society, Minneapolis.

Thompson, T., Davey, T.C., & Nering, M.L. (1998). Constructing adaptive tests to parallel conventional programs. Presented at the Annual Meeting of the American Educational Research Association, San Diego.

Wainer, H., (ed.) (1990). *Computerized Adaptive Testing: A Primer.* Hillsdale, NJ: Lawrence Erlbaum.

Way, W. D. (1998). Protecting the integrity of computerized testing item pools. *Educational Measurement: Issues and Practice*, 17, 17–27.

9
Computerized Classification Tests

Overview of the CCT Method

The computerized classification test (CCT) is the test-delivery method that provides the best approach to making classification decisions. Some testing programs only require a simple dichotomous categorical decision (such as pass/fail) while others may desire or need multicategorical decisions (e.g., high-pass/pass/fail). Computerized classification tests have been primarily used by certification and licensure organizations that credential professionals for employment in specialized areas (e.g., nuclear medicine technologists, registered dietitians, and registered nurses). These applications of CCT are for programs that are considered *high stakes* in nature, in that the certification or licensure is required for employment or practice and protection of the public. Most high-stakes programs require reasonably good numbers of examinees to support item pool development and maintenance.

It is important to note that classification testing has been in existence for a long time. Past literature (Glaser, 1963; Glaser & Nitko, 1971; Hambleton, Swaminathan, & Algina, 1976; Hambleton, Swaminathan, Algina, & Coulson, 1978; Popham, 1974; Safrit, 1977) has addressed the virtues of classification testing or criterion-referenced measurement (CRM). In the past, CRM placed an emphasis on the term *mastery testing*. The computerized administration of classification or mastery tests also has the capability to make multiple decisions at various points on a continuum of ability if necessary.

Test Procedures

Test Assembly

The CCT test assembly process is conducted by the computer program administering the test to the examinee. The primary concern is to administer items that meet the content and psychometric specifications following a set of rules. Items are selected for presentation to the examinee based on an item selection algorithm contained within the test administration software. The test assembly or item selection process for a CCT can be based on a variety of methods, depending on the methodology used to implement it. If a CAT approach is employed, the selection of items is guided by the current ability estimate of the examinee (i.e., items are selected based on the amount of information provided at the current ability estimate of the examinee).

Another method that attempts to measure an examinee's latent ability is a procedure based on the estimation of latent class models. Latent class models are probability statements about the likelihood of a vector of item responses being a function of an examinee's membership based on a latent categorical variable. They are similar in form to item response theory (IRT) models except that the latent variable is discrete instead of continuous. Most of the research in this area has been contributed by George B. Macready and C. Mitchell Dayton. Those who are interested in CCT using latent class models should refer to these references.

A second, general approach uses a statistical hypothesis framework and includes computerized mastery testing (CMT) (Lewis & Sheehan, 1990; Sheehan & Lewis, 1992) and the sequential probability ratio test (SPRT) introduced by Abraham Wald (1947). The CMT approach (Lewis & Sheehan, 1990; Sheehan & Lewis, 1992) relies on item clusters or packets, called *testlets*, that have been preassembled or constructed to have the same number of items that match content and psychometric specifications. The testlets are selected randomly during the administration of the CCT. In an SPRT classification test, items are selected based on the amount of item information at the passing score or decision point of the test. This feature changes the demands placed on the requirements for the item pool characteristics when compared with other test-delivery methods.

Scoring

The scoring of the CCT is determined by the method used to conduct the test. However, all methods rely on comparing examinee performance to a predetermined criterion level of performance. Two primary approaches have been employed in the administration of adaptive CCTs. A CCT may be scored using ability estimation as done in a CAT or using the SPRT. If a CAT approach is used, IRT ability estimates are obtained, along with the standard error of ability estimate. These values are used to compare to the latent passing score to determine a pass/fail decision. The stopping rule for a CAT is customarily defined as the point in the test at which the classification decision point or passing score falls outside of a given confidence level or credibility interval of the examinee's estimated ability. Typically, examinees are not permitted to change answers to previously answered items when items are selected at the target of the examinee's current ability estimate.

The examinee's performance also is assessed relative to a criterion level of performance in a CCT using the SPRT approach. However, unlike a CAT, the examinee's latent ability is not estimated directly. Instead, information about the examinee's performance is compared to two different points located above and below the passing score on the ability continuum. The SPRT uses this information to determine classification status (e.g., pass/fail) for examinees that clearly are above or below the decision point or points. The procedure can produce a scaled score or ability estimate after the test has been completed. More detailed information is provided later in this chapter in an example using the SPRT process.

Item Pool Characteristics

Adaptive tests, in general, tend to require large numbers of test items. However, the requirements for CCT are not as extensive as CAT when the selection algorithm chooses items based on information at the passing score. In this situation, it is best if the item pool has a large number of informative items that have maximum item information near the passing score. Therefore, CCT item pools do not need to be as large as CAT pools but they do need to be large enough to accommodate the psychometric and content specifications of the test. For most high-stakes testing programs, the acceptable or targeted maximum exposure rate (i.e., the percentage of time that an item should be administered) is 20%. This value can be used to estimate the number of items required to administer a CCT. If a CCT has a minimum test length of 100 items and a maximum exposure control target of 20%, the item pool needs to have at least 500 items to meet the requirements for the minimum test length. This minimum may be higher if the content specifications are complex. The item pool needs more items if the exposure control target is lower or the test length is longer.

Measurement Characteristics

Test Length

A CCT can make pass/fail decisions statistically with a very small number of items (e.g., less than 10). However, most test developers agree that tests of this length are not acceptable in most circumstances. Test length can be reduced to half the length of the paper-and-pencil format or even less and still maintain the accuracy of the classification decisions. Reductions in test length are determined by the quality of the item pool, whether the CCT is variable or fixed in length, and the complexity of the content specifications required for the test. A large item pool containing high-quality items allows test lengths to be considerably shorter than the traditional paper-and-pencil tests that they replace. Content specifications that include a high level of detail require more items to be presented in order to meet these specifications.

The determination of an appropriate test length is accomplished by performing computerized simulations of the testing environment. The simulation process permits the estimation of passing rates, decision error rates, and the degree to which content specifications have been met. Examinees whose abilities are further away from the passing score require fewer items on which to base a classification decision. On the other hand, examinees that possess abilities near the passing score require longer. The minimum and maximum test lengths can be manipulated during the simulation process to determine values that assist in minimizing classification errors, given other considerations such as item pool size and quality, seat time, and item exposure.

Research has shown that if the classification decision is made on the basis of an examinee's latent ability (i.e., a CAT), the test is more powerful if the selection of items is determined at the passing score level rather than at the examinee's estimated ability (Spray & Reckase, 1996). However, the SPRT method administers tests that are more efficient than the CAT. Specifically, the SPRT method provides test results that have comparable pass rates and classification errors to the CAT but requires fewer items.

Reliability

The evaluation of reliability for a CCT is based on statistics that provide information regarding the consistency of the decisions made in classifying examinees into two or more categories. The estimation of decision consistency and accuracy is facilitated during the computerized simulation of the CCT environment. Decision consistency is a reliability measure for criterion-referenced tests. It provides information concerning the stability or precision of decisions. Most decision consistency measures indicate the percentage or proportion of consistent decisions that would be made if the test could be administered to the same examinees over two occasions. Decision accuracy, on the other hand, is a measure of a test's ability to classify examinees correctly into the appropriate categories. A test with a low classification error rate has a high degree of decision accuracy.

Because an examinee's true classification status is never known precisely, it is impossible to determine a test's decision accuracy. However, based on assumptions pertaining to the ability distribution of the population of examinees taking the CCT, psychometricians can predict pass/fail rates, classification error rates, and consistency of classifications. Measures such as the proportion of consistent classifications, coefficient Kappa (i.e., the proportion of consistent classifications corrected for chance) (Cohen, 1960), and the proportion of correct classification decision made can be obtained through computer simulations.

Item/Test Security

A primary concern with any computerized test is the security of the items used in the testing process. Any CCT must address how the items will be protected from overuse. The determination of exposure control parameters can be accomplished during the computerized simulation process. Lewis and Sheehan (1990) and Sheehan and Lewis (1992) have employed the randomized selection of parallel testlets to meet this goal. Another approach is a modification of the Sympson-Hetter method, presented in detail in Chapter 10.

Set-Based Items

The CCT delivery method is capable of utilizing set-based items by selecting and then administering one or more of the items in a set. However, the administration of these items can decrease the efficiency of the test, because not all of the included items may be equally informative in the area of the passing score. If a set of items had been administered and calibrated previously on a paper-and-pencil administration, then some care must be taken if items are administered either as discrete items or in subsets of the original complete set. The characteristics of the items, as represented by the original calibrations, may no longer describe the discrete items or those appearing in subsets.

Practical Characteristics

There are a number of important considerations beyond those discussed so far that must be addressed when any classification test is delivered via computer. These include the examinee volume, the ease with which an exam can be maintained across dual platforms, initial development effort, accommodation of pretest items, examinee reactions, and the probable cost to the examinee of the computerized exam. Each of these factors is discussed next for the CCT.

Examinee Volume

Testing programs that wish to use IRT methodology in a CCT require large numbers of examinees to meet the requirements for item calibration. High examinee volumes also have an impact on the number of times items are seen. This, in turn, impacts designs regarding the CCT item pool to permit the rotation of item pools so that the items are not overly exposed.

Initial Development

Initial development for a CCT requires computerized simulation research to evaluate the quality of the item pool, item security, and accuracy of the decisions. This process requires use of skilled psychometric personnel to conduct simulations that meet the specifications and expectations of the test developer. These preparations require a fair amount of time for both the simulation process and evaluation of the item pool. The item pool also needs to be evaluated from the content specialists' perspective to ensure that items are current and accurate.

Dual Platform

It is possible to permit dual platforms for both computer and paper-and-pencil administrations using the SPRT process. Because SPRT CCT item selection is driven only by content specifications, item information, and item exposure control, a paper version of the CCT can be produced for offline administration. Paper versions of this test are set at the maximum test length but are scored using the SPRT process. Therefore, a decision on the pass/fail status of an examinee can be determined at the minimum test length or somewhere between the minimum and maximum test lengths. Before the implementation of this dual-platform process, the comparability of test results between the two platforms must be evaluated.

This is not true for CCT methods that use a CAT approach in making classification decisions. This approach requires a large amount of resources to ensure comparability, and the paper version would be unable to reproduce the adaptive format that is available via computer.

Pretest Items

As with other test-delivery methods, in order to support pool replenishment or replacement, continual item pretesting needs to be conducted with the CCT. Because many computerized classification tests are variable in length and adaptive in nature, it is difficult to predict exactly how many pretest items need to be administered to any one examinee. One approach is to administer the pretest items at the end of the test and allow the number of pretest items to vary according to the number of operational items an examinee takes. Another strategy is to fix the number of pretest items, administering them either at the end of or throughout the operational test, interspersed between operational items.

Examinee Reactions

Examinees are permitted to review items and even change answers throughout the testing process for those computerized classifications tests in which items are selected based on the amount of information at the passing score. For example, with CCT procedures such as the SPRT or CMT, examinee performance does not impact the selection of items and item responses to previous items can be changed at any time. Many examinees prefer to have this flexibility, considering it a highly valued testing option. In addition, some examinees prefer having shorter tests and the various CCT methods usually are able to reduce test lengths, given a strong item pool.

Cost to Examinee

The cost of developing and administering CBTs is often higher than typical costs for paper-and-pencil testing. Some portion of that cost is borne by higher examinee fees. The amount charged an examinee for any test is related to the developmental effort and expenses incurred by the testing company or certification/licensure board. Given the higher developmental effort needed for a CCT, the cost to the examinee often is more than a paper-and-pencil or CFT format.

Summary

A summary of the test procedures, measurement characteristics, and practical characteristics of the CCT delivery method is provided in Table 9.1. These features highlight the method's strengths and weaknesses. Overall, a CCT program requires some initial effort; this may be very intensive, especially if the item pool must be calibrated. Many of the critical decisions regarding the CCT can be answered only after extensive computer simulations. In spite of this drawback, the CCT approach is the test-delivery method of choice for many testing programs, particularly those concerned with making classifications of examinees to two or more categories. The most common use for a CCT is in the area of licensure and certification testing.

Table 9.1 Summary Features of the CCT Method

Test Procedures	Feature
Test assembly	IRT preferred, classical methods are an option
Scoring	Classification decision alone, or with a scaled score after test terminates
Item pool size	Medium
Measurement Characteristics	
Test length	Usually variable
Reliability	Consistency of classification
Item/test security	Item exposure control
Set-based items	Allowed with cautions
Practical Characteristics	
Examinee volume	Large (if IRT is used)
Initial development	Moderate effort
Dual platform	Possible
Pretest items	Easily handled
Examinee reactions	Relatively positive
Cost to examinee	May be high

An Example of the CCT Method

This section provides an explanation of the SPRT method for implementing a CCT and presents an example of a short test using the method. CCT methods that employ a CAT approach are simplifications of material presented in Chapter 8 and will not be presented in this chapter.

The SPRT CCT method has been shown to possess certain advantages over an ability estimation approach. The SPRT CCT:

- lessens the requirement that items in the pool must measure well at all ability levels (Kalohn & Spray, 1999);
- allows the option of permitting examinees to review previously answered items and change previous responses if desired (Kalohn & Huang, 1997);

- simplifies scoring (e.g., pass/fail score versus the calculation and scaling of ability estimates);
- simplifies the determination of item exposure control parameters and item overlap control; and
- may offset problems of multidimensionality in the item pool, the (IRT) latent ability space, or both.

The primary focus of the SPRT CCT is to make a decision regarding an examinee's competency compared to a standard. To do this, an item pool is needed that contains items possessing statistical characteristics that are optimal in differentiating between passing and failing examinees. This means that the item pool should contain items that provide adequate information in the area of the passing score, or if IRT is used the latent passing score, θ_p. This differs from item pools used in ability estimation, which need to possess items that provide a sufficient amount of information across the entire ability continuum.

Unlike a CAT or CCT that uses ability estimation, the SPRT CCT selects the next item to be administered based on item characteristics; it does not consider the response to the previous item by the examinee. The item selection criteria are based on item information at the passing standard, test blueprint constraints, and item exposure controls.

The SPRT Procedure

The sequential probability ratio test, or SPRT, was first proposed by Abraham Wald during the latter stages of World War II as a means of conserving Allied ammunition during test firing of production lots of ammunition. Prior to sequential testing, a fairly large quantity of live ammunition had to be fired in order to determine a simple binomial probability of unacceptable lots. This traditional *fixed sample* approach to testing required a predetermined number of rounds, N, to be fired and the proportion of unacceptable rounds to be observed. Using the sequential approach, rounds were fired only until a number of unacceptable rounds had been observed that would indicate, within a given statistical power and acceptable Type I error rate, what the unacceptable proportion was. In most cases, this (variable) number of rounds usually was smaller than the fixed sample required to reach the same conclusion with the same or less power and at the same error rate.

The SPRT was first suggested for mental testing via computer by Ferguson (1969a, 1969b) and later by Reckase (1983). Since this early research, the SPRT has been applied to a variety of classification tests.

The SPRT Hypotheses.

Statistically, the SPRT tests a pair of simple hypotheses.

Either

or $\left\{ \begin{array}{l} \text{examinee } i \text{ has latent ability} = \theta_0 \text{ (the null hypothesis)} \\ \text{examinee } i \text{ has latent ability} = \theta_1 \text{ (the alternative hypothesis).} \end{array} \right.$

Arbitrarily, we let $\theta_0 < \theta_1$ and refer to θ_0 as the level of ability beyond which we are $(1-\alpha)100\%$ certain that an examinee should fail the examination. In other words, the point θ_0 corresponds to the lowest possible passing level on θ, or it is the greatest lower bound of minimal competency that we are willing to tolerate.

Similarly, we refer to θ_1 as the level of ability beyond which we are $(1-\beta)100\%$ certain that the examinee should pass the examination. In other words, the point θ_1 corresponds to the highest possible passing level on θ, or it is the least upper bound of minimal competency that we are willing to tolerate.

Classification error rates are specified by α and β, where α is the rate of false positive classification errors, or the frequency with which we classify an examinee as passing the examination given that the examinee should truly fail, while β is the rate of false negative classification errors, or the frequency with which we classify an examinee as failing the examination given that the examinee should truly pass. We note that all classification examinations yield false positive and false negative errors. However, the SPRT is unique in that it can directly control these errors by specifying them in advance of testing.

Establishing the Four SPRT Parameters, θ_0, θ_1, α, and β

Based on our definitions above, we know that $\theta_0 < \theta_p < \theta_1$. The distance between θ_0 and θ_1 is called the indifference region. The larger the indifference region, the shorter the test, in terms of test length. However, there is a trade-off between length and classification accuracy. Examinees with $\theta_i > \theta_1$ or with $\theta_i < \theta_0$ will have shorter test lengths than examinees with $\theta_0 < \theta_i < \theta_1$. Examinees with true θ values in the indifference region will be classified with more error.

It is not unusual to fix α and β both at .05 or at .10. However, they need not be identical and only must satisfy $0 < \alpha < 1$ and $0 < \beta < 1$. For example, it could be possible to tolerate a higher negative positive error than a false positive error; thus, $\beta < \alpha$. This might occur in certification testing when public protection is an important outcome of the testing process. Once θ_0 and θ_1 have been established, θ_p is no longer needed to conduct the test, except to rank-order items based on maximum item information at θ_p.

Conducting the Test

If the items have been calibrated using a three-parameter logistic IRT model or 3-PLM, we can define $P(\theta)$ as the probability of answering an item correctly, given θ and the item's parameter estimates, $\hat{a}$, $\hat{b}$, and $\hat{c}$. Then $P(\theta)$ is the item characteristic function and $P(\theta_0)$ and $P(\theta_1)$ are two points of that function. If $Q(\theta) = 1-P(\theta)$, then $Q(\theta_0)$ and $Q(\theta_1)$ represent incorrect response probabilities at θ_0 and θ_1, respectively. Following each item response, the likelihood or probability that an examinee with $\theta_i = \theta_0$ has produced those responses thus far during the test is

$$L(x_1, x_2,..., x_k \mid \theta_0) = \pi_1(\theta_0)\pi_2(\theta_0)...\pi_k(\theta_0), \tag{9.1}$$

where

$$\pi_j(\theta_0) = P(\theta_0)^{x_j} Q(\theta_0)^{1-x_j} \tag{9.2}$$

or equivalently,

$$\log \pi_j(\theta_0) = (x_j) \log P(\theta_0) + (1 - x_j) \log Q(\theta_0) \tag{9.3}$$

where

$$\begin{cases} x_j = 1, \text{ if the item is answered correctly,} \\ x_j = 0, \text{ otherwise.} \end{cases}$$

The likelihood or probability that an examinee would have $\theta_i = \theta_1$ following each item response is

$$L(x_1, x_2,..., x_k \mid \theta_1) = \pi_1(\theta_1)\pi_2(\theta_1)...\pi_k(\theta_1), \tag{9.4}$$

where

$$\pi_j(\theta_1) = P(\theta_1)^{x_j} Q(\theta_1)^{1-x_j} \tag{9.5}$$

or equivalently,

$$\log \pi_j(\theta_1) = (x_j) \log P(\theta_1) + (1 - x_j) \log Q(\theta_1) \tag{9.6}$$

Scoring the Test

Once an item is selected and administered to an examinee, we can compute the likelihood under $\theta_i = \theta_0$ and the likelihood under $\theta_i = \theta_1$ (or equivalently, the logs of the likelihood functions). Next, we form a likelihood ratio (LR) of the two likelihood values,

$$LR = L(x_1 \mid \theta_1)/L(x_1 \mid \theta_0). \tag{9.7}$$

If LR is "large enough," we decide that an examinee with θ_i should pass.
If LR is "small enough," we decide that an examinee with θ_i should fail.
If LR is neither too large nor too small, we administer another item.

The likelihood ratio, LR, is actually compared to two boundary values, A and B. A is the upper boundary value and is approximately equal to $(1-\beta)/\alpha$, or equivalently,

$$\log(A) = \log(1 - \beta) - \log \alpha. \tag{9.8}$$

B is the lower boundary value and is approximately equal to $\beta/(1\_\alpha)$, or equivalently,

$$\log(B) = \log \beta - \log(1 - \alpha). \tag{9.9}$$

The likelihood ratio, LR (or the log of LR), is updated following the response to each item that an examinee is given, so that

$$LR = L(x_1, x_2, \ldots \mid \theta_1)/L(x_1, x_2, \ldots \mid \theta_0). \tag{9.10}$$

The test terminates when either $LR > A$, $LR < B$ {or equivalently when either $\log(LR) > \log(A)$ or $\log(LR) < \log(B)$} or a time limit or test length maximum has been exceeded. If the examinee has not been classified by the SPRT procedure when the time limit has been exceeded or the maximum number of items have been answered, some method must be used to determine how the examinee is classified. Typically, the (unsigned) distance between the LR and the boundaries is computed, and the shorter distance is used as the criterion on which to base the final classification decision.

Steps of an SPRT CCT

In this section, an example of a CCT using the SPRT approach is presented. The steps of this process include (1) determining the SPRT parameters, (2) preparing the items for selection and administration, (3) administering the items to the examinee, (4) calculating the log of the likelihood ratio, and (5) determining the decision status. In order to collect enough information to make a decision about an examinee's classification status, the examinee must receive many items. A CCT program will iteratively repeat steps 3 to 5 until the test terminates by making a decision, presenting the maximum number of test items, or time expires. In this example, we present a short test that can be processed by the reader manually.

Step 1: Determining the Parameters for the SPRT CCT

Prior to the administration of an SPRT CCT, we must know (a) the value of θ_p; (b) θ_0 and θ_0, and hence, the width of the indifference region; and (c) α and β. The value of θ_P is determined from results of a passing score study. We will demonstrate two methods for determining θ_P from passing score study results later. For this example, we assume that $\theta_P = -.40$. The width of the indifference region is arbitrarily set to be .70 and is symmetrical around θ_0. In other words, $\theta_0 = -.75$ and $\theta_1 = -.05$. These values also are arbitrary. In fact they need not be symmetrical around the latent passing score value, θ_p. The error rates for α and β have both been set to .10. This error rate was selected to provide an example that would produce a classification result quickly. The typical error rates used for a real SPRT CCT are based on acceptable error rates for a given testing program. In practice, these error rates typically are set at .05. The values of A and B {or the values of log(A) and log(B)}, the upper and lower boundaries of the test, can be determined by applying Equations 9.8 and 9.9, respectively.

By applying equations 9.8 & 9.9:

$$\log(A) = \log(1 - \beta) - \log \alpha \qquad \log(B) = \log \beta - \log(1 - \alpha)$$
$$\log(A) = \log(1 - .10) - \log (.10) \qquad \log(B) = \log(.10) - \log (1 - .10)$$
$$\log(A) = \log(.90) - \log (.10) \qquad \log(B) = \log(.10) - \log (.90)$$
$$\log(A) = (-.105) - (-2.303) \qquad \log(B) = (-2.303) - (-.105)$$
$$\log(A) = 2.198 \qquad \log(B) = -2.198$$

Step 2: Preparing Items for Selection and Administration

Calculate each item's information at θ_P, or $I(\theta_P)$ and the probability of a correct response at θ_0 and θ_1. The items are then ranked on $I(\theta_P)$ from highest to lowest. Refer to the appendix, Basics of Item Response Theory, for the formulas for item information. The results of these calculations and ranking are presented in Table 9.2. Items are selected for administration based on each item's $I(\theta_P)$.

Step 3: Administering an Item to the Examinee

In view of the fact that we do not have a real examinee for this example, we define the ability of our "examinee" to be a known value of θ. For this example, $\theta = 1.0$. This permits us to determine the probability of a correct response to the first item (and subsequent items) just as we do for θ_0 and θ_1. We then can determine whether the examinee answers correctly by selecting a random number between 0.0 and 1.0 (i.e., a uniform deviate or random number) and compare this number to the probability of a correct response. Think of a spinner with values from 0.0 to 1.0. After we spin the spinner, the arrow points to a number in the interval between 0.0 and 1.0. If the value of the spinner is less than or equal to the probability of a correct response for the examinee for the item being evaluated, the examinee answers the item correctly. If the spinner probability is greater than the probability of a correct response for the examinee for the item being evaluated, the examinee answers the item incorrectly. The scored response (x) for a correct answer is given a value of 1 and for an incorrect response, a value of 0.

For this example, we assume the first item is answered correctly and x is assigned a value of 1.

Step 4: Calculating the log of the likelihood ratio

There are two likelihood values that must be calculated for each item administered to an examinee, $LR(\theta_0)$ and $LR(\theta_1)$. Recall that

$$\log \pi_j (\theta_0) = (x_j)\log P(\theta_0) + (1 - x_j) \log Q(\theta_0)$$
$$\log \pi_j (\theta_0) = (1) * \log(.487) + (0) * \log(1 - .487)$$
$$\log \pi_j (\theta_0) = -.719$$

and

$$\log \pi_j (\theta_1) = (x_j)\log P(\theta_1) + (1 - x_j) * \log Q(\theta_1)$$
$$\log \pi_j (\theta_1) = (1) * \log(.876) + (0) * \log(1 - .876)$$
$$\log \pi_j (\theta_1) = -.123.$$

Subsequently,

$$\log(LR) = \log \pi_j (\theta_1) - \log \pi_j (\theta_0)$$
$$\log(LR) = -.123 - (-.719)$$
$$\log(LR) = .596.$$

This value is used in the next step.

Step 5: Determining the Decision Status

In this step we compare the $\log(LR)$ to the two boundaries $\log(A)$ and $\log(B)$. If the log of the likelihood ratio is greater than or equal to $\log(A)$ or less than or equal to $\log(B)$, testing ends. However, if the log of the likelihood ratio is between $\log(A)$ and $\log(B)$, another item is presented to the examinee. Because logs of the likelihood ratio are used, we simply add the log of the likelihood ratio for the next item and subsequent items administered to the examinee.

Steps 3, 4, and 5 are repeated until a decision is made or there are no more items remaining to administer. From the data presented in Table 9.2, we can observe that a total of 11 items were administered before a decision of passing was made based on the final log of the likelihood ratio of 2.25. This final ratio exceeded the upper bound, $\log(A)$, which was 2.198. Note that each correct answer increases the log of the likelihood ratio, while incorrect answers cause a decrease in the ratio.

It is important to note that this example was designed to provide a numerical example to explain the SPRT CCT process. There were no item exposure controls or content constraints used in this example. The implementation of an SPRT CCT requires the use of item exposure controls and content constraints to protect the security of the item pool. CCT requires a substantial number of items in the item pool to protect items from being overexposed. The item pool size needs to be at least five to seven times as large as the average number of items that are administered to examinees.

Summary of Example

This example illustrated the steps in the CCT delivery method. In addition to the developmental effort needed, the CCT method is best suited to exam programs that have moderately sized item pools available, test moderate to large numbers of examinees year-round, require only a moderate level of test security, benefit from test efficiency, and need classification decisions. For exam programs that do not fit this description, other test-delivery methods may have advantages that outweigh those of the CCT.

Table 9.2. Summary of Calculations for an SPRT CCT

θ_0	α	$\log(A)$	Width of the Indifference Region		
-.750	.10	2.197	.70		

θ_1	β	$\log(B)$	θ_P		
-.050	.10	-2.197	-.40		

Item Parameters						Probability Correct Response Examinee		Log of the Likelihood Ratio		
Item	$\hat{a}$	$\hat{b}$	$\hat{c}$	$I(\theta_P)$	$P(\theta_0)$ $P(\theta_1)$	with $\theta_t = 1.0$	SR*	Correct Response	Incorrect Response	Total Ratio
1	1.80	-.64	.12	1.70	.487 .876	.994	1	.59	-1.42	.59
2	2.00	-.16	.15	1.56	.249 .652	.984	1	.96	-.77	1.55
3	1.80	.83	.23	1.14	.659 .935	.997	1	.35	-1.65	1.90
4	1.88	.16	.19	.48	.228 .461	.948	0	.70	-.36	1.54
5	1.71	-1.51	.20	.25	.920 .989	.999	1	.07	-1.94	1.61
6	.88	-1.70	.31	.16	.866 .947	.988	1	.09	-.92	1.70
7	.63	-1.22	.24	.16	.714 .830	.935	1	.15	-.52	1.85
8	.68	-1.66	.22	.15	.797 .894	.965	1	.12	-.65	1.97
9	.92	-2.09	.14	.13	.906 .966	.993	1	.06	-1.02	2.03
10	.59	-1.74	.18	.13	.779 .873	.951	1	.11	-.55	2.14
11	.47	-1.94	.15	.09	.763 .846	.926	1	.10	-.43	2.25

* SR – Scored response

References

Cohen, J. (1960). A coefficient of agreement for nominal scales. *Educational and Psychological Measurement,* 20, 37–46.

Ferguson, R. L. (1969a). *Computer-Assisted Criterion-Referenced Measurement* (Working Paper No. 41). Pittsburgh: University of Pittsburgh, Learning and Research Development Center. (Eric Document Reproduction Series No. ED 037 089).

Ferguson, R. L. (1969b). The development, implementation, and evaluation of a computer-assisted branched test for a program of individually prescribed instruction. Unpublished doctoral dissertation, University of Pittsburgh. (University Microfilms No. 70-4530).

Glaser, R. (1963). Instructional technology and the measurement of learning outcomes. *American Psychologist,* 18, 519–521.

Glaser, R., & Nitko, A. J. (1971). Measurement in learning and instruction. In R. L. Thorndike (ed.), *Educational Measurement.* Washington, DC: American Council on Education.

Hambleton, R. K., Swaminathan, H., & Algina, J. (1976). Some contributions to the theory and practice of criterion-referenced testing. In DeGruijter, D. N. M., & van der Kamp, L. J. T. (eds.), *Advances in Psychology and Educational Measurement* (pp. 51–62). New York: John Wiley & Sons.

Hambleton, R. K., Swaminathan, H., Algina, J., & Coulson, D. B. (1978). Criterion-referenced testing and measurement: A review of technical issues and developments. *Review of Educational Research,* 48, 1–47.

Kalohn, J. C., & Huang, C. (June, 1997). The effect of changing item responses on the accuracy of an SPRT CAT for pass/fail classification decisions. Paper presented at the annual meeting of the Psychometric Society, Gatlinberg, TN.

Kalohn, J.C., & Spray, J. A. (1999). The effect of model misspecification on classifications made using a computerized classification test. *Journal of Educational Measurement,* 36, 46–58.

Lewis, C., & Sheehan, K. (1990). Using Bayesian decision theory to design a computerized mastery test. *Applied Psychological Measurement,* 14, 367–386.

Popham, W. J. (1974) Selecting objectives and generating test items for objectives-based items. In Harris, C. W., & Popham, W. J., (eds.), *Problems in Criterion-Referenced Measurement* (pp. 13–25). Los Angeles: University of California, Center for the Study of Evaluation.

Reckase, M. D. (1983). A procedure for decision making using tailored testing. In Weiss, D. J., (ed.), *New Horizons in Testing: Latent Trait Test Theory and Computerized Adaptive Testing* (pp. 237–255). New York: Academic Press.

Safrit, M. J. (1977). Criterion-referenced measurement: Applications in physical education. *Motor Skills: Theory into Practice,* 2, 21–35.

Sheehan, K., & Lewis, C. (1992). Computerized mastery testing with nonequivalent testlets. *Applied Psychological Measurement,* 16, 65_76.

Spray, J. A., & Reckase, M. D. (1996). Comparison of SPRT and sequential Bayes procedures for classifying examinees into two categories using a computerized test. *Journal of Educational and Behavioral Statistics,* 21, 405–414.

Wald, A. (1947). *Sequential Analysis.* New York: Wiley.

10
Item Pool Evaluation and Maintenance

Introduction

When testing programs indicate that they would like to move their current multiple-choice paper-and-pencil examinations to a computer-based testing program, they can consider several CBT options. These include CFT, ATA, CAT, and CCT. Ultimately, the decision to move a testing program to a CBT environment depends on many factors. These include the purpose of the test, the type of test, the status of current test specifications and classification of items, whether current exams are voluntary, current testing volumes, and the results of an item pool evaluation. This chapter focuses on the item pool evaluation process and item pool maintenance.

The evaluation of an item pool requires the involvement of two groups of experts, content and psychometric. Content experts are responsible for the evaluation of the item pool, paying particular attention to the quality of items from a content perspective. Psychometric experts are responsible for the evaluation of the quality of the statistical characteristics of the item pool in order to determine if a CBT is feasible. The item pool evaluation process involves three steps or processes. These are:

1. Item pool content review by content experts;

2. Assessment of item pool statistical characteristics; and

3. Simulation of CBT environment.

It is expected that most testing programs have the resources to complete the first step of the item pool evaluation process. However, many testing programs may not be in a position to evaluate their own item pools thoroughly and rigorously for possible implementation of CBT applications that are included in the remaining steps of the evaluation process. In this case, psychometricians who can perform this complex task should be consulted. The presentation of the material for Steps 2 and 3 assumes that such expert advice and technical assistance are available.

Once the CBT program is online and the program is operational, the item pool must be maintained. Item pool maintenance consists of updating the item calibrations from CBT administrations, calibrating and evaluating pretest items, monitoring item exposures, and possibly updating the standard reference set if or when a new test blueprint or content outline is introduced. Ongoing pool maintenance is a necessary process to ensure the best possible conditions for a CBT program.

Item Pool Evaluation

Item pool evaluation is a necessity for all testing programs, whether the test is presented in paper format or via computer. Ideally, testing programs should conduct regularly scheduled pool evaluations in order to maintain an item pool that is up to date and represents the state of the art for the particular domain it is designed to assess. Unfortunately, some testing programs do not regularly discard older items that are no longer appropriate. This lack of attention to the item pool makes the task of evaluating the item pool for CBT more time-consuming and complicated.

The item pool evaluation process provides valuable information to test developers about the current state of the item pool and the possibilities of administering a test using a given CBT method. While some aspects of the item pool evaluation are similar for most types of CBT, there are some differences among the various CBT methods presented in earlier chapters. These differences among the various CBT methods are highlighted in this chapter.

Item Pool Content Review

During an item pool review, content experts review all items in the pool to determine what items are suitable for inclusion in a CBT from a content perspective. For most testing programs considering CBT, this review process is lengthy and requires planning and the establishment of guidelines to be efficient and successful. One strategy is to assign small groups of content experts to review a portion of the item pool and to come to a consensus about the status of those items that they are assigned to review. Typically guidelines for reviewing items consist of questions that help focus the efforts of the content experts. Query-based guidelines are essential to assist the content experts in making decisions efficiently and accurately. Some suggested guidelines for this portion of the item pool evaluation process are presented in Table 10.1.

Each of the queries presented in Table 10.1 is a fairly common question that should be evaluated for any type of testing program conducting an item pool evaluation, regardless of presentation format (i.e., paper or computer presentation). The last question relates to items that may clue answers to other items in an item pool. Many testing programs refer to these "cueing" items as *enemies*. Items are enemies in the sense that they should not appear together on the same test for a given examinee. This is a relatively simple task for a fixed-form examination, given the limited number of items that are presented on an exam of this type. However, for CBTs constructed in real time, the computer program administering the test must have information that indicates item enemy pairs. The content experts also must review the item pool with the item enemy concept in mind throughout the entire evaluation process in order to identify these items. It is easy to see how this step of the evaluation process becomes very complicated with large item pools.

Table 10.1. Guidelines for Item Pool Content Review

---

1. Does the item measure content that is germane to the current test blueprint or test specifications?

2. Does the item contain information that is accurate and up to date (i.e., does it represent current content, laws, regulations, technology, etc.)?

3. Does the item possess correct content classification code(s) based on the current test specifications?

4. Does the item possess a correct response (i.e., is the key correct)?

5. Does the item cue the correct response for another item in the item pool? If so, those items should be identified to prevent the administration of these items on the same examination to an examinee.

In addition, the content experts must give special consideration to item sets. Recall that item sets are characterized by items that are preceded by a common stimulus or reading passage. The content experts have the discretion to determine how an item set is to be presented in the CBT environment. Specifically, the content expert can identify what group of items to present together in a set or how the set is to be split in order to produce multiple item sets that are attached to a common stimulus or reading passage. Based on this configuration the psychometric staff can incorporate each item set into the item selection and presentation process.

The content review process is a monumental task that requires a fair amount of commitment by numerous content experts. For the most part, this step can occur concurrently with Step 2, permitting some streamlining of the process. This allows the two groups of experts to perform these initial steps simultaneously. However, these first two steps must precede the process of simulating the CBT environment. This is essential to prevent repetition of the simulation process, because any changes in the composition of the item pool require repetition of the simulation process from the beginning.

Item Pool Statistical Review

The process of reviewing the statistical information about items in an item pool depends on the type of CBT to be developed and the type of item statistics that are used in assembling and scoring the CBT (i.e., classical versus IRT item statistics). This process is different for each of the four methods that have been presented in earlier chapters. The next sections present relevant information related to this review statistical process for each CBT method with an emphasis on CCT and CAT.

Computerized Fixed Tests

The statistical review process for CFTs is driven by the types of statistics that are maintained and used in the test assembly process. An important part of the review process is to determine if the item pool consists of enough items to assemble a form that is similar to the original or base form and meet the test specifications in terms of content and statistical characteristics. This review process requires a close look at each item's difficulty, discrimination, and response analysis, comparing the item's performance to items from the base form. Items that deviate significantly from the statistical item characteristics from the base form most likely would not be used in the creation of a new CFT.

Automated Test Assembly

The statistical review process for tests created using the ATA procedure is driven by the types of statistics that are maintained and used in the test assembly process. Item pools under ATA approach must contain more items for the construction of multiple test forms than a CFT. Review of the item statistics for ATA must consider those statistics that pertain to item difficulty, discrimination, and response analysis. As in the CFT analyses, a review of an item pool to be used for ATA should compare each item's statistics to items from a base form. The review also includes the analysis of IRT item parameter estimates if IRT is used in the automated test assembly process.

Information pertaining to the review of IRT model selection and the review of item statistics is presented in detail in the next section. Although the primary focus of the following section is on CAT and CCT, the IRT item review section is applicable to any testing program that uses IRT in the development of a test, regardless of the mode of administration.

Computerized Adaptive Tests and Computerized Classification Tests

Most tests that use either CAT or CCT employ IRT item statistics to determine (a) selection of items to be presented to examinees and (b) reported scale scores, if desired. The evaluation process of an IRT-based item pool consists of several steps. If an IRT model has already been selected and implemented, it is important to review documentation to ensure that the model is appropriate. If there is not sufficient historical documentation to determine if this was done, then a complete review of the model currently selected must be conducted to determine its adequacy. Testing programs in the process of determining which model to use need to consider many factors in selecting or reviewing a selected model. The next sections address issues that are important to consider when selecting or assessing an IRT model for use with either CAT or CCT.

IRT Model Selection

In any item pool evaluation for CBT, it is necessary to review the status of the items in the pool with respect to the quality of the IRT item calibrations. Although a testing program does not have to be based on any particular IRT model, there are advantages to having all of the items in the pool calibrated with an IRT model and scaled to a common metric. The selection of an IRT model is influenced by many factors, including psychometric theory, item format, testing philosophy, organization politics, and testing organization preference. Prior to beginning this step, it is beneficial for the psychometric consultants to meet with representatives of the testing program to share information about possible CBT options, given the factors that may impact the selection of the IRT model. This prevents any misunderstanding about the intent of the testing program's examination and assists in focusing the future work of the psychometric experts. It is important to determine which model is the best given all of the factors that may impact the final decision. Regardless of the final decision, it is crucial that the implementation of the selected model adhere to the model's assumptions and rules as closely as possible.

An important point to consider in the selection of an IRT model is that one IRT model is *not*, by itself, better than another. The most important aspects of selecting a model are (1) understanding what is required to implement the model and (2) recognizing from the examination that the data and model are compatible. Once a model is selected, the model has assumptions and rules that must be followed. Violations of these assumptions or rules have an impact on the accuracy of the examination process. The magnitude of the error depends on the model's sensitivity to a particular violation. One commonly observed violation is to permit items that don't fit a model to be used in a CAT or CCT. Using a model inappropriately could result in poor measurement and inaccurate decisions once the testing program is online. For example, Kalohn and Spray (1999) found that misclassification errors increased when a one-parameter IRT model was used to fit item responses from a three-parameter logistic model when misfitting items were permitted to be used in a CCT. This is problematic because the primary purpose of a CCT is to make decisions regarding the classification status of examinees. Increases in classification errors should not occur when errors can be prevented through correct IRT model specification or the correct application of the IRT model that has been selected.

If the item pool has been calibrated, it is always a good idea to determine if the model used in the calibration process was appropriate. It may not be possible to obtain item response data from previously calibrated items in order to check the goodness of fit of the model to the data. In this case, the psychometric staff may have to assume that the model is appropriate and simply proceed from that point. However, if response data are available, or if the pool has not yet been calibrated, a careful assessment of the quality of the calibrations is a necessary *initial step* in the item pool evaluation process.

Evaluating the Convergence of the Calibration Process. An evaluation of the overall quality of the calibration process is helpful in deciding whether to accept the fitted estimates. BILOG and other item calibration programs provide output pertaining to the estimation process itself. This output should be evaluated before a decision to accept a model is reached. For example, it is helpful to know whether the calibration process, which consists of numerous computational iterations to reach a solution, converged or ended properly. Evaluation of the convergence process, either by careful study of the convergence indicators or by visual inspection of a plot such as the one in Figure 10.1, provides further evidence of good model fit. Important features to observe in Figure 10.1 are that the log of the likelihood function continues to decrease during the calibration process and that the largest change in the item parameter estimates decreases with each iteration. Instances have been observed in which this function has decreased during the early iterations of the calibration process but then begins to increase. Usually, this is indicative of items that are either poorly performing or miskeyed. The removal of these items or the correction of the answer key usually corrects the problem, resulting in a likelihood function that converges appropriately.

Assessing Goodness-of-Model-Fit. Several statistical indices can be used to help determine whether an item fits a particular item response model. However, like many statistical tests, these measures are sensitive to sample size. Large samples almost always reject all models for lack of fit, while small samples rarely reject any model. An additional approach to statistical tests of evaluating model fit involves a graphical evaluation.

Plots of the fitted item characteristic curve (ICC) or $P(\theta)$ versus the observed response curve are very helpful in evaluating overall model fit quality. They are also helpful in ascertaining whether the model fits in crucial areas along the latent ability or θ scale. For example, it may be important to determine if the model fits around the area of the latent passing score, θ_P, for CCT. Figure 10.2 shows a plot of an estimated ICC (i.e., the fitted model) versus the empirical response curve for a given item. These curves were plotted from output generated by the calibration software program, *BILOG*. This output includes the expected frequencies of correct responses as predicted from the fitted model and the proportions of correct responses actually observed. Although a test of model fit is also part of that computer output, many researchers prefer to perform a

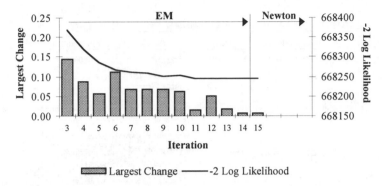

Figure 10.1. An Example of a Convergence Plot Derived from *BILOG* Output

simple visual inspection of the fit before accepting or rejecting the parameter estimates.

A visual inspection of the individual calibrated items reveals how well a particular model fits each item's responses. A plot of a poorly fitting ICC is illustrated in Figure 10.2. It is apparent from the plot that this item did not differentiate among candidates across the entire ability continuum and did not fit the model. Additional information about the item, in terms of test form information, sample size, classical item statistics indices, IRT item parameter estimates, standard errors of estimate, and a goodness-of-fit index also are included in the summary information. Further analysis of this item by content experts indicated that this item was miskeyed. In contrast, Figure 10.3 shows an item with good fit characteristics.

Figures 10.2 and 10.3 illustrate items where it is relatively easy to determine the status of fit for each item. However, many items require a more detailed review of the plot and associated data. Figure 10.4. depicts such an item. The observed curve is approximated fairly well by the estimated curve. The fit is not as good as in Figure 10.3 but it is still acceptable. This conclusion is based not only on a review of the plot but also of the item statistics presented above the plot. In light of this information, it is apparent that this item should perform well.

Approximating Item Calibrations. An item pool may consist of a mixed collection of items in which some have actual item calibrations while others only have classical item statistics, such as p-values and point-biserial correlation coefficients. When this situation occurs, it is possible to use approximation methods to link or scale the items without calibrations to those that have been calibrated. The resulting calibrations are only approximate, but Huang, Kalohn, Lin, and Spray (2000) have shown that these approximations work reasonably well in some testing situations.

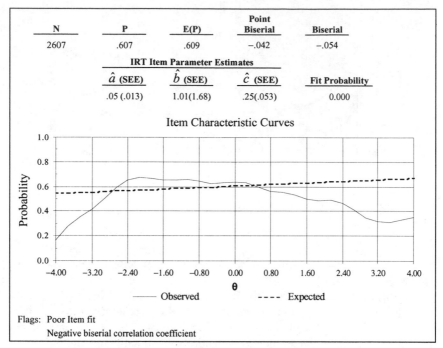

Figure 10.2. An example of an Item with Poor Model Fit

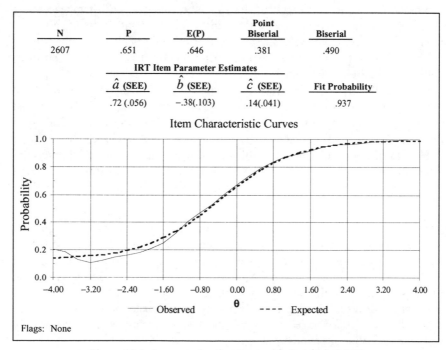

Figure 10.3. An example of an Item with Good Model Fit

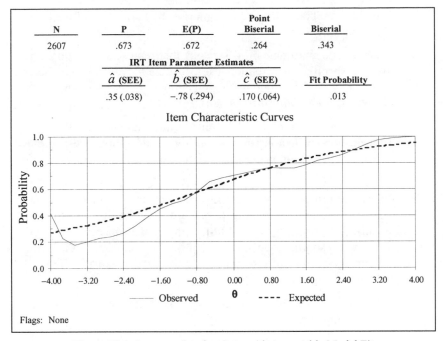

N	P	E(P)	Point Biserial	Biserial
2607	.673	.672	.264	.343

IRT Item Parameter Estimates

$\hat{a}$ (SEE)	$\hat{b}$ (SEE)	$\hat{c}$ (SEE)	Fit Probability
.35 (.038)	−.78 (.294)	.170 (.064)	.013

Figure 10.4. An example of an Item with Acceptable Model Fit

IRT Model Fidelity

Once an IRT model has been selected and an item pool has been successfully calibrated, the next step is to simulate the performance of a typical operational, paper-and-pencil form of the exam. This is done for two reasons: The simulation allows the psychometricians to (1) use the IRT model, selected to calibrate the item pool, to compute the expected values of several test characteristics and to compare the expected results to those observed in operational administrations of the test; and (2) to estimate certain properties of the test results that usually are unknown, such as the proportion of true or accurate classification decisions or the accuracy of the estimation of ability. This latter point is important because, for a real-life operational administration of a test form, the true classification rate (and, hence, the classification error rate) of the test or true examinee ability is never known. The simulation of the fixed form for purposes of estimation is performed in order to determine how well the current test is classifying or measuring candidates. In most cases, we do not want to recommend that a testing program substitute a CBT that will yield a greater classification or estimation error than the paper-and-pencil test it was designed to replace.

Simulation of a Fixed-Length, Paper-and-pencil Test. The steps necessary to simulate a previously administered (paper-and-pencil) operational test form are as follows. Further details concerning computerized simulations are provided later in this chapter, under the heading, Simulation of the CBT Environment.

1. Use the k calibrated items that comprise the fixed form of the exam for administration.

2. Draw a random sample of N θ-values that represent the examinees from a specified distribution used to obtain the item parameter estimates in the calibration computer program (usually denoted by the phrase *prior ability distribution*).

3. Administer the items one by one to each *examinee* as described previously by comparing the probability (P) of a correct response to that item to a uniform-random deviate or $U(0,1)$ drawn *pseudorandomly* by the computer.

4. Score the test for each examinee based on total number of items correct (or whatever scoring procedure is normally used for this exam); if the test is a pass/fail test, compare the resulting scores, X, for each examinee against the pass/fail score, P_X (i.e., the percentage-correct rate required to pass) and make the pass/fail decision.

5. Compare the expected score distribution with the simulated observed score distribution.

6. For CCT, evaluate the errors in classification (i.e., the number of examinees with true passing abilities who were scored as failing the test and the number of true failing examinees who were scored as passing the test). For CAT, determine errors in the estimation of latent ability.

7. Compute test statistics such as average observed test score, standard deviation of observed test score, reliability (KR-20), and distribution of observed test scores; and compare these to the actual results from the previous test form administrations. Additionally, for CCT compute pass/fail rates and decision consistency estimates for the proportion of agreement and Cohen's kappa.

If the results of the fixed form simulation appear to match those that were actually observed in a previous operational administration of the form, then the model can be assumed to be adequately describing the examinee-item interaction. If the results do not match, then it will be important to review assumptions that were included in this process. Differing results may be due to an incorrect assumption related to the latent ability distribution or the selection of an incorrect model for the calibration process. The cause of the differences needs to be resolved before going forward with any further work. Once this has been resolved, the results of any subsequent CBT simulations based on this model can be accepted, and classification error rates or the accuracy of ability estimates can be compared to those achieved in the paper-and-pencil fixed-form format.

Evaluating Maximum Item Information

Prior to conducting computerized simulations of the CBT environment, it is beneficial to review the overall quality of the item pool in terms of maximum item information (i.e., Fisher information). Item information, a function of the latent ability, θ, provides a numerical estimate of (1) where along the θ-scale an item measures and (2) how well that item differentiates between examinees. The point at which an item measures *best* is that point (θ_{max}) at which the information function ($I\{\theta\}$) of that item reaches a maximum, or Max ($I\{\theta\}$). Plots of the points, $[(\theta_{max}, \text{Max } (I\{\theta\}))]$, are called *maximum information plots*. These should be done routinely for each item in the pool and for each item within each content area in the pool. These plots identify strengths and weaknesses with an item pool because most items are selected for administration on the basis of an item's estimated maximum information.

Examples of maximum information plots appear in Figure 10.5. The maximum information plot for Pool A illustrates a pool of items that (a) are dispersed fairly well and (b) possess items that have relatively high maximum information across a broad range of the ability metric. This pool could be suited for a CAT, in which the assessment goal is to estimate an examinee's ability as accurately as possible.

The plot for Pool B is different from that of Pool A in the distributional characteristics of maximum item information. Pool B contains items with smaller values of maximum information; they also are more concentrated in the area of θ from -1.0 to 1.0 than Pool A. Based on this plot, Pool B may be better suited for a classification test; there is a higher density of items around any latent passing score in the interval $[-1.0, 1.0]$ than other areas on the ability metric.

Standard Reference Set

Another part of the preparation process consists of assembling a standard reference set (SRS) of items either from one or more previously administered paper-and-pencil forms of the test or from a set of items that follows the desired examination blueprint and psychometric specifications. If the SRS is constructed from the pool, it is important to include both content experts and psychometricians in the item selection process so that an SRS is selected that meets all specifications related to the content outline and the statistical specifications for the examination. Once an SRS has been assembled, relative information functions for the SRS and the entire pool can be plotted for comparison. The relative information function calculated by determining the average amount of item information based on a set of items (e.g., the SRS or pool) over a range of θ. The two curves in each of these plots can be compared with one another to determine if the item pool is similar to the SRS. If the two curves differ too much, the pool may not be able to support any type of computerized adaptive testing. If this occurs, it may be possible to reevaluate the item pool, eliminating and adding items to create a pool that is more representative of the SRS, provided that the revised pool has a sufficient number of items. The plot in Figure 10.6 illustrates an item pool and SRS that are acceptable in terms of their similarities.

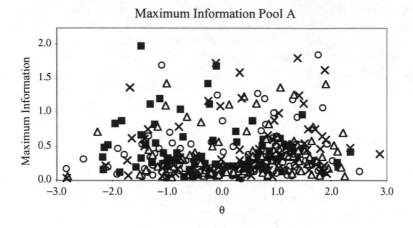

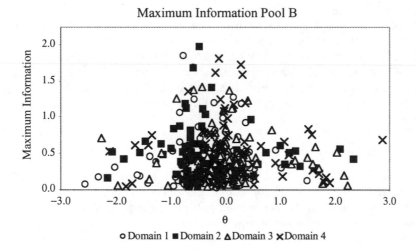

o Domain 1 ■ Domain 2 ▲ Domain 3 ✕ Domain 4

Figure 10.5 Maximum Information Plots or Pool A and Pool B

Simulation of the CBT Environment

Earlier in this chapter, we discussed simulation of a fixed-length paper-and-pencil test so that certain unobservable test characteristics, such as classification accuracy, could be estimated. In a similar manner, before placing a testing program online, it is important to conduct simulations of the proposed CBT environment to determine how the CBT will function and to predict certain outcomes based on the assumptions of the environment

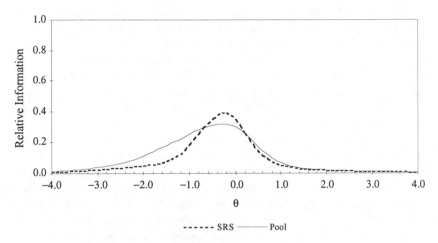

Figure 10.6 Plots Comparing the SRS and Pool Information Functions

By environment, we mean (a) the type of CBT administered, (b) assumptions regarding the examinees and/or their abilities being measured by the test, and (c) assumptions about the items, including the item-by-examinee interaction. Some CBT methods do not necessarily require simulations. For example, the CFT often consists of a single fixed form and, unless there was interest in estimating some characteristic of the test that could not be observed first-hand (e.g., classification accuracy), there may not be a need to simulate the administration of a single fixed form. However, there could be some interest in predicting the outcome of administering the CFT to, say, a different population of examinees from previous administrations of the test form. A simulation of the administration of the CFT to this population would answer questions such as "How many examinees would be expected to pass?" "What would the classification consistency and accuracy rates be?" "What is the expected score distribution" and "What are the expected characteristics of the test?" (e.g., the mean observed score, the variance of observed scores, and the expected reliability of the test).

For ATA test forms, a simulation would reveal how many multiple forms could be assembled, what kind of test overlap rates would be observed, and what the statistical properties of these tests would be.

Simulations for the CCT and CAT environments are essential to predict how a particular set of specifications functions for a given test. The next section presents information specifically on the simulation of the CCT and CAT environments.

Simulation of the CCT and CAT Environments

Many testing programs that consider the move to CCT or CAT want to shorten their current tests because they have heard that a computerized adaptive test can replace their current fixed-form exam and may decrease the length of the test for most, if not all, of their candidates. Computerized simulations of a CAT or CCT can be used to evaluate if an adaptive test can replace the previous fixed form of the exam. Recall that a critical requirement of any CBT is that it retain at least the same measurement accuracy and precision that it had as a longer paper-and-pencil exam. Simulations can help determine whether a particular item pool can support a shorter test without sacrificing measurement accuracy and precision.

Note that there are many conditions that are assumed to hold for simulation results to be trusted. First, the statistical model describing the item-by-examinee interaction must be assumed to be known and correct. In most cases this implies that a particular IRT model has been adopted appropriately to describe the item-by-examinee interaction and that the item parameters from the model have been estimated accurately. If the IRT model is the typical one-, two-, or three-parameter model, estimation of the item parameters requires the adoption of a unidimensional latent ability, θ, and the assumption of local independence. Secondly, a specified distribution of the latent ability of the examinees must be assumed. Thirdly, the assumptions underlying the CBT item pool must be met.

Once the item and examinee properties or values have been specified and the item pool is established, scored responses to the items can be generated with the use of a computer program. Most general simulation programs perform the steps listed here. These steps are similar to those described earlier in this chapter for the computerized simulation of a fixed-length paper-and-pencil test.

1. Draw a value of the latent variable, θ, from the specified distribution of latent ability, $g(\theta)$. Often $g(\theta)$ is assumed to be a standard normal distribution, or $N(0,1)$. This is the default distribution used by the computer program, *BILOG*, for example.

2. Compute $P_i(X = x \mid \theta_j, a_i, b_i, c_i)$ where θ_j is the value of the latent ability for examinee j, a_i, b_i, and c_i are the known item parameters for item i and X is the response to the item. Either $X = x = 1$ (for a correct response) or (usually) 0 if the item is answered incorrectly.

3. Draw a random number from the uniform distribution, $U[0,1]$. Call this value u.

4. Compare u to $P_i(X \mid \theta_j, a_i, b_i, c_i)$.

    If $u \leq P_i(X \mid \theta_j, a_i, b_i, c_i), X = x = 1$.

    If $u > P_i(X \mid \theta_j, a_i, b_i, c_i), X = x = 0$.

5. Continue to "administer" n items to this examinee. When the test is complete for this examinee, return to Step 1 and administer the test to another examinee.

Comparing Simulation Results to Expectations

Comparison of the simulation results to the expectations that have been defined in the test specifications is an important step. It is at this point where the test developer can determine the viability of a test given all of the specifications. For example, suppose that the ideal requirements for a test state that it should administer no more than 40 items, have a reliability not less than .90, and administer no item to more than 20% of all examinees. An initial simulation may show that a test of 35 items can reach the desired reliability but only at the cost of allowing some items to be administered too frequently. The next simulation may experiment with increasing test length to 38 items while simultaneously either increasing pool size or making exposure control stricter. The results of this simulation may either confirm that all requirements are now met or suggest changes that are evaluated by subsequent simulations.

Simulations may reveal that ideal test requirements are unrealistic and unobtainable. Test developers would always prefer that tests be shorter, more accurate, and more secure. Simulations make it clear what is in fact possible and allow the compromise between competing goals to be made on informed and rational grounds.

Finalizing Test Specification

The iterative simulation process ends when test developers are either satisfied that the test is likely to perform as specified or resigned to the fact that their specifications and expectations must be lowered. In the latter case, it is certainly best to know that test performance will be disappointing before a test is operationally administered on computer. Whatever the simulations reveal, their result is the set of test specifications that produce the most satisfactory characteristics. These specifications are carried forward to operational use.

At this point in the preparation process there are some differences between CCT and CAT. The next sections of this chapter will focus on the remaining simulation steps for CCT and CAT separately. The processes discussed in these sections are closely tied to the previous chapters where the specifics of CCT and CAT have been presented.

Preparation Steps for CCT Simulation

The four parameters presented in Chapter 9 on CCT must be defined before the simulations of an SPRT CCT can begin. These are α, β, and the two boundaries of the indifference region, A and B (or equivalently, $\log\{A\}$ and $\log\{B\}$). Additionally, content specifications, minimum and maximum test lengths, the expected latent-ability distribution of the complete examinee population, and the maximum item-exposure rate that will be tolerated must be known. Values for α and β typically are equal to one another, unless there is a compelling reason to fix one error rate larger or smaller than the other. They usually are set to some reasonable error tolerance (e.g., 05). The indifference region boundaries θ_0 and θ_1 are usually set to be equidistant from θ_P.

Determination of the Latent Passing Score (θ_P)

The next step involves establishing the passing score on the latent scale, θ_P, that will be used in evaluation of the quality of the item pool. The latent passing score usually is assumed to be equivalent to the passing percentage used in the fixed-length simulation described earlier, or P_X. There are two approaches that may be used to determine θ_P, a graphical procedure and a computational procedure.

Graphical Procedure. First, plot the function $\frac{1}{k}[\,\Sigma P(\theta)]$ versus θ, where the sum is over the k items from the fixed-length test described earlier for the SRS. The function $\frac{1}{k}[\,\Sigma P(\theta)]$ is called the test characteristic function, or TCF. The SRS serves as the reference form on which θ_P is established.

Next, locate the point P_X on the vertical axis and the TCF (i.e., the percentage-correct score required to pass the test; 67% in Figure 10.7), and draw a horizontal line until it intersects the TCF. Then draw a vertical line perpendicular to the θ-axis. The point at which the vertical or perpendicular line intersects the θ-axis is θ_P, or approximately 0.40, the latent passing score that corresponds to P_X.

Computational Procedure. The second method requires calculation of the probabilities of the TCF to a much finer degree in order to determine what value of θ corresponds to the passing standard, P_X. Values of θ are substituted into the TCF until a match occurs to the P_X value (see Table 10.2). This is comparable to finding the θ solution to the equation

$$\frac{1}{k}\sum_{j=1}^{k} P(\theta) = P_X. \tag{10.1}$$

In Table 10.2, two values of θ have been marked with asterisks to identify where the probability is 67%. The comparable passing score on θ, the latent ability metric, is equivalent to $-.397$.

Item Exposure Control.

After the definition of the initial set of SPRT parameters (i.e., *starting parameters*), exposure control rates or parameters must be determined for each item in the pool. Item-exposure control may involve a relatively simple approach, such as simple randomization, or a more complicated one, involving estimation of optimal exposures given the other items in the pool. An example of determining item exposure controls was described by Sympson and Hetter (1985) for ability estimation CAT and has been adapted for the SPRT CCT. In the Sympson-Hetter method, an item's exposure control parameter is the

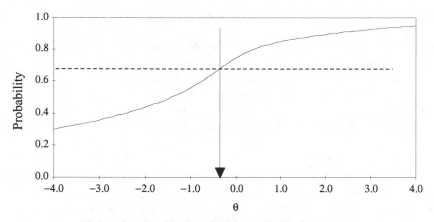

Figure 10.7. Graphical Method for the Determination of θ_P

Table 10.2. Results of the Computational Method for Determining θ_P	
θ	Probability
−0.405	0.6683
−0.404	0.6685
−0.403	0.6687
−0.402	0.6689
−0.401	0.6691
−0.400	0.6693
−0.399	0.6695
−0.398	0.6697
* −0.397	0.6699
* −0.396	0.6701
−0.395	0.6703

percentage of time an item is administered once it has been selected. The process of determining exposure controls is iterative and requires the use of software that simulates the actual testing environment. That is, all of the parameters for the SPRT CCT must have been defined and the algorithms applied in this process must be the same algorithms that will be used in the actual testing environment. In the approach suggested by Sympson and Hetter (1985), an initial exposure control parameter of 1.0 is used for all of the items in the pool. With each successive iteration, the exposure controls for the items are adjusted until they stabilize between consecutive simulation runs. Items selected frequently will have low exposure control parameters, while items selected rarely will have high exposure control parameters (i.e., their administration does not have to be limited). For the SPRT CCT, this process can be accelerated by using an initial exposure control parameter that is equal to the target for the maximum item exposure rate. This reduces the number of iterations to find the optimal exposure controls by about 50%. Software developed to determine the exposure control parameters essentially takes the test administration software and provides a computing environment that repeats the simulation process until the item exposure parameters begin to stabilize, as evidenced by the minimal differences in the parameters for two consecutive simulation runs.

Once the acceptable exposure controls have been established, the simulation can be run to determine classification error rates, average test length, consistency of classification, percentage of examinees force-classified, actual item exposure rates, test overlap, and how well the test specifications were met. At this point, the parameters for the SPRT CCT can be adjusted to improve the decision accuracy. Then exposure control parameters must be determined again before a simulation can be run to evaluate how the new parameters function. It is important to note that any changes to any of the SPRT CCT parameters or to the item pool itself necessitate the estimation of new item exposure controls. This is critical because any change that impacts how items are selected and administered has a direct impact on final total exposure rate of items.

SPRT CCT Simulation Evaluation

Several outcome measures can be evaluated from these simulations. The average variable length of the test can be calculated for the examinees, and a decision can be made as to the feasibility of shortening the test. Estimates of test accuracy and precision can be obtained, so that the simulated CBT can be compared to the fixed-length paper-and-pencil test simulated earlier. An important question to answer is, "Will the CBT provide at least the same measurement accuracy and precision that the paper-and-pencil test provided?" Other measures, such as estimates of the passing percentage or percent of examinees who are predicted to pass the exam can be calculated. Simulations also provide data to evaluate the quality of the item exposure control parameters that have been established, as well as the ability of the CBT and item selection algorithms to meet or match test content specifications.

Preparation Steps for CAT Simulations

These preparations are similar to those used in CCT, but the procedures do not focus on a specific passing point on the θ-metric. The termination of a CAT is determined by the minimum and maximum test lengths and the accuracy of the examinee's ability estimate. In a CAT the measure of the accuracy of an ability estimate is the standard error. An acceptable standard error of the ability estimates must be decided on before CAT simulations can proceed.

One primary difference between CCT and CAT is that the determination of the exposure control parameters must be conditioned on θ. In CCT, selection of items is focused on the amount of information an item possesses at the latent passing score. For CAT, the selection of items also is based on item information, but it is the amount of information at the current ability estimate of the examinee that dictates item selection. During the simulation process, the exposure control parameters must be evaluated at each θ point to prevent examinees at the same ability levels (i.e., at a given value of θ), the receipt of similar sets of items, resulting in a high degree of overlap between tests. This is of particular concern in areas where the density of the θ distribution is low (e.g., near the tails of the θ distribution). This process is referred to as a conditional approach to item exposure control.

Prior to conducting CAT simulations, not only must the acceptable level of accuracy be determined for the ability estimates, but there are other test parameters that must be established. These include (1) the minimum and maximum test lengths, (2) maximum item exposure control target, (3) a method for establishing the exposure control parameters, and (4) the maximum acceptable test overlap rate.

Methods for Determining Exposure Control Parameters.

Probabilistic item *exposure control parameters* are used in the Sympson-Hetter method for item exposure control (Sympson & Hetter, 1985) as well as in various adaptations of it, such as the Conditional Sympson-Hetter (Stocking & Lewis, 1995; Thomasson, 1995), the Davey-Parshall (Davey & Parshall, 1995; Parshall, Davey, & Nering, 1998) and the Tri-Conditional methods (Nering, Davey, & Thompson, 1998). All of these methods use the same basic approach of conducting a series of preliminary CAT simulations in order to successively obtain the exposure control parameters that subsequently are used in operational testing to limit item exposure to a prespecified target. As a result of these simulations, each item is assigned a specific exposure control parameter that will protect it more or less from overexposure, based on the frequency with which that item tends to be selected for administration. In this sense, the Sympson-Hetter method is seen to "condition" on the individual item. (The Conditional Sympson-Hetter additionally conditions on examinee ability, while the Davey-Parshall also conditions on test context. The Tri-Conditional method combines these approaches, conditioning on the item, ability, and test context.) The basic Sympson-Hetter simulation procedure described here can be extended for these other methods.

The exposure control parameters for the individual items are obtained through a series of simulations conducted prior to operational testing. In order to conduct these preliminary exposure control simulations a "maximum target exposure rate" must first be determined. This testing program goal specifies the maximum proportion of times that it is desired for an item to be administered. For example, it may be decided that 15% is the maximum proportion of exams on which any item should appear. After this target rate is defined, initial values for the exposure control parameters must be established. In some testing programs, the item exposure control parameters (which range between 0 and 1) are initialized to 1, and the values are allowed to decrease during the simulations. In other applications, the exposure control parameters are initialized to the target maximum rate and may be allowed to either increase or decrease during the simulations.

Once these values are determined, a large number of adaptive test administrations are simulated, using an assumed distribution of examinee ability. Following each simulation, the number of times each item is administered is tallied and compared to the target maximum exposure rate. If an item is administered too many times (i.e., a greater proportion of times than the target maximum rate), its exposure control parameter is decreased. One method for decreasing the exposure control parameter is to multiply the current value by .95. An item that has been administered too rarely may be adjusted upward (to a maximum of 1), by multiplying the current value by 1.04. This upward adjustment can keep an exposure control parameter from being overly reduced due to its chance overfrequent occurrence in a single simulation. It is also a necessary potential adjustment for those simulations that have initialized the exposure control parameters to the target maximum rate. One definition of a "too rare" use of an item is less than half of chance administration (e.g., for a 300-item pool and a 30-item test, chance administration for an item would be 10% and excessively low administration would be 5%).

Throughout the series of simulations, items that are selected but not administered are put aside and rendered unavailable for reselection, unless the item pool becomes exhausted. The exposure control parameter adjustments continue through a cycle of simulations, with those items selected frequently assigned more restrictive exposure control parameters, and items that are less frequently selected assigned more relaxed exposure control parameters. In each new cycle, the adjusted exposure control parameters are used, and their relative effectiveness at controlling item exposure is evidenced. The cycle ends when the exposure control parameters have stabilized and no items exceed the target maximum exposure standard.

The final set of item exposure control parameters can be used operationally, just as the temporary exposure control parameters were used during the preliminary simulations. The exposure control parameters are incorporated into the item selection algorithm and selected items are only administered with the probability given by their exposure control parameter. During an operational CAT, a given item first is identified as the best item to be administered next to a given examinee, using any optimal item selection criterion (with or without content constraints). After the item has been selected, a uniform $(0,1)$ random number is generated. This random number is then compared to the selected item's exposure control parameter. If the exposure control parameter for the selected item is greater than the random number, the item is administered. Otherwise, the item is not administered, and a new item must be selected. The end result is that an item is only administered a given proportion of the times after it is selected for administration, with that proportion specified by the item's exposure control parameter.

Principles of Conducting CAT Simulations

In order to conduct simulations of a CAT program, several test assembly decision rules must be established. The test must be designed to be either a fixed-length or a variable-length CAT. If the CAT is to be a fixed-length exam, then the total number of items must be determined. However, if a variable-length CAT is decided on, then both the minimum and maximum number of items must be established. Attention must also be given to the content constraints for the exam program; these often are based on the test specifications used to assemble the paper-and-pencil version of the exam. The method for controlling content within the CAT also must be determined. For example, the item selection algorithm can be programmed to select a given proportion of items from each content category (e.g., 12% of the items are to be drawn from content category A). Content alternatively can be constrained by selecting items to satisfy target information rates for each content category (e.g., 12% of the total test information for examinees at ability level .8 are to come from content category A). Finally, target goals for individual item administration rates, and for total test overlap need to be determined.

Once the set of CAT characteristics has been determined for a given exam, the simulations can begin. These simulations are based on a large number of simulated examinees from a specified assumed distribution of ability. Given that many of the test assembly rules are competing, it is likely that several attempts must be made. The simulated CAT is evaluated to determine whether satisfactory results were found for such test elements as total test length, test precision, content coverage, and item exposure and overlap rates. If the average CAT resulting from a given set of criteria is unsatisfactory, then some adjustments to the rules must be made. Then the CAT simulation is run again, and the new results are evaluated. This process ends when a reasonable compromise between criteria is reached, or when all critical rules are satisfied without resulting in unacceptable performance on the other criteria. (If it becomes necessary to adjust the exposure control criteria, then the preliminary simulation phase, described in the previous section, needs to be rerun. Once the exposure control parameters from that phase have been obtained, they can be used to rerun the CAT simulations in this stage of test development.)

Summary of the Item Pool Evaluation Process

The results of the item pool evaluation can be used to help testing programs make important decisions regarding the type of CBT program that would be best for their program. If the item pool evaluation suggests that an adaptive CBT program cannot be supported, one possible alternative is to have multiple fixed-length exams available for online administration. Recall that the process of constructing multiple fixed-length test forms is called automated test assembly or ATA (see Chapter 7). An evaluation of an item pool for a possible ATA application simply consists of running the ATA software program or programs to determine if multiple forms can be constructed from the pool and, once constructed, if these multiple forms (a) have adequate protection from item overexposure and high test overlap rates, (b) have the appropriate content distribution in terms of the test blueprint or content outline, and (c) can be considered *equivalent* in terms of defined psychometric criteria.

Item Pool Maintenance

Item pool maintenance consists of four primary tasks: (1) updating the item calibrations from online CBT administrations, (2) calibrating and evaluating pretest items, (3) monitoring item exposures and making adjustments accordingly, and (4) possibly updating the standard reference set if and when a new test blueprint or content outline has been introduced or the operational pool has been changed. Most of the activities associated with the maintenance of a live item pool are program-specific. That is, the tasks performed depend on the specific needs and CBT program requirements of that particular CBT application. However, some activities can be generalized to most CBT testing programs.

Online Calibration

Concerns about obtaining item calibrations from online CBT programs depend on the type of CBT being used. For CAT programs, items are selected for administration based on current estimates of ability. Therefore, there is a restriction of ability range for some of the CAT items, which may affect the item calibrations (Stocking & Swanson, 1993). For CCT programs, items are administered at the passing score, and theoretically all examinees can receive all items. Therefore, restricted range is not an issue with CCT.

A potentially more serious problem arises when the initial item pool has been calibrated from paper-and-pencil administrations, and the items somehow interact with the CBT environment significantly to change the examinee-item interaction. For traditional multiple-choice text-based items, this may not be much of a problem. However, items that depend on extensive graphics or those that require responses other than the traditional multiple-choice alternatives may operate differently online. If the item calibrations from online administrations appear to differ significantly from those in the initial pool, the online calibrations should replace the paper-and-pencil calibrations in the item pool. If this happens frequently, the entire item pool may change, requiring a reevaluation of the entire pool. It is suggested that online calibrations be performed and evaluated, in terms of their discrepancies from the original item parameter estimates, only after enough data have been collected to ensure that calibration differences are real and not simply due to examinee sample sizes or estimation error. This may translate into an item calibration cycle that spans several years.

Pretest Item Calibration

Pretest or *tryout* items are usually introduced into online CBT administrations in order to stock the item pool with new items that reflect changes in content or are intended to replace or augment weak areas within the pool. The problem of calibrating pretest items so that they can be used online differs from those associated with the calibration of operational items. Usually, pretest items can be administered to all examinees, regardless of their ability levels so that there is no problem with range restriction. However, pretest items tend to be administered to fewer examinees than operational items, and small sample sizes can lead to large item parameter estimation errors.

The typical method of calibrating pretest items is to perform the calibration along with the calibration of the operational items that also were administered. This can lead to a *sparse matrix* situation where the responses from the N examinees who have taken the operational items plus some number of pretest items are calibrated together in the same computer run. The matrix of item responses has to consist of N rows and $O + p$ columns, where O equals the number of operational items administered totally to the N examinees and p equals the number of pretest items administered totally to the N examinees. Because each examinee does not receive the same operational items nor (usually) the same pretest items, the number of columns, $O + p$, exceeds the number of actual item responses from each examinee. The remainder of the columns must be identified as *not presented* items or items to be ignored in the calibration process. This N by $(O + p)$ calibration problem may become too large for many calibration software programs to handle. In addition, there is always a danger that the calibration of the p pretest items somehow may contaminate the calibration of the O operational items. After all, pretest items are, by their very nature, in the early stages of development and refinement. Calibrations on items that do not function well or may be miskeyed can affect the entire process.

An alternative approach is to consider the O_i operational item parameter estimates as fixed or known (by using the previously known estimates of the parameters) and to calibrate the pretest items one at a time using the posterior distribution of θ, given the responses to the operational items to estimate the ability of the examinee taking the pretest item. This amounts to solving the pretest item calibration as a *regression* problem with the single value of θ replaced by an estimate of the posterior density of θ, given the operational item responses, X_i, or h $(\theta|X_i)$, $i = 1, 2, \ldots O_i$. Not only does this approach eliminate the size of the *sparse matrix* problem; it also allows the calibration of the single pretest item to be performed on relatively small sample sizes. This is due to the fact that (1) only a single item actually is being calibrated at any one time and (2) ability is assumed to be fixed or known (i.e., h $(\theta|X_i)$ is given). The approach just described frequently produces estimates of item parameters that cannot be satisfactorily obtained by other more traditional methods.

Determination of Item Exposure Rates

Once the pretest items have been calibrated, they can be put aside until it is convenient to integrate them into the operational pool. This integration process occurs infrequently because changes in the operational pool require new pool simulations to update item exposure rates. It makes more sense to withhold all of the pretest items and introduce them into the operational pool systematically, for example, on a yearly basis. Once they have been included in the operational pool, the pretest items can be used in subsequent simulations to determine their individual item exposure rates. The inclusion of these new items into the pool also will affect the exposure rates of those items already in the pool (i.e., these will have to be reestimated using the entire new pool).

Updating the Standard Reference Set

If the test blueprint or content outline has been changed, or if a new passing standard has been established, a new standard reference set must be used to locate the new passing standard on the θ-scale. If new content areas have been added to the test blueprint, or even if current areas have been retained but only the percentages of items to be used on the CBT have been changed, the changes can alter the reference set and, hence, the passing standard. Obviously, once a new standard reference set has been developed or a new passing standard has been established, computer simulations will have to be run again to estimate new item exposure rates as described earlier.

Summary

A complete and intensive evaluation of an item pool is required before a decision to move an existing program to CBT is made. Essential steps in this evaluation process have been considered in this chapter. Major steps include: item pool content review by content experts, assessment of item pool statistical characteristics, and simulation of the CBT environment. This process helps to identify the strengths and weaknesses of an item pool and facilitates the selection of an appropriate CBT method. Once a testing program is online, it is imperative that planning take place to ensure that the item pool is maintained by periodic evaluation and stocked with newly pretested items.

References

Davey, T., & Parshall, C. G. (1995, April). New algorithms for item selection and exposure control with computerized adaptive testing. Paper presented at the annual meeting of the American Educational Research Association, San Francisco.

Huang, C., Kalohn, J. C., Lin, C., & Spray, J. A. (2000). *Estimating Item Parameters from Classical Indices for Item Pool Development with a Computerized Classification Test.* (ACT Research Report) Iowa City: ACT, Inc.

Kalohn, J. C., & Spray, J. A. (1999). The effect of model misspecification on classifications made using a computerized classification test. *Journal of Educational Measurement*, 36, 46–58.

Nering, M. L., Davey, T., & Thompson, T. (1998). A hybrid method for controlling item exposure in computerized adaptive testing. Paper presented at the annual meeting of the Psychometric Society, Champaign-Urbana.

Parshall, C. G., Davey, T., & Nering, M. L. (1998, April). Test development exposure control for adaptive testing. Paper presented at the annual meeting of the National Council on Measurement in Education, San Diego.

Stocking, M. L., & Lewis, C. (1995). *A New Method of Controlling Item Exposure in Computerized Adaptive Testing.* (Research Report 95–25). Princeton, NJ: Educational Testing Service.

Stocking, M., & Swanson, L. (1993). A method for severely constrained item selection in adaptive testing. *Applied Psychological Measurement,* 17, 277–292

Sympson, J. B., & Hetter, R. D. (1985). Controlling item-exposure rates in computerized adaptive testing. *Proceedings of the 27th Annual Meeting of the Military Testing Association* (pp. 973–977). San Diego: Navy Personnel Research and Development Center.

Thomasson, G. L. (1995). New item exposure control algorithms for computerized adaptive testing. Paper presented at the annual meeting of the Psychometric Society, Minneapolis.

11
Comparison of the Test-Delivery Methods

Overview

The purpose of this chapter is to highlight some of the considerations in choosing a test-delivery method. First, a brief summary of test-delivery methods is provided, followed by a discussion of aspects of a testing program on which the test-delivery models can be compared. The various elements of a testing program that were discussed in each of the individual test-delivery method chapters are used here as grounds for comparison across methods.

These considerations are test procedures, measurement characteristics, and practical characteristics. The test procedures include test form assembly, scoring method, and item pool characteristics. Measurement characteristics include elements such as test length, reliability, test security, and the ability to accommodate set-based items. Practical characteristics include examinee volume, initial efforts required for development, ability to sustain dual platforms, ability to accommodate pretest items, and cost.

In addition to these aspects of a testing program, other considerations are used as grounds for comparison. These include relevant pool maintenance issues, examinee concerns, software considerations, and the ease with which innovative item types can be supported.

Summary of Test-Delivery Methods

Each of the test-delivery methods addressed previously in this volume is summarized briefly here. These delivery methods are computerized fixed testing, automated test assembly, computerized adaptive testing, and computerized classification testing.

Computerized Fixed Tests

Recall that a computerized fixed test (CFT) is a fixed-length fixed-form computerized test that is analogous to traditional paper-and-pencil testing. Typically, previously administered paper-and-pencil forms are directly transferred to a computerized environment and administered as though they were still in the more traditional format. Thus, the development of a CFT from a traditional paper-and-pencil program usually can occur within a relatively short time frame. Computerizing a fixed test form offers the examinee several advantages over the previous paper-and-pencil testing. For example, the examinees have more options for scheduling test dates and they can obtain immediate feedback regarding their test performance. A CFT can be used to determine pass/fail status, provide diagnostic information, or obtain an estimate of the examinee's ability in some norm-referenced sense. Multiple fixed forms can be used but they must be designed to have comparable statistical properties or comparable passing scores across forms.

Automated Test Assembly for Online Delivery

The automated test assembly process produces multiple test forms that are equivalent in some sense. If the test assembly process has required the test forms to have comparable difficulty and variability for each examinee, the tests, and thus the results, would be interchangeable. This would eliminate the need for separate passing scores for each form or post-administration equating. Such tests are called *preequated tests*. ATAs have the same advantages over paper-and-pencil testing that the computerized fixed tests offer. Furthermore, they offer improved test security when testing volumes are high and item sharing among examinees is a concern.

Computerized Adaptive Tests

The CFT and ATA test-delivery methods are not equipped to meet the needs of the individual test taker. However, the very nature of the computerized adaptive test, or CAT, makes it ideal for constructing or *tailoring* the items to the individual examinee. A CAT is particularly ideal for obtaining a norm-referenced score, one that distinguishes between examinees along an interval score scale. The CAT usually is variable in length, although there are exceptions to this.

In terms of adaptive variable-length tests, the choice between a CAT and a CCT often comes down to (1) the purpose of the test; (2) the strength, width, and depth of the item pool; and (3) examinee preferences for item review. If the primary purpose of the CBT is to classify examinees into mutually exclusive categories, the CCT accomplishes this task more efficiently than a traditional adaptive CAT (Spray & Reckase, 1996). On the other hand if the primary purpose is to rank-order examinees over the entire score scale, then a CAT is preferred.

Computerized Classification Tests

The computerized classification test, or CCT, is intended to make a gross classification of each examinee into one of two or more mutually exclusive categories, such as the criterion-referenced decision *pass/fail*. Like the CAT delivery method, the CCT is adaptive. However, in CCTs examinees typically do not receive scores beyond their placement into a classification. Because of this targeted goal, the CCT is the most efficient way of selecting and administering the appropriate items to make accurate and precise classification decisions.

Test Procedures

The foundational test procedures of test form assembly, scoring method, and requirements for item pools characteristics are discussed here. The differences across test-delivery methods in terms of these test procedures are considered.

Test Assembly

Test assembly refers to the psychometric methods used to construct a test. For example, CFT forms usually are constructed using classical item statistics, such as item difficulty indices or p-values and discrimination or point-biserial correlation coefficients. A CFT also may be constructed on the basis of the content specifications of an existing test blueprint with little attention paid to item statistics. Because the test form is fixed (i.e., because items are not selected to be best in any sense), the items and therefore the test score may not be optimal for all examinees, the "one test fits all" philosophy. Such a test form *could* be constructed to measure best at, say a particular point on the score metric, such as at the passing score. However, this is not typically done. Thus, the CFT is not likely to be the most efficient delivery method to use, in terms of measurement precision.

In the ATA method, multiple test forms constructed to be equivalent in some sense are assembled offline for online delivery later. These test forms are assembled according to content and statistical requirements. Like the CFT, tests that have been constructed using ATA methods may not be optimal for individual examinees but might be constructed to measure well at a particular point on the ability or score scale (e.g., at the passing score). ATA methods allow for both classical and IRT construction methods, while the adaptive tests, CAT and CCT, usually require IRT calibrations of the items.

The ramifications of an IRT-based program are many. First, if they have not been previously calibrated, items must be analyzed using an item calibration program that provides estimates of the items' characteristics. This implies that the item response data from previously administered test forms be accessible. In addition calibration requires fairly large examinee samples and access to calibration software. IRT-based programs typically also involve some input and oversight from trained psychometric personnel. There are ways in which an item pool can be calibrated even if only a portion of the items have response data (Huang, Kalohn, Lin, & Spray, 2000). However, these calibrations must be considered *temporary* until enough data have been collected from online testing to update the item calibrations.

For adaptive delivery methods, test assembly may more directly be conceptualized in terms of item selection. In CATs, items are selected to produce a maximally efficient and informative test, resulting in examinee scores. Conversely, in CCT item selection the goal is to classify examinees into one or more mutually exclusive groups, and individual examinee scores are usually not provided. In both cases, tests are assembled interactively, as the examinee responds to individual items. Further, tests may be designed to be either variable- or fixed-length.

Scoring

Examinees and program directors tend to prefer simple, straightforward scoring such as percentage-correct, number-correct, or percentile rank. Often the number-correct score is transformed into a *scale score* using a simple linear transformation. For example, a number-correct score of X can be *standardized* by subtracting the mean or average number-correct score in the group and dividing by the group's standard deviation of X. Fixed-length computer-based tests such as the CFT usually report scores as either percent- or number-correct, or a simple scaled score conversion is used. ATA exam programs that are classically based can also be scored using standard number-correct methods.

Computerized classification tests that are targeted to the cut-score usually report pass/fail status and may provide an overall scaled score of the number or percent correct or an IRT ability estimate for the entire test and various content areas.

The scoring of a CAT is more complex, however. Under a CAT (and under a CCT as well), examinees are administered different test items. The number-correct score is not appropriate for a true CAT because the examinees, at least in theory, should receive about the same number-correct, around the 50 to 60% range. Instead, estimates of the examinee's true ability, θ, can be obtained and then scaled. Preferred score scales are those that do not appear to *look like* number-correct or percent-correct scores (i.e., they are not on a 0-to-100 or 0-to-1 scale). Other CAT scoring methods have used the estimate of the latent trait, θ, to obtain a percent-correct score on the entire item pool or on a reference or subset of items. However, these estimates of percent correct can be confusing to examinees, especially if they know or have a good idea about how many items they did, in fact, answer correctly on the CBT.

Item Pool Characteristics

Many times the type of CBT delivery method to be used is dictated solely by characteristics of the current item pool, primarily the quality and quantity of items. CFTs have the simplest item pool requirements in that many CFTs are constructed from a relatively small number of available items. Furthermore, if there *is* no item pool per se but rather only enough items for one form exist, then the CFT is the obvious choice. (Alternatively, the test program could be maintained in paper-and-pencil mode as additional items are developed and pretested.)

On the other hand, if a pool appears to be able to support multiple forms with a tolerable amount of test overlap (or if a sufficient number of additional items are written), then the ATA method makes sense. In the ATA method there is an assumption concerning the item pool from which the tests are constructed. It is assumed that the item statistics on which the ATA process depend, are representative of the items as they will appear online. This assumption may be untenable in situations in which items near the end of a test were not reached by a majority of examinees. Such items would have higher difficulty or p-values (i.e., would be easier) if these items appeared earlier on the computerized version of the test. Thus, the item would no longer function as its difficulty index would predict. It is usually assumed that the item statistics on ATA forms are invariant to item position on the test and to test context effects. A context effect could include the way in which a graphic image might appear on the computer display or the interaction of other items with a particular item (e.g., one item providing a clue to the answer of another item).

Requirements are greater for computerized adaptive testing programs. The CAT item pool must measure well across a wide range of abilities. In other words it must include many items that measure high- and low-ability examinees as well as those in the middle of the ability range. Depth (or a large number of items in the pool that actually have a chance to appear on a CBT) is also critical for test security reasons. CAT programs tend to be very demanding in terms of the size of the item pool required, due to uneven item exposures, to the fact that CATs are frequently used for high-stakes exam programs, and to their availability in continuous or on-demand test setting.

In terms of the item pool, a CCT requires items to measure well (i.e., to discriminate well between those who should pass and those who should fail) at the passing score (or scores, if more than one decision point is used). Therefore, the items in a CCT pool should have the greatest amount of information at or near the passing score (or scores). In other words the CCT pool should have depth at or near the passing scores. Items that measure well at the extremes of the ability scale are not important in the CCT decision. Pool depth also is critical in ensuring that test overlap and individual item exposure are minimized.

For the CCT item pool, items that are optimal at distinguishing between the two or more score classifications are preferred. Items do not have to measure well at all potential ability levels; however, items that measure well at the decision point or points are critical to the CCT process. The basic rule of thumb is, "The more items that measure well at the passing score or decision point, the better."

Measurement Characteristics

Test-delivery methods can be analyzed in terms of the ease with which they can support testing programs with specific measurement characteristics. The measurement characteristics considered here as grounds for comparison across delivery method include aspects of test length, methods for estimating test reliability, needs for test security, and support for set-based items.

Test Length

The CFT and ATA methods produce tests of a fixed length, while CAT and CCT can produce either fixed- or variable-length tests. The concept of adaptivity implies that items are selected to maximize the solution to the CBT measurement problem for each examinee. This in turn leads to selection of a minimum number of test items for each examinee, resulting in different test lengths for different individuals. If a fixed test length requirement is imposed on the CCT or CAT, it results in different levels of precision for different individuals. This may or may not be acceptable to a given testing program. Given the interaction between test length and reliability, and the conflict between measurement efficiency and content constraints, satisfactory test lengths are often determined through simulations conducted during the test development process.

Reliability

The reliability of a test pertains to the test's measurement precision. Regardless of the type of CBT administered, the test results should be as precise as possible within whatever constraints or boundaries are imposed. The precision reported should be one that is pertinent to the test's purpose. For example, if the exam is a CFT, the test program may elect to report a measure of internal consistency such as KR-20, which is an overall or average measure of precision. In ATA, a measure of the test's internal consistency may be used as a construction constraint or target. A CAT that is designed to obtain an estimate of an individual's θ ability should report the precision of the θ estimate. On the other hand, tests that classify examinees into categories are required to have a high proportion of classification consistency (i.e., a proportion of consistently classifying examinees as passing or failing the test over more than one administration). The reliability index reported in CCTs is thus often decision consistency.

Item/Test Security

Item or test security is a function of anything that tends to result in the same items being administered to many examinees. For example, deeper item pools usually result in better security than more shallow pools, for obvious reasons. Also, few content requirements (and in fact, fewer constraints in general) result in more item *choices* for administration. By their very nature, the CFT will reveal the same items to all examinees unless more than one fixed form is used. Consequently, it is important to consider examinee volumes and security needs when using a CFT. The ATA method can produce test forms that have a controlled test overlap rate through multiple forms. Within both the CAT and CCT methods, the item selection algorithms used include item exposure control methods in order to control test security to some extent.

Set-Based Items

An item *set* consists of a group of items that usually refer to the same stimulus material or stem. Items in a set can either be forced to appear in total or can be selected to appear as a subset. All of the CBT methods allow set-based items to appear on tests. They can easily be included in the fixed-form CFT and ATA methods. For the adaptive CAT and CCT methods, forcing certain items to be administered solely on the basis of requiring all or a subset of the items in a set may result in longer tests or tests of less precision.

Practical Characteristics

Additional elements of a test program concern certain practical characteristics, such as the examinee volume, the extent of the initial development likely to be required, the ease with which the program can be maintained on dual platforms, aspects of item pretesting, and the cost to the examinee. Test-delivery methods vary in their needs and methods for addressing these practical concerns.

Examinee Volume

Examinee volume refers to the number of examinees who take a test. Typically, volumes are reported by year, testing cycle, or administration. Small-volume programs (e.g., fewer than 500) may be able to tolerate a single, fixed test form, especially if there is little danger of item sharing between examinees or candidates. Further, even if a single fixed form is used, the items on that form can be *scrambled* or presented in a random order to each examinee to increase security. In order for a CFT test form to be secure, examinee volumes usually have to be rather small to justify a single form. Security would be enhanced if several forms of the test, such as those provided under the ATA method, could be constructed and administered randomly to examinees. Thus, for programs with small examinee volumes, either the CFT or the ATA method would be suitable.

Programs with moderate volumes (e.g., around 1000 to 2000) or large volumes (more than 2000) require multiple fixed forms or a larger pool of items from which to assemble multiple forms online. Therefore, either the ATA method for fixed forms or the adaptive methods, CAT or CCT, are appropriate for these larger volumes.

Initial Development

Initial development activities refer to the amount of work, time, and expense required to begin constructing or assembling computer-based tests. Often, items already exist from previous administrations of paper-and-pencil tests. Although there is no guarantee that the items will behave when administered online as they did in the paper-and-pencil format, at least they provide some foundation on which to build an item pool.

The number of items that a testing program requires is based on many elements. Among the most critical are the stakes of the testing program and how frequently the exam is offered (i.e., a few times a year, occasional testing windows, or continuous testing). The number of examinees needed to pretest items is based primarily on the psychometric test model used. IRT methods require more examinees for pretesting than do classical test methods. The three-parameter IRT model requires more examinees than the one-parameter, or Rasch, model. Because of these elements, the CFT method is often the least demanding test-delivery method in terms of needing the fewest items and examinees, while the adaptive, variable-length CAT and CCT are often the most demanding. The ATA method offers a viable compromise because the method can be used to construct tests based on classical item characteristics.

Initial development activities also include conducting any preparatory computerized simulations. These simulations of test conditions are not necessary for the CFT but are for the ATA, CAT, and CCT methods. Within these delivery methods, the most extensive simulations are probably needed for CATs and the least for ATAs.

Dual-Platform Capabilities

Some programs provide two simultaneous administration formats or platforms (i.e., administer some exams on computer and some in paper-and-pencil format) for their examinees. Supposedly, the test scores from either administration mode should be interchangeable, meaning that an examinee should not be penalized or advantaged for taking the test in either mode. The CFT method handles dual-platform needs best followed by ATA multiple forms.

The two adaptive methods, CAT and CCT, do not handle dual-platform requirements easily. When these adaptive exams are administered as variable-length, it is more difficult to support a dual administration platform. However, it can be done.

Pretest Accommodations

Recall that a pretest item is one that is undergoing a tryout phase. Usually, the tryout or pretest item is not integrated into the examinee's final test score. The pretest item must be administered to a sufficient number of examinees before stable estimates of the item's characteristics, such as its difficulty and discrimination, can be calculated and the item becomes operational for future administrations.

The key to the development of good items via pretesting is to ensure that the examinee responds to the pretest item as though it were an operational or scored item. That is, the examinee should not be able to detect the tryout nature of the item from the item's position on the test or in the item's stem or list of alternatives. For many paper-and-pencil tests, pretest items are placed at the end of the operational test, so that, if the test is timed or has time limits and the examinee runs out of time, it will affect only the pretest items and not the operational or scored items. This is an easy task for tests of fixed length, but it is more difficult for variable-length tests such as CAT or CCT.

However, it still is possible to pretest a certain number of items on a variable-length CAT or CCT. For example, if a program's CCT required a minimum number of 50 and a maximum number of 70 items to be presented, then those examinees who complete the test in 50 items would be required to respond to 30 pretest items. Those who finished after 70 items would only have to answer 10 pretest items. This would ensure that each examinee had to respond to a total of 80 items. Other examinees that completed the test in fewer than 70 items but more than 50 would be given the appropriate number of pretest items to equal 80 items total.

Interspersing or embedding pretest items throughout the variable-length adaptive test is difficult because the number of items required of a particular examinee is never known until test administration has been completed. Research concerning attempts to predict CAT length online for the purpose of administering embedded pretest items has met with equivocal results (Davey, Pommerich, & Thompson, 1999).

Cost

The cost of a CBT (initially to the testing program, but often then indirectly to the examinee) consists of many elements such as item development, software programming, and administration fees. Some cost sources, including these three, differ across test-delivery methods. To determine the cost of computerizing an exam, either overall or per examinee, these and additional factors need to be analyzed.

The number, and thus the cost, of items needed for a test program is related to test-delivery method. In most cases, a CFT is the least demanding in terms of the item development cost, followed by the ATA, the CCT, and finally the CAT.

The cost of software programming is also likely to vary across delivery method. More complex software, such as might be required for test-delivery methods using complex, adaptive item selection, typically results in greater cost. In this case, the adaptive tests, (i.e., the CAT and CCT) will have higher development costs.

Finally, the cost of administering a computerized test may also vary across delivery method, as it is often related to *seat time,* the amount of time scheduled for an examinee to use a computer and take a computerized exam. In fixed-length exams such as those provided in the CFT and ATA methods, it is easier to determine the cost per examinee. While variable test length sometimes makes it more difficult to estimate computerized administration time and costs, the more efficient delivery methods, such as the CAT and CCT, are likely to have an advantage over nonadaptive methods.

Other Considerations

Finally, selection of a test-delivery method for a given testing program should also take into account several additional considerations, including pool maintenance issues, examinee issues, software issues, and the inclusion of innovative item types.

Pool Maintenance Issues

The CFT method is typically the least demanding test-delivery method in terms of pool maintenance activities, due to its small pool size and its frequent use in low-stakes settings. ATA procedures require more extensive maintenance activities, including updating the content and statistical properties or indices of the items.

As with the ATA method, the CAT method requires extensive item pool maintenance activities before going online and after the testing program is fully underway. The pool must consist of items that measure well across *all* of the ability levels of *all* possible examinee candidates. Thus, the CAT item pool has to be relatively large to support a variety of potential examinees. CAT items usually are calibrated using IRT computer software, which can be expensive and time-consuming to run. Item calibration work also requires some knowledge of modern psychometrics or test theory, and large samples of examinees typically are required to obtain good calibrations. The same assumptions concerning the stability of item statistics hold in the CAT item pools as they did in the ATA item pool. A longer amount of time may be necessary to get a CAT program up and running than either a CFT or an ATA program. In addition to the item calibrations, each item must have exposure control parameters to prevent the overexposure of items that the CAT algorithm identifies as optimal. Calculating each item's exposure control parameter also takes time and knowledge of the simulation process. The CCT item pool requires almost as much maintenance as the CAT item pool, but it may require fewer items. However, item exposure control still must be determined for each item in the pool.

Examinee Issues

Examinees' reactions to computer-based testing are related to their overall comfort level with computers and to specific elements of the different test-delivery methods. If given a choice, examinees usually prefer shorter tests to longer ones. Thus, they may prefer adaptively administered exams (e.g., CAT or CCT) for this reason. However, examinees also strongly prefer to be able to go back in the test to review their items and possibly change their responses, and to preview upcoming items in order to pace themselves and appropriately allot time to each item. These are standard features in paper-and-pencil tests and are usually provided in CFTs and ATAs. However, these navigational features are most often not provided in CATs. CCTs afford the opportunity to either provide or not provide the option of item review.

When several examinees take a variable-length CBT at the same time and the same site, there is a great possibility that some of them will complete the test before others. In fact some of the examinees may have to be administered the maximum number of items before their testing session ends, while others in the same room may complete their testing session after seeing only the minimum number of items. Examinees have reported that variable stopping times have added to their anxiety about the test and CBTs in general.

Finally, examinees tend to understand the scoring of the fixed-length fixed-form CBT better than the adaptive variable-length test.

Software Issues

It is obviously important that the CBT administration software be well-designed and error-free, regardless of the test-delivery method used. One software issue that differs across test-delivery methods is the software complexity. The item selection and administration process will be far less complex for fixed test form methods such as the CFT and ATA. While the ATA method may require complex psychometric software for the assembly of the multiple exam forms, that process can occur prior to actual test administration. For both of these methods, this aspect of the CBT software is quite straightforward. Adaptive delivery methods such as the CAT and CCT, on the other hand, typically have very complex item selection algorithms. This has implications for the quality-control phase of test development and software evaluation as well as for the need to ensure psychometric expertise in developing the software.

A second, and related, aspect of software complexity concerns the navigational features provided in the user interface. CBTs that restrict examinees to viewing each item a single time (i.e., that do not allow reviewing or previewing of items) actually have simpler user interfaces. Almost all CATs have this greater simplicity, while some CCTs and almost all ATAs and CFTs require more complex interfaces in order to enable examinees to move throughout an exam relatively freely. While examinees prefer this flexibility, it does necessitate more complexity in the interface, which has implications for the level of software use training that must be provided.

Innovative Item Types

The relative ease with which innovative item types may be incorporated into a CBT program differs depending on a number of elements, including the dimension of the innovation and the facility with which that type of dimension can be handled by the CBT administration software and hardware. The aspect of innovative item types that is most relevant in comparing test-delivery methods, however, may be task complexity. Innovative item types with low task complexity can be used relatively freely across delivery methods. Conversely, item innovations that result in high task complexity can be used most easily in a nonadaptive exam. In fact, a highly complex computerized simulation of a performance-based task can be conceived of as a novel test-delivery method standing on its own. In any case, it is clearly a more challenging proposition to add highly complex, perhaps interactive items, to an adaptive CBT than to a fixed-form program.

Summary

One of the basic premises of this book is that any test-delivery method has particular strengths and weaknesses, and a testing program should carefully select the delivery method that best satisfies its goals and needs. The four methods of CFT, ATA, CAT, and CCT are only some of the test-delivery methods that may be considered. Within this chapter these methods have been compared on several important elements, including testing procedures, measurement characteristics, practical characteristics, and other considerations. Table 11.1 provides a brief summary of some of the highlights of this discussion. This should make clear some of the advantages and disadvantages of each delivery method, and help guide test developers in the selection of an optimal method for a specific exam program.

Table 11.1. Summary of Features of the Test-delivery Methods

Test Procedures	CFT Features	ATA Features	CAT Features	CCT Features
Test assembly	Classical or IRT methods	Classical or IRT methods	IRT methods; tests are assembled in real time	IRT preferred, classical possible
Scoring	Number correct or proportion correct	Number correct or proportion correct	IRT ability estimates or scaled scores	Classification decision alone, or scaled score
Item pool size	Typically small	Small or large	Large	Medium
Measurement Characteristics				
Test length	Fixed	Fixed	Fixed or variable	Usually variable
Reliability	Usually internal consistency	Usually internal consistency	Standard error of ability estimates	Consistency of classification
Item/test security	Minimal provisions	Creates multiple forms to minimize test overlap	Minimize test overlap across examinees	Item exposure control
Set-based items	Easily addressed	Easily addressed	Easily implemented, but degrades efficiency	Easily implemented, but degrades efficiency

Table 11.1. Summary of Features of the Test-delivery Methods (cont'd)

	CFT Features	ATA Features	CAT Features	CCT Features
Practical Characteristics				
Examinee volume	Typically modest	Any size	Large	Large (if IRT is used)
Initial development	Modest effort	Minimal effort unless item pool is to be calibrated	Substantial effort	Moderate effort
Dual platform	Easily handled	Easily handled	Possible but difficult and expensive	Possible
Pretest items	Easily handled	Easily handled	Easily handled	Easily handled
Cost to Examinee	Modest for CBT	Modest but test lengths usually are not reduced	High relative to conventional tests	May be high

References

Huang, C., Kalohn, J. C., Lin, C., & Spray, J. A. (2000). *Estimating Item Parameters from Classical Indices for Item Pool Development with a Computerized Classification Test.* (ACT Research Report) Iowa City: ACT, Inc.

Davey, T.C., Pommerich, M., & Thompson, T.D. (1999). Pretesting alongside an operational adaptive test. Paper presented at the annual meeting of the National Council for Measurement in Education, Montreal.

Spray, J. A., & Reckase, M. D. (1996). Comparison of SPRT and sequential Bayes procedures for classifying examinees into two categories using a computerized test. *Journal of Educational and Behavioral Statistics*, 21, 405–414.

Appendix
Basics of Item Response Theory

Introduction

Although mental testing has a long history, it acquired a rigorous statistical foundation only during the first half of the last century. This introduced the concepts of parallel test forms, true scores, and reliability. By quantifying certain aspects of how tests perform, these developments, which have come to be called *classical test theory*, allow us to determine whether tests are useful, accurate, or better or worse than one another. Classical test theory is focused primarily on test scores rather than the individual test questions or items that comprise those scores. Furthermore, examinees are also dealt with in the aggregate, as members of groups or populations, rather than as individuals. Some simple examples may make these distinctions clearer.

Reliability is the classical test theory index of how precisely a test measures examinee performance. Loosely defined, it is the expected correlation between pairs of scores that would be obtained if each member of a group were tested twice. A reliability coefficient is dependent on a particular examinee group; a test can be more reliable with some groups than with others. However, reliability cannot be attached to any particular member of a group. Surely some examinees are measured more precisely than others are, but reliability does not recognize these differences.

The same is true of the classical measure of item difficulty. The item difficulty index, or p-value, is simply the proportion of examinees in a given population who would be expected to answer an item correctly. An item with a p-value of .60 is expected to be answered correctly by roughly 60% of the examinees that attempt it. But this is not to say that 60% of *any* group of examinees will answer correctly. Clearly, sixth-grade and first-grade students will approach the same problem with differing degrees of success. So the p-value also depends on a particular reference population. Neither can the p-value be attached to any particular examinee. The difficulty index is averaged over all examinees in a population. But brighter examinees obviously answer any item correctly more often than less able examinees. Again, classical test theory has few answers to offer.

Item Response Functions

Item response theory (IRT) has developed over the last 40 years to extend the concepts of classical test theory down to the level of individual examinees and test items (Birnbaum, 1968; Lord, 1980). A central idea is the *item response function*, which relates the probability of examinees answering particular items correctly to their general level of latent ability (usually denoted by the Greek symbol theta, or θ). A sample function from an arbitrary item is shown in Figure A.1.

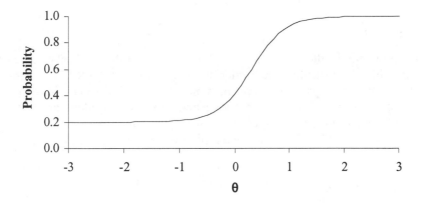

Figure A.1. Item Response Function

Several features of this function are notable. The first is that it is continually (monotonically) increasing, meaning that the probability of a correct response increases uniformly with the latent ability level of the examinee. Although this is not the case with every item, it's true often enough to make the assumption tenable. Second, the function asymptotes at 1.0 on the upper end and .20 on the lower. The upper asymptote implies that very capable examinees will always answer correctly. Again, this does not hold uniformly, but it is generally reasonable to assume. The nonzero lower asymptote indicates that even very low-performing examinees have some probability of a correct response. This is characteristic of multiple-choice items, which can be answered correctly by chance guessing. Finally, the function is seen to rise at different rates across different latent ability levels. An item is said to be *discriminating* over regions where the response function ascends steeply. This means that small differences in latent ability map to large differences in the probability of a correct response. A discriminating item is able to distinguish between two examinees that differ little in latent ability

Response functions, also known as *item characteristic curves* or ICCs, are usually modeled as *logistic ogives,* which take the form

$$\text{Prob}(u_i = 1|\theta) = P_i(\theta) = c_i + \frac{1-c_i}{1+\exp\{-1.7a_i(\theta - b_i)\}} , \qquad \text{(A.1)}$$

where the *examinee parameter*, θ, indexes the latent ability of the examinee, with higher values indicating higher performance. Each of the *item parameters*, $a_i, b_i,$ and $c_i,$ control some aspect of the item response function's shape. The attributes of these item parameter are described next.

Item Parameters

Difficulty (b)

The b parameter is often considered the IRT analogue of the classical p-value as an index of item difficulty. The b value sets the location of the ICC's inflection point, or the point at which the curve rises most steeply. Easier items have lower b values and response functions that are generally shifted left along the θ scale. Probabilities rise to nearly one even at lower latent ability levels. Conversely, difficult items have larger b values and response functions that are shifted to the right.

Discrimination (a)

The a parameter dictates how steeply the ICC rises at its point of maximum discrimination, or at $\theta = b$. Larger a values produce the steeper response functions associated with more discriminating items.

Lower Asymptote (c)

The c parameter governs the height of the lower asymptote, or the probability of a very low-performing examinee answering correctly. A nonzero lower asymptote is generally required for multiple-choice items, which can be answered correctly by chance.

Likelihood Function

Response functions describe how examinees interact with individual items. However, they also provide a basis for describing and making inferences about the test scores built from the responses to individual items. The key to extending inferences from single responses to test scores is the *likelihood function*. Likelihood functions express the probability of examinees producing a given pattern of correct and incorrect answers to series of items, given that their latent ability truly takes on some fixed value. Some notation and a simple example may make this definition more concrete.

Suppose an examinee answers a series of n items labeled 1, 2, ..., n. We can denote the responses to these items as u_1, u_2,...,u_n, where u_i is set to either 1 or 0 depending on whether the ith item is answered correctly or incorrectly, respectively. The *response vector* $\underline{U}$ = <u_1, u_2, ..., u_n> then encodes the examinee's pattern of responses to the n items answered. The likelihood function is the probability of observing the pattern of responses for that particular examinee with a known level of latent ability, $\theta = t$, or

$$\text{Prob}(\underline{U}=< u_1, u_2,...,u_n> \mid \theta = t). \tag{A.2}$$

This probability can be computed as a product of the individual item response probabilities. Consider a very simple test consisting of only two items. Only four response patterns are possible for this test: Both items answered correctly, both items answered incorrectly, the first item answered correctly and the second incorrectly, and the first item answered incorrectly and the second correctly. These patterns read as follows:

$$\underline{U} = < 1, 1 >$$
$$\underline{U} = < 0, 0 >$$
$$\underline{U} = < 1, 0 >$$
$$\underline{U} = < 0, 1 >$$

From the response functions for these two items, we know the probabilities of a correct answer to each item, given that the latent ability level θ takes on some value t. These are denoted as $P_1(t)$ and $P_2(t)$. The other important probabilities are those of incorrect answers to these items. Because an answer must be either right or wrong, the probability of an incorrect answer is the complement of the probability of a correct answer. Notationally, $Q_i(t) = 1 - P_i(t)$. Then, under the circumstances outlined later, the joint probability of a series of responses can be computed as the products of the probabilities of the individual responses. In the simple example:

$$\text{Prob}(\underline{U} = < 1, 1 > \mid \theta = t) = P_1(t)\, P_2(t)$$
$$\text{Prob}(\underline{U} = < 0, 0 > \mid \theta = t) = Q_1(t)\, Q_2(t)$$
$$\text{Prob}(\underline{U} = < 1, 0 > \mid \theta = t) = P_1(t)\, Q_2(t)$$
$$\text{Prob}(\underline{U} = < 0, 1 > \mid \theta = t) = Q_1(t)\, P_2(t)$$

A notational trick allows this to be extended to tests of any length n as:

$$\text{Prob}\langle \underline{U} \mid \theta = t \rangle = L\langle \underline{U} \mid t \rangle = \prod_{i=1}^{n} P_i(t)^{u_i} Q_i(t)^{1-u_i} \tag{A.3}$$

The $P(t)$ terms are included in the product when $u = 1$ while the $Q(t)$ terms are included when $u = 0$.

Figure A.2 shows that likelihood functions provide a means for estimating the latent ability of examinees based on their pattern of responses across a test. The graph sketches the likelihood functions for the four possible response patterns to the simple two-item test. Very proficient examinees are seen most likely to produce the (1,1) pattern while low-latent-ability examinees will probably get both items wrong. Examinees with middle-range true proficiencies are about equally likely to answer in any of the four possible ways.

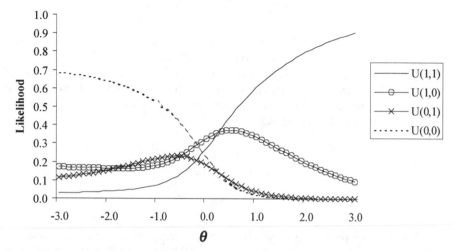

Figure A.2. Likelihood Functions for Four Response Patterns

Recall that the likelihood function is the probability of observing a series of responses, *given* that the examinee's latent ability truly took on a particular value. What we would like to do is reverse the order of conditionality and make inferences about an unknown latent ability level, given an observed series of responses. There are several ways to do this, but all make the important assumption that the item parameters (a, b, and c) are themselves known (or at least have been previously estimated). In the case of an adaptive test, item parameters would have been estimated (a process known as *calibration*) prior to operational administration of the test. With conventional tests, both item and latent ability parameters can be estimated simultaneously from the entire set of response data. A variety of stable and generally easy-to-use software programs are available to perform item calibration. For a more detailed discussion of the methods of obtaining estimates of θ, see Chapter 8.

Item Information and Test Information

Item information and test information are concepts important to IRT in a general sense and critical to computerized adaptive testing. Closely related to the slope of the response function, the item information function characterizes how much measurement discrimination an item provides at each point along the latent ability scale. This is important to know when deciding which items to administer during an adaptive test. As detailed later, the goal of most adaptive testing procedures is to select items that provide substantial information across regions where it is believed an examinee's true latent ability lies.

The information function for the response function in Figure A.1 is shown in Figure A.3. The interpretation of this function is fairly intuitive: Information is high where the response function is steep or where the item discriminates well among examinees with similar latent ability. Information is low where the response function is flat (horizontal) and examinee discrimination is minimal. An item's information function suggests at what latent ability level the item would be most productive, in terms of the measurement precision at that latent ability level. Under ideal conditions, items would only be administered to examinees if those items were the most informative items at the examinee's current estimated latent ability level.

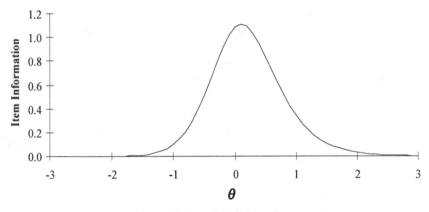

Figure A.3. Item Information Function

Information can be accumulated or added across items in a test to produce the test information function. Test information is interpreted identically to the item information functions that comprise it. Information is high across latent ability ranges where a test provides substantial measurement precision and low where a test measures less precisely. In fact, the precision of both maximum likelihood and Bayes latent ability estimates can be inferred directly from the test information function. The test information function therefore can be considered as the IRT analog of test reliability. However, it has the important advantage of being specific to or conditional on each latent ability level rather than averaged or aggregated across levels. Thus, it acknowledges that test precision varies along the latent ability scale.

Model Assumptions

Like most models, item response theory makes a number of assumptions to simplify the very complicated interactions between examinees and test items. It cannot be reasonably argued that any of these assumptions are strictly true. However, it's not necessary for a model to conform exactly with reality in order to be useful. Indeed, most models are useful precisely because they offer idealized and therefore clearer descriptions of what are, in fact, messy and complex situations. It is only necessary that the predictions and inferences drawn from a model prove accurate and valid enough to be valuable. The importance of assumptions lies in the fact that predictions and inferences will tend to be accurate to the extent that the model fits real data. Fortunately, decades of experience in applying IRT in a variety of contexts and situations have generally revealed that the assumptions made are true enough, often enough.

Three major assumptions are generally identified. These are described and their importance evaluated in turn.

1. Response Functions are Logistic. The functional form of response functions assumes that response probabilities change across latent ability levels in a way that can be fit by a logistic curve. This assumption is not as restrictive as it might appear, because the three-parameter logistic model (with item parameters a, b, and c) is a remarkably flexible family of functions, capable of taking on a wide variety of different shapes. Furthermore, it is really only necessary that the function fit well over the fairly narrow latent ability range in which most examinees fall. The most restrictive aspect of the assumption is that the logistic function must increase as latent ability increases. Although it seems reasonable that examinees that are more able should always have a better chance of answering an item correctly than do less able examinees, this does not uniformly hold true. However, exceptions are rare and even when they occur, the logistic curve does an adequate job of interpolating the data. Difficult multiple-choice items are those most likely to be poorly fit by logistic curves. Such items are often difficult because one of the incorrect answers looks plausible to many examinees. At very low latent ability levels, examinees don't know enough to get trapped and so mainly guess, answering correctly at chance levels. But middle-range examinees are drawn almost exclusively to the plausible distracter, and so answer correctly at considerably less than chance levels. More able examinees can see past the distracter and choose the correct answer with increasing probability, causing the true response function to ascend.

2. Responses are Independent when Conditioned on Latent Ability. This assumption, often called *local* or *conditional independence,* is perhaps the most subtle (and least understood) concept in IRT. Recall that likelihood functions are computed as simple products of the individual response probabilities for the items in a test. However, the joint probability of a series or pattern of events (such as the answers to a series of items) is equal to the product of the probabilities of the individual events only when those events are independent of one another.

Coin tosses are the classic example of independent events. The probability of a single *head* occurring remains at one-half and does not change depending on whether a *head* was also observed on the previous toss. Even after ten consecutive *heads,* the probability of an eleventh on the next toss is that same one-half or .5.

But conditional independence does not claim that responses are completely random occurrences like tosses. Responses are certainly dependent (correlated) across examinees; examinees who get some items right are likely to get others right as well. What conditional independence does maintain is that for any particular examinee, responses are independent once latent ability is conditioned on. In practical terms, this means that nothing contributes to the prediction of whether a particular response is correct or not beyond knowledge of the examinee's latent ability. As a concrete example, suppose we were trying to predict an examinee's response to the second item on a test. Knowing the examinee's latent ability (and the item parameters) allows the response function to be evaluated and the probability of a correct answer to be determined. This probability, like the probability of a *head,* does not change given the additional information that the first item was answered correctly. It is a function only of the examinee's latent ability.

Like the assumption that response functions are logistic, the assertion of conditional independence is not as restrictive as it may appear. Empirically, conditional independence has been checked by an assortment of statistics applied in a variety of settings. The usual finding is that independence holds strongly enough and often enough to allow IRT models to adequately fit and describe data.

3. Unidimensionality. The item response models described here and in common use today characterize examinees by only a single latent ability parameter. It can be reasonably (and accurately) argued that this grossly oversimplifies what really happens when an examinee is confronted with a test item. In fact, even the simplest items draw on and require numerous skills or traits in order to be correctly solved. Examinees differ from one another in numerous ways along multiple dimensions. Even so, it is again the case that an assumption does not need to be strictly true in order to make the model tenable. Experience has shown that what IRT models require for adequate fit is simply that a test yields reasonable scores, however determined. It is certainly possible to construct a test from such a disparity of items measuring such a medley of topics that scores are uninterpretable and meaningless. Such a test would be badly fit by a unidimensional IRT model. However, as long as number-right scores remain reasonable and valid, a unidimensional model, approximate though it may be, is likely to fit well.

Summary

The model assumptions, along with other concepts introduced here, such as item response functions, likelihood functions, and information functions, are the basic elements of IRT. They can be used to handle many complex measurement problems, not the least of which is adaptive computer-based testing. Further information on IRT can be found in Lord (1980) and in Hambleton and Swaminathan (1985). Discussion of how IRT is used within computer-based testing is included throughout this text.

References

Birnbaum, A. (1968). Some latent trait models and their use in inferring an examinee's ability. In Lord, F. M., & Novick, M. R. *Statistical Theories of Mental Test Scores.* Reading, MA: Addison-Wesley.

Hambleton, R. K., and Swaminathan, H. (1995). *Item Response Theory: Issues and Applications.* Boston: Kluwer Nijhoff.

Lord, F. M. (1980). Applications of Item Response Theory to Testing Problems. Hillsdale, NJ: Lawrence Erlbaum.

Index

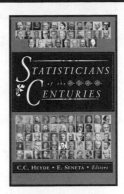